MAN'S ESTATE

MAN'S

ESTATE

Masculine Identity in Shakespeare

Coppélia Kahn

University of California Press / Berkeley / Los Angeles / London

University of California Press
Berkeley and Los Angeles, California

University of California Press, Ltd.
London, England

Library of Congress Catalog Card Number: 79-63547
ISBN 0-520-03899-1

Printed in the United States of America

1 2 3 4 5 6 7 8 9

FOR GABRIEL

The boy of act one is the mature man of act five. All in
all. In *Cymbeline,* in *Othello* he is bawd and cuckold. He
acts and is acted on. Lover of an ideal or a perversion,
like José he kills the real Carmen. His unremitting intellect is the hornmad Iago ceaselessly willing that the
moor in him shall suffer.

JAMES JOYCE, Ulysses

Contents

Acknowledgments   xi

ONE   Introduction   1

TWO   Self and Eros in *Venus and Adonis*   21

THREE   "The Shadow of the Male": Masculine
Identity in the History Plays   47

FOUR   Coming of Age: Marriage and Manhood in
Romeo and Juliet and *The Taming of the Shrew*   82

FIVE   "The Savage Yoke": Cuckoldry and
Marriage   119

SIX   The Milking Babe and the Bloody Man in
Coriolanus and *Macbeth*   151

SEVEN   The Providential Tempest and the
Shakespearean Family   193

Index   227

Acknowledgments

Writing a book about Shakespeare requires, at the least, both perseverance and presumption. In the years I have spent on this task, the poet's own searching, tolerant, relentlessly keen insight into human nature has sustained me as well as my labor. So my first debt is to William Shakespeare.

If he is "not of an age but for all time," then he is also for our time. He portrays struggles for self-definition like our own. Among the great writers of the pre-industrial, pre-scientific past, he speaks most perceptively to our modern experience. He does so, I think, because he more than any other writer was aware that he lived in a patriarchy—an awareness we are beginning to share when we look at our own world. In our marriages, our families, our public lives, we reenact or reassess or protest against patriarchal habits of mind that Shakespeare observed in his society four hundred years ago. It is no wonder we see ourselves reflected in his art.

I have many other debts to friends and colleagues that I am happy to acknowledge here. First, to my extended family of Shakespearean scholars, whose work on sexuality, marriage, and the family in Shakespeare has been a catalyst for mine: Madelon Gohlke, Carol Thomas Neely, Murray Schwartz, Richard Wheeler, and especially C. L. Barber, who died on March 26, 1980, as this book was going to press. His extraordinary insight and his nurturant presence enriched all who knew him.

Conversations with Lee David Brauer have also helped me understand my ideas about Shakespeare. Of those who read part or all of my manuscript, I owe the most to Sherman Hawkins, Miriam Miller, Joseph W. Reed, Jr., and Elise Snyder. At the least, they saved me from later embarrassment; at the most, they clarified my prose and deepened my thought. I took less advice than they gave.

From the time of my apprenticeship at the University of California at Berkeley, Norman Rabkin has been my friend and mentor. His rare generosity and wit have buoyed my spirits; his writings have given me a robust example of learning ever in touch with life. Judd Kahn improved many parts of this book with his lucid, sympathetic criticism, and gave his time and understanding in countless other ways. Doris Kretschmer of the University of California Press encouraged the project from its beginning and guided it through publication. Richard S. Field, Curator of Prints at the Yale University Art Gallery, helped me find and choose the jacket illustration. Wesleyan University provided research funds, and Alice Pomper and Judith Gray typed the manuscript with intelligence and good grace.

Some portions of this book have been published previously, and I am grateful for permission to reprint them in revised versions. Chapter 2, "Self and Eros in *Venus and Adonis*," first appeared in *The Centennial Review*. The essays on *The Taming of the Shrew* and *Romeo and Juliet* that make up chapter 4 were both originally published in *Modern Language Studies*. The essay on *Taming* also appeared in *The Authority of Experience: Essays in Feminist Criticism*, ed. Lee Edwards and Arlyn Diamond, copyright © 1977 by the University of Massachusetts Press, as *"The Taming of the Shrew:* Shakespeare's Mirror of Marriage." The essay on *Romeo and Juliet*, titled "Coming of Age in Verona," was reprinted in *The Woman's Part: Feminist Criticism of Shakespeare*, ed. Gayle Green, Carolyn R. S. Lenz, and Carol Thomas Neely, copyright © 1980 by the Board of Trustees of the University of Illinois. Chapter 7, "The Providential Tempest and the Shakespearean Family," appeared in *Representing Shakespeare: New Psychoanalytic Essays*, ed. Coppélia Kahn and Murray Schwartz, published by Johns Hopkins University Press, 1980. My thanks also go to Wesleyan University, Davison Art Center, Middletown, Connecticut, for permission to reproduce *Venus and Adonis* by Giorgio Ghisi.

In quoting Shakespeare, I have cited whenever possible the new Arden editions, general editors Harold F. Brooks and Harold Jenkins; otherwise I have used *The Complete Signet Classic Shakespeare*, ed. Sylvan Barnet (New York: Harcourt Brace Jovanovich, 1963; rpt. 1972). Quotations from the works of Sigmund Freud, when taken from *The Standard Edition of the Complete Psychological Works of Sigmund Freud*, ed. James Strachey, 24 vols. (London: Hogarth Press, 1953–1974), will be cited as *Standard Edition*.

Middletown, Connecticut
June, 1980

CHAPTER ONE

Introduction

Problems of sexual identity, family relationships, and
gender roles fill Shakespeare's work, from the
sundered twin brothers who find themselves by
finding each other to the prime duke who renounces
sibling rivalry and reclaims a patrimony through his
rough magic. His male characters are engaged in a
continuous struggle, first to form a masculine
identity, then to be secure and productive in it. In the
action of his plays and poems, he explores the
unconscious attitudes behind cultural definitions of
manliness and womanliness, and behind the mores
and institutions shaped by them. Leontes' horns,
Macbeth's "unmannerly breech'd dagger," Kate's
hand beneath her husband's foot, and Coriolanus's
wounds are prismatic and ambivalent images at the
center of works that examine sexual identity as
shaped by the patriarchal culture in which the
playwright lived.

Shakespeare and Freud deal with the same subject:
the expressed and hidden feelings in the human heart.
They are both psychologists. While Shakespeare had
no formal theory of the unconscious, he possessed
extraordinary and sophisticated insight into it, insight

2 INTRODUCTION

that cannot be explained by humors psychology or the lore of melancholy. In this book, my intention is to use psychoanalytic theory to understand Shakespeare's conception of identity. Like all critics, I bring to the texts I interpret some conceptual apparatus originating outside them. Rhetoric, iconography, stage history, Christian doctrine—these are some of the modes of interpretation that have been applied to Shakespeare. Any such critical approach can be justified only by its results, by whether it can contribute as much to our understanding as its rivals, and more than our unaided intelligence. The following pages may not satisfy the reader who thinks that "common sense is psychology enough,"[1] and they probably will not help the clinician seeking confirmation of theory in literature. I am not trying to psychoanalyze individual characters, but to discover dilemmas of masculine selfhood revealed in the design of the works as a whole. "Hamlet may not have an Oedipus complex, but *Hamlet* does."[2]

We do not see Hamlet at his mother's breast, or Leontes learning to walk. Yet we can be confident, from the resonance of the poet's imagery and characterization, that he thought of them as human beings whose adult selves were shaped by the experience of growing up within a family. They speak in its modes of eating and spitting out, they echo its delusions of omnipotence and fears of abandonment. Their utterances and their conflicts spring from the residue of early life. While it would be reductive to translate the intricate action of a Shakespearean play into the terms of infantile experience, oedipal or pre-oedipal, seeing that experience as the *source* of the action helps us understand its inner coherence. Coriolanus, for example, comes to political maturity at the historical moment when the plebs challenge the patricians' absolute power, sees the hungry mob as the shadow of his own emotionally starved self as a child, and responds to it accordingly. The political complexity of his situation is not the result of his

1. Frederick Crews, "Literature and Psychology," in *Relations of Literary Study: Essays on Interdisciplinary Contributions,* ed. James Thorpe (New York: Modern Language Association, 1967), p. 76.
2. Crews, *ibid.,* p. 85.

childhood, but his way of handling it is crucially shaped by that childhood.

The process of forming an identity, which is central to Shakespeare's work, has been vividly illuminated by such post-Freudian ego psychologists as Margaret Mahler, Edith Jacobson, Erik Erikson, D. W. Winnicott, and others. Their theories and clinical observations have helped me to understand the vicissitudes of Shakespearean manhood. I shall summarize them here before bringing them to bear on the plays themselves. What follows is by no means a comprehensive account, but rather my own synthesis, an eclectic weaving together of ideas about the growth of identity that seem best to fit the Shakespeare I know. Up to the point at which gender identity becomes crucial to my argument, I shall use the masculine pronoun as the conventional though misleading referent for everyone, male or female, growing into a sense of identity during the first three years of life.

Identity has two sides. One faces inward, to the core of the individual, to his own confidence in being uniquely himself, and in the consistency and stability of his self-image through space and time. The other looks outward, to his society; it rests on his confidence in being recognized by others *as* himself, and on his ability to unify his self-image with a social role. The formation of identity begins at birth and continues throughout life, but there are two points when it crystallizes: around the third year and in adolescence. At these times, certain milestones of growth are reached without which the individual cannot function normally. Identity continues to develop throughout life, in response to particular crises and in concert with passage from one stage of life to the next.[3] The key to this process is the attainment of separation from the original, undifferentiated unity of the child and its mother. This unity is essential for the sense of security it provides,

3. I am indebted to the works of Erik Erikson for this broad formulation of identity. See his "The Problem of Ego Identity," in *Identity and the Life Cycle: Selected Papers* (New York: International Universities Press, 1959), pp. 101–164; *Identity: Youth and Crisis* (New York: W. W. Norton, 1968), especially pp. 22–23, 50; *Childhood and Society* (New York: W. W. Norton, 1974), *passim*.

without which there can be no viable identity. But without separation, and the emotional growth dependent on it, there can be no close and meaningful relationships with others, no mature selfhood, and no sexual identity as a man or a woman. The physical separation of the child from its mother at birth does not bring about a psychological separation of equal severity.[4] In the first month of life, though the baby is profoundly dependent on his mother, he experiences her feeding, touching, and holding without awareness of her as a separate person. When he cries for the breast, it comes, and he greedily receives its satisfactions, but under the delusion that it is himself. Deriving pleasure primarily from his internal physical sensations of well-being, asleep or in a sleeplike state most of the time, psychologically speaking he resembles a chick in its shell; he carries his nourishment within himself. From the second month, he becomes dimly aware of something outside himself that satisfies his needs, but behaves as though he and it are "an omnipotent system—a dual unity within one common body."[5] As his sensory apparatus develops and he becomes attuned to the sights and smells, sounds and touches of the world, he realizes a dim demarcation of his body from the rest of the world—"the peripheral rind of the ego."[6] Along with the central "core" of body sensation developed earlier, this "rind" constitutes the primitive basis on which his sense of self can begin to form.

A face takes shape in the baby's penumbra of sensations, the human face in motion. Though he smiles back at it, he doesn't actually recognize it. As his smile shows, he now perceives that his needs are satisfied by something outside him-

4. The following description of symbiotic union and the separation-individuation process has been freely adapted from chapters 3 through 7 of *The Psychological Birth of the Human Infant: Symbiosis and Individuation*, by Margaret S. Mahler, Fred Pine, and Anni Bergman (New York: Basic Books, 1975), pp. 39–120. Based on extensive observation of normal infants (up to age three) with their mothers in a playroom setting, the description and analysis of the children's interaction with their mothers and their environment is far richer in detail, subtlety, and theoretical complexity than I can indicate here.
5. Mahler *et al.*, pp. 44.
6. Sigmund Freud, "The Ego and the Id" (1923), *Standard Edition* 19, p. 26.

self, but he still sees that something as existing within the shell of self-and-mother, a dual unity in which he is omnipotent. Though strikingly more alert and responsive to people, sensations, and things, he still has not differentiated "I" from "non-I."[7]

This can only be accomplished with the mother's sensitive, loving help, which she provides by "mirroring" her child to himself, and by playing with him. In mirroring, which is her characteristic way of holding her baby, of touching, feeding, and especially of looking at him, she gives him back an image of himself that D. W. Winnicott has described best:

> What does the baby see when he or she looks at the mother's face? I am suggesting that, ordinarily, what the baby sees is himself or herself. In other words the mother is looking at the baby and *what she looks like is related to what she sees there*. All this is too easily taken for granted. Many babies . . . have a long experience of not getting back what they are giving. They look and they do not see themselves.[8]

The emotionally absent or the narcissistic mother looks at her baby, but does not see him; thus she deprives him of his first, crucial, two-way exchange with the world.

In playing with her child, the mother allows him to experience a sense of magical omnipotence like that he enjoyed at the breast, but also helps him to gain control of the actual world—exploring, testing, risking—in an atmosphere of warm intimacy. She adapts to the baby's wishes, but introduces her own as well.[9] Thus she enables him to move from the kind of primitive identification with her that he began to experience at the breast in fantasies of incorporating her or merging with her, to the more sophisticated selective identification of imitating her or being *like* her while also being himself. These selective identifications allow him to com-

7. For the important distinction between the unspecific social smile and the specific preferential response to the mother, see Mahler *et al.*, pp. 46, 52.
8. D. W. Winnicott, "Mirror Role of Mother and Family in Child Development," in his *Playing and Reality* (New York: Basic Books, 1971), pp. 111–118.
9. D. W. Winnicott, "Playing: A Theoretical Statement," in *Playing and Reality*, pp. 38–52.

promise between his desire to remain symbiotically fused with her and his conflicting need to be independent from her.[10]

A further stage of separation and individuation is marked by what Winnicott calls the transitional object, familiar to many of us in the form of a ragged blanket. The child assumes dominion over it and alternately cuddles and mauls it, refusing to allow the slightest change or most generous substitute. He endows it with a special vitality, but then gradually loses interest in it, though without repressing, forgetting, or mourning it. Winnicott's description of its function brings out the paradox of the mother's role in the child's growth:

> The object is a symbol of the union of the baby and the mother (or part of the mother). This symbol can be located. It is at the place in space and time where and when the mother is in transition from being (in the baby's mind) merged in with the infant and alternatively being experienced as an object to be perceived rather than conceived of. The use of an object symbolizes the union of two now separate things, baby and mother, *at the point in time and space of their state of separateness*.[11]

The child can finally accept realistic boundaries between himself and his mother only if he finds a temporary means of denying them psychically. And his ability to find a means compatible with his own growth and the demands of reality—in other words, one that isn't regressive or hallucinatory—depends on the experiences of being mirrored and of playing, experiences of trust and reciprocity, that he first has with his mother.

---

10. Edith Jacobson, *The Self and the Object World* (New York: International Universities Press, 1964); see especially pp. 62–66. The following statement summarizes the interrelationship of identification and object relations in the growth of the self:

> In fact, the child cannot establish emotional investments in other persons as objects which are different from his own self until he is able to experience his own identity; and since active strivings to acquire likenesses to others are also motivated by the discovery of differences from them, these strivings cannot develop either until the child has become aware of such differences. (p. 63)

11. D. W. Winnicott, "The Location of Cultural Experience," in *Playing and Reality*, pp. 96–97; see also "Transitional Objects and Transitional Phenomena," in the same volume, pp. 1–25.

But even the normal child who has, in the clinical phrase, a "good enough" mother feels considerable anxiety during the next-to-last stage of separation and individuation during the second year of life. His growing awareness of separateness from his mother combines with his increasing mobility, to produce an ambivalence from which he will never, perhaps, be completely free. Previously buoyant and seemingly elated at his first steps away from his mother, he now realizes his smallness and helplessness; he finds that the cost of his new-found mastery is the loss of that magical omnipotence he felt when he didn't see himself as distinct from his mother. Naturally, he wants both to push his mother away and to cling to her; he watches her movements and follows her about, or darts away from her with the expectation of being sought and scooped up in her arms.[12] The "good enough" mother will both adapt to and frustrate her child's exasperating needs; she will be neither intrusive and smothering nor distant and demanding. She will neither belittle her toddler's grandiose aims nor indulge them too far. No one has expressed the ordinary miracle in such intuitive equilibrium of response better than Kierkegaard:

> The loving mother teaches her child to walk alone. She is far enough from him so that she cannot actually support him, but she holds out her arms to him. She imitates his movements, and if he totters, she swiftly bends as if to seize him, so that the child might believe that he is not walking alone. . . . And yet, she does more. Her face beckons like a reward, an encouragement. Thus, the child walks alone with his eyes fixed on his mother's face, *not* on the difficulties in his way. He supports himself by the arms that do not hold him and constantly strives towards the refuge in his mother's embrace, little suspecting *that in the very same moment that he is emphasizing his need of her, he is proving that he can do without her,* because he is walking alone.[13]

12. Mahler *et al.*, pp. 76–108, describe this and other revealing behavior as part of the interesting subphase of separation-individuation, "rapprochement," marked by the child's effort to resist and undo his separateness from the mother as he becomes more aware of it.
13. Quoted in Mahler *et al.*, pp. 72–73, from *Purity of Heart* (1846), by Søren Kierkegaard (New York: Harper and Row, 1938).

In contrast, the mother who conveys her own fears to the child, adopts a critical attitude toward his faltering efforts, or in general infantilizes him by encouraging passivity floods him not just with the terror of the endeavor itself but more importantly with the paralyzing magnitude of his need for her, which he experiences as being engulfed by her. When this happens, separation and individuation are blocked and the child is thrust back into a regressive attempt to reestablish symbiotic union.

At this point the father's role in the child's growth toward identity, as a powerful support against reengulfment of his ego into maternal union, becomes crucial. The child wants both to regain the omnipotence he felt when merged with her and to retain his new autonomy separate from her. The father is untainted by such conflict. Unlike the mother, he needn't be distinguished in the child's mind from a primitive realm both blissful and threatening, but rather is clearly part of the real world of things and people. He becomes significant for the child around the eighteenth month, when the child is experimenting with especially challenging forms of upright-ness, locomotion, and dexterity. At this time, the mother is hardly able to keep up with her child's idealized, all-giving image of her; in contrast, the father is a stable island of exter-nal reality: identifying with him can help the child manage separation more easily.[14]

The child who has a "good enough" mother does learn, by his third year, to negotiate between the poles of his ambiva-lence about separation. He does so in two ways. First, he is able to retain a mental image of his mother when she is absent—an image increasingly distinct from his mental rep-resentation of himself. He remains constant to this maternal image as his primary object of love, and refuses to exchange it for another even when it temporarily fails to gratify him. This capacity for attachment to the mother as an object separate from the self, as opposed to an identification with her that

14. Ernest L. Abelin, "The Role of the Father in the Separation-Individuation Process," in *Separation-Individuation: Essays in Honor of Margaret S. Mahler,* ed. J. B. McDevitt and C. F. Settlage (New York: International Universities Press, 1971), pp. 229–252.

blurs boundaries between the child and her, marks the beginning of a true sense of identity. Second, he is able to unify the good and bad aspects of this maternal image—the satisfaction he feels when it gives him what he wants and the rage or fear he feels when it does not provide or is absent—into one whole representation, without splitting off the bad part and feeling persecuted by it.[15]

Now I turn to those aspects of separation and individuation peculiar to the boy, and will use the masculine pronoun with a sharp sense of sexual difference. The awareness of being a man or a woman—gender identity—coexists with the awareness of being a separate individual. Freud thought that gender identity began to develop only after the onset of the phallic phase, which coincides with the oedipal phase, around the age of four, and that consciousness of gender depended, for both sexes, on discovering the penis.[16] His theory has, of course, undergone much revision: some opposing its phallocentrism; some claiming that a core of body awareness in both girls and boys derived from their own sensory experiences arises during the first year of life; some building on much clinical observation that shows gender awareness before the second year.[17]

But the most important revision for my purposes is based on the simple fact that most children, male or female, in Shakespeare's time, Freud's, or ours, are not only borne but raised by women.[18] And thus arises a crucial difference between the girl's developing sense of identity and the boy's.

15. Edith Jacobson, *The Self and the Object World* (cited in note 10), p. 63.
16. Sigmund Freud, "The Infantile Genital Organization" (1923), *Standard Edition* 19, pp. 139–145.
17. For objections to penis envy as central to female identity, see the useful collection of essays on femininity by Freud and others, paired with critical comment by a variety of authors, *Women and Analysis: Dialogues on Psychoanalytic Views of Femininity*, ed. Jean Strouse (New York: Grossman, 1974); on body awareness, Phyllis Greenacre, "Early Physical Determinants in the Development of the Sense of Identity," *Journal of the American Psychoanalytic Association* 6 (1958): 612–627; on early awareness of gender identity, Mahler *et al.*, pp. 104–106.
18. See Dorothy Dinnerstein, *The Mermaid and the Minotaur: Sexual Arrangements and Human Malaise* (New York: Harper and Row, 1977), and espe-

For though she follows the same sequence of symbiotic union, separation and individuation, identification, and object love as the boy, her femininity arises in relation to a person of the *same* sex, while his masculinity arises in relation to a person of the *opposite* sex. Her femininity is reinforced by her original symbiotic union with her mother and by the identification with her that must precede identity, while his masculinity is threatened by the same union and the same identification. While the boy's sense of *self* begins in union with the feminine, his sense of *masculinity* arises against it.[19] (Though I have distinguished here, for the sake of clarity, between identity and gender identity, between a sense of self and a sense of masculinity or femininity, in much of life—and much of Shakespeare—this distinction is artificial.)

Thus for him the task of separation and individuation carries an added peril, which Robert Stoller states succinctly:

> While it is true the boy's first love object is heterosexual, he must perform a great deed to make this so: he must first separate his identity from hers. Thus the whole process of becoming masculine is at risk in the little boy from the day of birth

cially Nancy Chodorow, *The Reproduction of Mothering: Psychoanalysis and the Sociology of Gender* (Berkeley and Los Angeles: University of California Press, 1979). Both offer searching and provocative critiques of this division of labor within the family. Chodorow's book, published after I had completed my manuscript, provides fresh support for my thesis from an object-relations perspective.

19. Chodorow is particularly helpful in distinguishing the critical tasks of identity formation for boys as opposed to girls. Citing studies of male-dominated societies in which women exclusively care for children in a father-absent setting, she argues that

> masculinity and sexual difference ("oedipal" issues) become intertwined with separation-individuation ("pre-oedipal" issues) almost from the beginning of a boy's life. . . . the early period is sexualized for boys in a way that it is not for girls so that phallic-masculine issues become intertwined with supposedly nongender-differentiated object-relational and ego issues concerning the creation of a sense of separate self. (pp. 106, 107)

Concerning the resolution of the oedipal stage, she states:

> Compared to a girl's love for her father, a boy's oedipal love for his mother, because it is an extension of the intense mother-infant unity, is more overwhelming and threatening for his ego and sense of (masculine) independence. (p. 131)

on; his still-to-be-created masculinity is endangered by the primary, profound, primeval oneness with mother, a blissful experience that serves, buried but active in the core of one's identity, as a focus which, throughout life, can attract one to regress back to that primitive oneness. That is the threat lying latent in masculinity. . . .[20]

As another psychoanalyst puts it, for the boy the critical threat to masculinity is not, as Freud maintains, castration, but en-gulfment by the mother, and his critical task in establishing his masculinity is not an oedipal one but a pre-oedipal one of "dis-identifying" from his mother and "counter-identifying" with his father, interdependent and complementary pro-cesses.[21] According to Freud, the boy's discovery of the dif-ference between his genitals and the girl's is crucial, for it eventually produces castration fear, and leads him to define a woman as a castrated man.[22] But according to the later theory on which I rely, men first know woman as the matrix of all satisfaction, from which they must struggle to differentiate themselves in order to be men.

The polarization of social roles and behavior into mas-culine independence, power, and repression of feeling as opposed to feminine dependence, weakness, and tenderness, and the consequent devaluation of femininity by men (and

20. Robert J. Stoller, "Facts and Fancies: An Examination of Freud's Concept of Bisexuality," in Strouse, *Women and Analysis* (cited in note 17), p. 358.

21. Ralph Greenson, "Dis-Identifying from Mother: Its Special Impor-tance for the Boy," *International Journal of Psycho-analysis* 49 (1968): 370–374.

22. Sigmund Freud, "Some Psychical Consequences of the Anatomical Distinction Between the Sexes" (1925), *Standard Edition* 19, pp. 241–259. Freud argues here and in "Female Sexuality" (1931) that the girl also faces special problems in establishing her femininity; she must give up the wish for a penis, forsake clitoral for vaginal pleasure, and renounce her mother as a primary love object and turn to her father instead. See Chodorow's critique and revision of this theory, especially chapter 7, "Object Relations and the Female Oedipal Configuration," pp. 111–129, in which she argues that "a girl's libidinal turning to her father is not at the expense of, or a substitute for, her attachment to her mother" (p. 127). Thus it is during adolescence, when she has already formed her gender identity as a woman, that she undergoes "a struggle for psychological liberation from her mother" (p. 136), trying to establish a sense of self rather than of gender. For the boy, these issues of self and gender are intermingled in the separation-individuation period of in-fancy. The girl's problems, however, are not my concern here.

women as well) may arise, then, as "a quite nonbiological defensive maneuver against an earlier stage: closeness and primitive identification with mother."[23] A man whose separation from the mother was problematic or incomplete has not fully secured his masculine identity. No matter how much status or power his sex *per se* allows him, he is likely to feel anxious when he is called upon to "be a man" as husband or father. Once again, he finds himself dependent upon a woman to confirm his identity. And so he may reenact, in disguised or displaced forms, the original crisis of his masculine identity, ambivalently seeking forms of merger or separation that echo it.

Shakespeare's interest in masculine identity centers on this adult struggle to achieve a second birth into manhood. Whatever the details of his own experience, he lived as a man in Elizabethan times and knew first hand at least some of the male anxieties and fantasies he depicts. Moreover, he lived in a patriarchal society that exacerbated male anxieties about identity. Though he accepts conventional arguments for patriarchy, perhaps because he sees no preferable alternative, he objects to the extreme polarization of sex roles and the contradiction underlying it. In its outward forms, patriarchy granted near-absolute legal and political powers to the father, particularly powers over women. Yet in unacknowledged ways it conceded to women, who were essential to its continuance, the power to validate men's identities through their obedience and fidelity as wives and daughters. Shakespeare's works reflect and voice a masculine anxiety about the uses of patriarchal power over women, specifically about men's control over women's sexuality, which arises from this disparity between men's social dominance and their peculiar emotional vulnerability to women.

Patriarchal power belongs not so much to men in general as to the father acting as the head of a family. The aristocratic or middle-class family of Shakespeare's day is better described

23. Robert J. Stoller, "The 'Bedrock' of Masculinity and Femininity: Bisexuality," in *Psychoanalysis and Women,* ed. Jean Baker Miller (New York: Penguin, 1973), p. 275.

as a household consisting of parents and children, together with other kin, boarders, and perhaps apprentices and servants.[24] Its authoritarian structure stems from the father's dominance:

> This sixteenth-century aristocratic family was patrilinear, primogenitural, and patriarchal: patrilinear in that it was the male line whose ancestry was traced so diligently by the genealogists and heralds, and in almost all cases via the male line that titles were inherited; primogenitural in that most of the property went to the eldest son, the younger brothers being dispatched into the world with little more than a modest annuity or life interest in a small estate to keep them afloat; and patriarchal in that the husband and father lorded it over his wife and children with the quasi-absolute authority of a despot.[25]

The willingness of women to be married to husbands of their fathers' choice, and to be sexually faithful to their husbands in bearing legitimate male heirs—in both ways serving the continuation of patriarchy—is the invisible heart of the whole structure. In most instances, single men didn't manage estates or head workshops; men who lacked sons extinguished their family lines. Marriage and fatherhood were "the entry to full 'membership' in society."[26]

Moreover, patriarchy as a family structure and a way of defining sex roles was indistinguishable from patriarchy as the basis of all social thinking. All political writers took from Aristotle the analogy between family and state, and all forms of social control were construed in terms of obedience to the king or magistrate as to the father, the head of the family. In treatises on government, commentaries on Scripture, and systems of theology, authority was grounded in the father. Most Elizabethans first encountered patriarchal doctrine in their catechisms, when they were taught that all authorities— masters, teachers, magistrates, and princes—were to be hon-

24. Lawrence Stone, *The Family, Sex, and Marriage in England, 1500–1800* (New York: Harper and Row, 1978), p. 7.
25. Lawrence Stone, *The Crisis of the Aristocracy, 1558–1641*, abridged ed. (New York: Oxford University Press, 1967), p. 271.
26. Peter Laslett, *The World We Have Lost: England Before the Industrial Age*, 2nd ed. (New York: Scribner's, 1971), p. 12.

ored and obeyed like fathers. William Tyndale's *The Obedience of a Christian Man* (1528), John Knox's *The First Blast of the Trumpet against the Monstrous Regiment of Women* (1558), and Sir Thomas Smith's *De Republica Anglorum* (1583) are just three of the many treatises and pamphlets of Shakespeare's day that characterize social order as based on the patriarchal order of the family.[27] Sir Robert Filmer's *Patriarcha* (ca. 1635–1640), intended as a defense of "the natural power of kings," bases its whole argument on the natural power of the father within the family. Reasoning from Scripture with a dogged literalness common in his time, Filmer pictures all human society as "a family, and a family descended from one single male individual, Adam." His authority, Filmer argues, descended through his sons generation by generation to the kings reigning at the present.[28]

Patriarchy, then, was regarded as the natural order of things. But like other kinds of "natural order," it was subject to historical change. Lawrence Stone has recently argued for an increase in the power of the husband and father over his wife and children during the time Shakespeare wrote, making the father "a legalized petty tyrant within the home."[29] Between 1580 and 1640, Stone claims, two different forces converged to heighten paternal power, one political and one

27. Gordon J. Schochet, *Patriarchalism in Political Thought: The Authoritarian Family and Political Speculation and Attitudes Especially in Seventeenth Century England* (New York: Basic Books, 1975), discusses the catechism and reviews patriarchally-based political thought during Shakespeare's lifetime; see especially pp. 37–53.

28. Peter Laslett, "Introduction," in Sir Robert Filmer, *Patriarcha and Other Political Works,* ed. Peter Laslett (Oxford: Basil Blackwell, 1949), p. 27. Filmer lived from 1588 to 1653. His treatise circulated in manuscript during his lifetime, and was only published in 1680. It is hard to say whether it expresses the mainstream of patriarchal ideology or its excess; nonetheless, the patriarchal family that formed his paradigm of society *was* the prevailing family structure.

29. Lawrence Stone, *The Family, Sex, and Marriage* (cited in note 24), p. 7. Stone's argument for the increase in patriarchal power is part of a larger and more controversial argument not relevant to my main point, concerning changes in family structure and affective relations over several centuries. I hold simply that since Shakespeare wrote during a time in which the father's already considerable powers over his family were extended and intensified, he might have been particularly aware of and sensitive to male anxieties concerning the patriarchal role.

religious. As the Tudor-Stuart state consolidated, it eroded ancient baronial loyalty to the family line above the immediate
family, in the effort to replace it by loyalty to the crown. As
part of the same campaign, the state also encouraged obedience to the *paterfamilias* in the home, according to the traditional analogy between state and family, king and father.
James I stated, "Kings are compared to fathers in families: for
a King is truly *parens patriae,* the politic father of his people."[30]
Therefore, the state had a direct interest in reinforcing patriarchy in the home.

Concurrently, Puritan fundamentalism—the literal interpretation of Mosaic law in its original patriarchal context—
reinforced patriarchal elements in Christian doctrine and
practice as well. As the head of the household, the father took
over many of the priest's functions, leading his extended family of dependents in daily prayers, questioning them as to the
state of their souls, giving or withholding his blessing on their
undertakings. Though Protestant divines argued for the
spiritual equality of women, deplored the double standard,
and exalted the married state for both sexes, at the same time
they zealously advocated the subjection of wives to their husbands, on the Scriptural grounds that the husband "beareth
the image of God." Heaven and home were both patriarchal.
The Homily on the State of Matrimony, one of those issued
by the crown to be read in church weekly, quotes and explicates the Pauline admonition,

> Let women be subject to their husbands, as to the Lord; for the
> husband is the head of the woman, as Christ is the head of the
> church.[31]

In effect, a woman's subjection to her husband's will was the
measure of his patriarchal authority and thus of his manliness.

Stone singles out other indications that the father's power
within the home was increasing. Severe physical punishment

30. Quoted from *Political Works of King James I,* ed. C. H. McIlwain
(Cambridge, Mass., 1918), p. 307, in Lawrence Stone, "The Rise of the Nu-
clear Family in Early Modern England," in *The Family in History,* ed. Charles
E. Rosenberg (Philadelphia: University of Pennsylvania Press, 1975), p. 54.

31. "An Homily of the State of Matrimony," *The Two Books of Homilies
Appointed to Be Read in Churches,* ed. John Griffiths (Oxford, 1859), p. 505.

of children by parents and schoolmasters became widespread, its purpose being "to break the will of the child in order to enforce his subjection to his parents' will," mainly in their later choice of his occupation and his wife. This choice was dictated in most cases by the desire to strengthen the estate passed on from father to son. In the course of the sixteenth century, lawyers found a way to break entails (which decreed by law the disposition of the estate), possibly in response to their clients' desires. Without the constraint of entail, the head of the family could threaten or reward his children as he chose, according to the way he sliced up their patrimony. The marks of deference toward parents expected even of adult children were regarded by observers as extreme compared with other countries. They were the routine, visible reminders of patriarchal power: children knelt daily to receive the paternal blessing, full-grown sons doffing their hats and daughters standing patiently to address their parents in the most formal terms of respect.[32]

Though a man coming of age in Shakespeare's day enjoyed enormous prerogative compared to a woman,[33] he also assumed an enormous burden of authority and power that depended on his being an actual or potential father, which in turn depended on his taking a wife. Thus, the ambivalence he had felt as a child toward his mother—his need to define his masculinity in contrast to her femininity, and his complementary fear of reengulfment into an undifferentiated unity with her—was likely to be reawakened in manhood. Ample possibility of "counter-identifying" with his father existed, of course, when he assumed the father's role in his own house-

---

32. Stone, "The Rise of the Nuclear Family," pp. 36–49, especially p. 41.
33. The exclusion of women (with the sole exception of Elizabeth I) from public life in government and the professions follows from the fact that

> a woman's legal right to hold and dispose of her own property was limited to what she could specifically lay claim to in a marriage contract. By marriage, the husband and wife became one person in law— and that person was the husband.

Widows had few rights, either (Stone, The Family, Sex, and Marriage [cited in note 24], p. 195). For some idea of the scope of commercial activity pursued by middle-class women, see Alice Clark, The Working Life of Women in the Seventeenth Century (London: Routledge, 1919).

hold or succeeded to his father's estate and carried on his father's public identity.

It is time to draw together the psychological and the historical strands of my argument. Shakespeare's men face two problems in achieving their manhood. The first arises in so many cultures as to seem universal. Men originally learn their sexual identities by differentiating their masculinity from the femininity of their mothers, but must as adults reunite with women in marriage to fulfill their roles in society. After a profound separation from women, they must enter into a profound union with them. Patriarchy presents a second problem: though it gives men control over women, it also makes them dependent on women indirectly and covertly for the validation of their manhood. Paradoxically, their power over women also makes them vulnerable to women.

This book will discuss how Shakespeare perceived, explored, and sometimes attempted to resolve these problems of masculinity. Each chapter focuses on a particular crisis; most discuss several works centered on it. The successive chapters follow the ages of man: the first deals with adolescence and the last, in large part, with fatherhood and mortality, while the intervening chapters take up the relations between fathers and sons as mediated by lineal succession, and between husbands and wives as defined by marriage. But the book does not proceed chronologically through the canon; rather, sometimes by pairing works from different periods and sometimes by surveying a motif running through many works, it tries to be faithful to Shakespeare's perception, borne out by common and clinical experience, that time and change revive the past, old patterns recurring in new ways. The late tragedies, whose heroes are men in the prime of life —Macbeth, Coriolanus, Othello, Timon, Antony—heighten the tensions between masculine and feminine that emanate from early life, and in many instances portray them as unresolvable. Throughout, I have tried to reconcile the historical facts of sex roles in patriarchal society as reflected in the works, with the psychological motivations, defenses, and conflicts revealed in their action and their poetry.

In the second chapter, I interpret the early narrative poem *Venus and Adonis* as depicting the masculine self in flight from sexual desire that would both challenge and nurture it. The poem's action constitutes an adolescent *rite de passage* in reverse. When Adonis rejects Venus's invitation to love, he refuses entry into manhood, because he perceives Venus as a quasi-maternal figure threatening to devour him. He responds to this threat by retreating into a spurious narcissistic autonomy. Inevitably, this attempt to remain a boy forever fails, and Adonis's death symbolically depicts its result: regression, as Venus's metaphorical "child," the flower sheltered forever in her bosom, to a state of total merger in which he has no separate identity.

The two history play tetralogies are the topic of chapter 3. They take place in a masculine world of war and politics in which identity is defined by kinship relations with other men, to the virtual exclusion of women. Thus the plays illustrate a counter-identification with the father, which takes the form of lineal succession—the passing on of identity from father to son. In the first tetralogy, masculine identity begins as the son's emulation of the father in a feudal context and ends as vengeance in the father's name, which ultimately destroys the family. In the second, Shakespeare envisions a departure from the iron rule of paternal priority, and makes identity formation a reciprocal process between father and son. By reestablishing hereditary succession, Hal assumes his identity and lifts the cloud of guilt from his father.

Chapter 4 explores marriage, the basic institution of patriarchy, as presented in *Romeo and Juliet* and *The Taming of the Shrew*. In tragic and comic modes, these plays present marriage as a passage to manhood. Through the feud in *Romeo and Juliet*, Shakespeare delineates the hold of the patriarchal family on its children, and contrasts two opposing modes of validating manhood: phallic violence on behalf of the father, and sexual union with woman. In *The Taming of the Shrew*, he makes Petruchio a caricature of male violence and male dominance, and the taming action a farce. At the same time, he celebrates marriage as the authentication of Petruchio's manhood by Kate's submission to him. Both plays illustrate how women, handed on from fathers to husbands, mediate male rivalry.

Continuing this examination of marriage, chapter 5 discusses the psychosocial meanings of cuckoldry. Showing how
it arises from a confluence of misogyny, the double standard,
and patriarchal marriage, the chapter first broadly surveys the
cuckoldry motif throughout Shakespeare, and then focuses on
works in which it is central or particularly important. In
Othello, cuckoldry becomes an affair between men, who as
actual or potential cuckolds unite in defensive alliance against
women as betrayers. In *Hamlet,* the obliquely stated fact that
King Hamlet is a cuckold tarnishes the hero's idealized image
of his father and complicates the task of avenging him. In *The
Merry Wives of Windsor,* the cuckold's horns suggest his subjugation to "the savage yoke" of marriage, which mocks virility
by making men vulnerable to betrayal by their wives.

A paradox of sexual identity in *Macbeth* and *Coriolanus*
forms the topic of chapter 6. [The two virile heroes of these
plays are really unfinished men—boys, who fight or murder
because they have been convinced by women that violence
will make them manly. In their tragic careers they recapitulate
the original separation process by forming a negative bond of
hate or envy with a rival who is psychologically either a twin
or an ego ideal, a bond as close and ambivalent as that which
they still maintain with the mother. A corollary confusion in
the sexual identities of these women is also explored. Volumnia and Lady Macbeth, having excised the feelings their cultures associate with women, become half men themselves in
trying to transcend their femininity vicariously through men.
The more the heroes try to surpass or destroy their rivals and
thus prove their masculinity, the greater their fusion with the
willful women who drive them on.

The final chapter sets the masculine quest for selfhood in
the context of the family and the life cycle, charting the passage from being a son to being a father. It discusses five plays
patterned on the separation, reunion, and symbolic rebirth of
family members, taking this action as a reenactment of original separation. In the first two plays, *The Comedy of Errors* and
Twelfth Night, through narcissistic merger with a twin similar
to a mirroring mother, and the confusion and sexual license it
gives rise to, the protagonists fall in love and move away from

their families and into their adult identities. In the last three plays, *Pericles, The Winter's Tale,* and *The Tempest,* the protagonist is a father, and his daughter, like the twin in the earlier plays, lifts him out of his past in his original family; she enables him to accept his fatherhood and his mortality. Pericles and Leontes are restored to their completed nuclear families, but Prospero, though his renunciation of revenge implies a decisive break with his oedipal past, is restored to his dukedom, not his family. *The Tempest* stresses the subordination of female sexuality to male power, not a filial harmony between them. Thus at the end of his career, Shakespeare does not resolve the masculine dilemma of how to reunite with woman after separating from her, but leaves us with a realistic sense of its stubborn continuance.

Shakespearean criticism has usually assumed that the plays present universal experiences equally true for men or for women. To a great extent—perhaps the greatest—they do. But much of their enduring value also lies in how they present specifically masculine experience. Today we are questioning the cultural definitions of sexual identity we have inherited. I believe Shakespeare questioned them too, that he was critically aware of the masculine fantasies and fears that shaped his world, and of how they falsified both men and women. I hope in the following pages to contribute to the growing body of cultural criticism examining sex roles and the institutions behind them, by providing new insights into Shakespeare and historical perspective on how our own culture defines masculinity.

CHAPTER TWO

Self and Eros
in *Venus and Adonis*

"Art thou a woman's son and canst not feel
What 'tis to love, how want of love tormenteth?"
Venus and Adonis, 201–202

When Shakespeare altered the myth of Adonis, making
its hero refuse an invitation from the goddess of love,
he gave his poem an extraordinary pattern of action.[1]
It became a *rite de passage* in reverse. As an archetypal
event in youth, the *rite de passage* marks "the complete
symbolic separation of the male adolescents from the
world of their youth, especially from their close
attachment to their mothers."[2] At the same time, this
separation marks the youth's new sexual and social
identity as a man, whose future love-choices will be
women not his mother. The Adonis of Shakespeare's
poem is caught between the poles of intimacy and
isolation: intimacy with Venus, which constitutes
entry into manhood, and the emotional isolation of
narcissism, which constitutes a denial of growth,
change, and the natural fact of mortality that
underlies them. But Adonis's self-absorption and

1. This chapter appeared in a longer version, "Self and Eros in
Venus and Adonis," in *The Centennial Review* 20 (Fall 1976):
351–371.
2. S. M. Eisenstaedt, "Archetypal Patterns of Youth," in *The
Challenge of Youth*, ed. Erik H. Erikson (Garden City, N. Y.:
Doubleday, 1965), p. 33.

claims of autonomy actually mask an intense need for dependency, a wish to escape the risk and conflict involved in having a separate identity, a wish symbolically fulfilled in his metamorphosis into the flower that Venus treats as her child.

A similar conflict is strongly implied in the first seventeen of Shakespeare's sonnets, possibly written about the same time as *Venus and Adonis*.[3] There the speaker urges the beautiful youth contracted to his own bright eyes to love and procreate, as Venus urges Adonis, and warns him that in his refusal to love he will become "the tomb / Of his self-love." In the *Metamorphoses,* in the sonnets, and in *Venus and Adonis,* narcissism is specifically a crisis of identity which occurs in youth. Ovid's Narcissus and his Shakespearean successors are male adolescents, poised between youth and manhood, forced to confront the emerging imperative of mature sexuality, but reluctant to answer it and define themselves as men by making love to women.

This theme was richly explored in Shakespeare's source, Ovid's *Metamorphoses.* Brilliantly improvising on several Ovidian tales, Shakespeare portrays the conflict between Venus and Adonis as a conflict between eros and death fought within the narcissistic self. The boyish Adonis, whom Venus, the very incarnation of desirable femininity, presents with an enviable chance to prove his manhood, sternly rejects that opportunity, meets death in the boar hunt, and, metamorphosed into a flower, ends up as a child again, sheltered in Venus's bosom. Shakespeare's characterization of Venus and Adonis, and the coherence of the narrative, can best be understood in terms of this dilemma.[4]

3. Michael Goldman's discussion of "the unsounded self, surely the great motif in early Shakespeare" in *Venus and Adonis,* the sonnets, *Lucrece,* and other early works, touches on the kind of narcissism I examine here; see his *Shakespeare and the Energies of Drama* (Princeton: Princeton University Press, 1972), chapter 2, "The Unsounded Self," pp. 12–32.

4. Most critics explain the central conflict and narrative action as illustrating a philosophical or moral theme. T. W. Baldwin, *On the Literary Genetics of Shakespeare's Poems and Sonnets* (Urbana, Ill.: University of Illinois Press, 1950), finds a Platonic argument in the poem in which Love and Beauty, the forces sustaining creation, are menaced by chaos. Kenneth Muir, *"Venus and Adonis:* Comedy or Tragedy?" in his *Shakespeare the Professional and Related Studies* (Totowa, N. J.: Rowman and Littlefield, 1973), sees it as an Ovidian refutation of neo-Platonic and Puritan arguments against the flesh. Exploring

The following interpretation will center on four major questions suggested by the poem. Why does Adonis refuse to love Venus? Why does he choose the boar instead, and what does the boar signify? What does his metamorphosis mean? In answering these questions, I will explore Shakespeare's use of Ovid to portray narcissism as a masculine defense against the fear of woman—woman perceived as an engulfing maternal presence by a youth not fully separated from that presence.

Before I proceed, I want to distinguish between the context in which I use the concept of narcissism and other contexts for

---

the metaphor of the hunt, Don Cameron Allen argues that through it Shakespeare presents a moral lesson against yielding to passion, in "On Venus and Adonis," in Elizabethan and Jacobean Studies Presented to F. P. Wilson, ed. Herbert Davis and Helen Gardner (Oxford: Clarendon Press, 1959), pp. 110–111. Robert P. Miller, "Venus, Adonis, and the Horses," English Literary History 19 (1952): 250–264, calls the poem "a mythological re-enactment of man's fall to sin," but in a later article, "The Myth of Mars' Hot Minion in Venus and Adonis," English Literary History 26 (1959): 470–481, sees the poem in less moralistic terms, closer to mine. Hereward T. Price holds that the imagery embodies the tragic paradox of "Nature with herself at strife," mirroring "the problem of the dissonances that destroy harmony in the moral order of the world," in "The Function of Imagery in Venus and Adonis," Papers of the Michigan Academy of Sciences, Arts and Letters 31 (1945): 275–297. Several critics avoid these overschematized approaches. Norman Rabkin, "Eros and Death," in his Shakespeare and the Common Understanding (New York: Free Press, 1967), pp. 150–162, reads the poem as a myth exploring the neo-Platonic opposition between sensual and spiritual love, and A. C. Hamilton, "Venus and Adonis," Studies in English Literature 1500–1900 1 (1961): 1–15, believes it "an allegory of the myth of creation and the fall." Both are sensitive to the problematical aspects of the poem, as is S. Clark Hulse, "Shakespeare's Myth of Venus and Adonis," PMLA 93 (1978): 95–105, who shows how Shakespeare "holds his conflicting attitudes toward love in an aesthetic balance" by recourse to iconographic techniques. In Elizabethan Erotic Narratives: Irony and Pathos in the Ovidian Poetry of Shakespeare, Marlowe, and Their Contemporaries (New Brunswick, N.J.: Rutgers University Press, 1977), William Keach offers a well-rounded reading of the poem as "a tragic parody of the Platonic doctrine that love is the desire for beauty." Though he does not deal with the poem's psychology, his interpretation coalesces with mine when he argues that "beauty's destruction [is] made inevitable by its own death-seeking efforts to avoid involvement with possessive, threatening sexual love." The few interpretations that do not take a moral or philosophical approach are Rufus Putney, "Amour with Humor," Philological Quarterly 20 (1941): 533–554; J. W. Lever, "Venus and the Second Chance," Shakespeare Survey 15 (1962): 1–8; and most recently, William Sheidley, " 'Unless it be a boar': Love and Wisdom in Shakespeare's Venus and Adonis," Modern Language Quarterly 35 (March 1974): 3–15.

it. In Shakespeare's day, the story of Narcissus was allegorized in accordance with various traditions. For instance, in a surviving medieval interpretation, the fate of its hero illustrated the folly of trusting in riches, beauty, and things of this world.[5] Renaissance mythographers read it variously as an argument "reproving most prodigious lusts"; as a fertility myth in which Adonis is the sun and Venus the earth, their love bringing forth rich fruit despoiled by the boar, which is winter; as a tale illustrating the transience of youth and beauty, or the awesome and many-sided force of love, "comic, sensual, and violent."[6] The common meaning of the term today arises from the idea that Narcissus loved his own beauty; in most dictionaries, narcissism is defined as self-love, excessive admiration of oneself or interest in all that pertains to oneself.[7]

As a psychoanalytic concept, however, narcissism has subtler and more inclusive reference to the effect of self-love on one's relations with others. Freud first used it in 1910, in discussions of homosexuality, characterizing it as the choice of love objects modeled on the self rather than on the mother.[8] Later he differentiated between this sense of the word and "primary narcissism," normal when satisfactions experienced in the body itself are the object of libido.[9] Since Freud, an extensive and complicated controversy over the concept has arisen, involving the serious theoretical questions of when and

5. See Douglas Bush, *Mythology and the Renaissance Tradition in English Poetry*, new rev. ed. (New York: W. W. Norton, 1963), pp. 47–48, and for the Narcissus theme in courtly love poetry, Frederick S. Goldin, *The Mirror of Narcissus in the Courtly Love Lyric* (Ithaca: Cornell University Press, 1967).

6. Hulse (cited in note 4) is especially interesting and persuasive on the multivalent meanings of the myth in Renaissance commentaries and painting; see particularly pp. 95–98.

7. See the *American Heritage Dictionary of the English Language*, *Webster's New World Dictionary of the American Language*, and the *Oxford English Dictionary*.

8. Sigmund Freud, *Three Essays on the Theory of Sexuality*, Standard Edition 7, p. 145n.; *Leonardo da Vinci and a Memory of His Childhood*, Standard Edition 11, p. 50.

9. Sigmund Freud, "On Narcissism: An Introduction," *Standard Edition* 14, pp. 73–107.

how the ego is formed and the role that object relations play in its formation.[10]

Whatever the theory of its etiology, however, a paradox lies at the center of narcissism: the one who seems to love himself does not really have a self and thus is not capable of loving himself or others. The narcissist lacks a coherent, stable, realistic image of himself as distinct from others:

> He has not become a securely independent person—not created a core of himself—and unless he becomes an independent person he cannot himself in turn love. . . . Such separation as the narcissist achieves will remain uncertain and he will always be more than willing to put it off.[11]

His apparent preference for himself over others, his superior attitude or claims of autonomy, are actually defensive attempts to keep this inner deficiency secret, even from his conscious self. They enable him to withdraw into himself, to avoid the risk of opening up to others in the challenge, conflict, and frustration of normal intimacy. According to Michael Balint,

> A truly narcissistic man or woman is in fact a pretense only. They are deeply dependent on their environment, and their narcissism can be preserved only on the condition that their environment is willing or can be forced to look after them.[12]

In such relationships as he does pursue, the narcissist seeks total, unquestioning reassurance and acceptance, and finds ordinary demands from others threatening. I refer to "the narcissist" only for convenience, for narcissism is a component of many neurotic illnesses, as well as a trait of many healthy

10. Some theorists understand narcissism as an adaptation to the stresses of relationships with others, and some regard it as a structural fault in the ego. For the former, see Heinz Kohut, *The Analysis of the Self* and *The Restoration of the Self* (New York: International Universities Press, 1971 and 1977); for the latter, Otto Kernberg, *Borderline Conditions and Pathological Narcissism* (New York: Jason Aronson, 1975).

11. Grace Stuart, *Narcissism: A Psychological Study of Self-Love* (London: George Allen Unwin, 1956), p. 45. This book provides a useful account of narcissism in myth and in some post-Freudian psychoanalytic thought.

12. Michael Balint, *The Basic Fault: Therapeutic Aspects of Aggression* (London: Hogarth, 1958), p. 55.

people.[13] Not only in the character of Adonis, but as a narrative and poetic whole, *Venus and Adonis* reveals its nature.

I. ADONIS

It has long been known that Shakespeare took the narrative outline of his poem from Ovid's tale of Venus and Adonis. But his fidelity to the Ovidian conception of eros as a psychological force, an inescapable imperative that creates and destroys, hurts and delights, has not been adequately recognized. Nor has the significance of his alterations to the source material been noted. He actually created the character of Adonis and the conflict between him and Venus not from the tale of Venus and Adonis, but from the stories of Narcissus and of Salmacis and Hermaphroditus, which are dominated by the figure of the youth who refuses to love a woman and suffers for it.[14] Shakespeare worked in fruitful harmony with

13. I am also indebted to Karl Abenheimer, "On Narcissism," *British Journal of Medical Psychology* 20 (1944): 322–329; Philip Slater, *The Glory of Hera: Greek Mythology and the Greek Family* (Boston: Beacon Press, 1968); and to Miriam Miller, for the understanding of narcissism on which my interpretation of *Venus and Adonis* is based.

14. T. W. Baldwin, *On the Literary Genetics of Shakespeare's Poems and Sonnets* (cited in note 3) has systematically presented evidence for Shakespeare's borrowings from Ovid. His conclusions are the opposite of mine, however, for he argues that Shakespeare was mainly interested in portraying Venus as female wooer, and only used the Narcissus story to heighten that motif. Douglas Bush, *Mythology and the Renaissance Tradition* (cited in note 5), pp. 138–140, briefly outlines Shakespeare's use of Ovid. He notes that Venus as wooer and Adonis as reluctant lover are modeled on Salmacis and Hermaphroditus, and that "the somewhat similar story of Narcissus and Echo may also have been in the poet's mind" (p. 139), but takes the idea no further. More recently, J. D. Jahn, "The Lamb of Lust: The Role of Adonis in Shakespeare's *Venus and Adonis*," *Shakespeare Studies* 6 (1970): 11–26, takes note of parallels between the characterization of Adonis and of Ovid's Narcissus and touches on Adonis's self-love, holding that he is "a male coquette," "afraid to risk physical contact," but focuses on his behavior rather than the motivation for it. W. A. Streitberger, "Ideal Conduct in *Venus and Adonis*," *Shakespeare Quarterly* 26 (1975): 285–291, mentions that Shakespeare used the stories of Salmacis and Hermaphroditus and of Narcissus and Echo from Ovid, but does not develop the point. Hulse (cited in note 4) argues that Ovid's comparison of Adonis to a flower underlies both the meaning and the narrative structure of Shakespeare's poem: "The realization that Adonis is Beauty, which fadeth like the flower, explains his peculiar, unmotivated death. Beauty fades, flowers wither, no matter what. . . . Narratively, he must die to be-

Ovid, taking from him the theme of self in conflict with eros that gives his poem a firm psychological coherence.[15]

The story of Deucalion and Pyrrha in Book I of the *Metamorphoses* is a symbolic statement of Ovid's conception of eros. Sole survivors of the first iniquitous race of men, which Jove destroyed in the flood, this innocent and worshipful couple are advised by the oracle of Themis, goddess of justice,

> Go hille your heads, and let your garments slake,
> And both of you your Graundames bones
>   behind your shoulders cast.
>
> (I, 451–452)[16]

Horrified at this commandment to desecrate the sacred worship of their ancestors, at last they realize that the earth is their mother, that the stones of earth are her bones. When they do as Themis commands, the stones become the men and women of a new human race. The story insists that our primary obligation is to the Great Mother; the goddess of justice hands down only one law, the law of generation, which is conditional on an act of destruction. Born of mothers who must die, nourished by the fruitful earth, we all in turn must love, procreate, and die. It is the only norm Ovid recognizes, and in Shakespeare's poem, it is Venus's most compelling argument for love: "Thou wast begot, to get it is thy duty" (168).

Eros regulates nature, but, paradoxically, eros creates anarchy. Anyone, god or mortal, may be struck with desire for

---

come that flower, and what that flower means is that he must die" (p. 97). In contrast to Hulse, I find Adonis's death psychologically motivated, and read Ovid's story as a narrative version of that motivation.

15. For a rich and sensitive introduction to the unique Ovidian ambivalence of violence, urbanity, and pathos, see William Keach (cited in note 4), chapter 1, "Ovid and 'Ovidian' Poetry," pp. 3–35.

16. This and all subsequent quotations from Ovid's *Metamorphoses* (except one, to be given in Latin) will be given in Golding's translation; Shakespeare probably made use of both his translation and the original Latin version. I have used *Shakespeare's Ovid, Being Arthur Golding's Translation of the Metamorphoses,* ed. W. H. D. Rouse (Carbondale, Ill.: Southern Illinois University Press, 1961), and Ovid, *Metamorphoses,* with an English translation by Frank Justus Miller, 2 vols. (London: William Heinemann, 1936; Cambridge, Mass.: Harvard University Press, 1936).

anyone else, and whatever the cost, even to an innocent victim, that desire must be satisfied. One group of stories emphasizes the inexorable character of sexual passion by treating incest and homosexuality at length. Though Ovid often affects, usually through the persona of a narrator, a decorous horror of such perversions, he no doubt does so only to amuse an audience he assumes to be as sophisticated and unshockable as himself. We share the author's knowing smile rather than the narrator's pious judgment. Ovid as author regards men and women as creatures of nature, and to him nothing in nature is unnatural. Thus he relates with a sympathy born of tolerance the story of Byblis, who loved her brother Caunus and in her crazed passion was turned into a fountain; of Iphis, a girl raised as a boy who loved the bride chosen for her and, in answer to her prayers, was changed into a man; of Adonis's mother Myrrha, who, horrified at her own passion, slept with her father and was changed to an ever-weeping tree. No moral scheme governs the denouements of these stories: a capricious fate either gratifies or denies, legitimates or punishes the forbidden wishes.

Though eros is the only constant Ovid recognizes, he is too much of a realist to believe it reigns unchallenged. As the stories I have mentioned make clear, conflict is inherent in love. The illicit lovers deplore their unnatural desires, but cannot help loving. Lust struggles with love, perversion with normal affection. Similarly, Shakespeare announces "Nature with herself at strife" as a theme in the second stanza of the poem. The idea of a conflict in which neither side is right, in the sense of being more reasonable, more natural, or morally more justifiable, is as basic to Shakespeare's poem as it is to Ovid's. The beauteous war of red and white repeatedly reminds us of this conflict. If in nature roses and lilies have equal claims, do not desire and rejection, blushes and pallor, Venus and Adonis? Because eros itself is potentially destructive as well as creative, the human reaction to it is necessarily ambivalent, compounded of joy and fear, loathing and desire.

Yet in Adonis's rejection of Venus there is something more than natural. He does not merely shun her as a particular woman, for she is a goddess and represents love, no matter

how realistically Shakespeare portrays her. Rather, in re-
pudiating her he repudiates love itself. His reasoned arguments are less convincing than his emotional stance: a cold
and harsh withdrawal from the very idea of sexual union. Im-
pervious to her erotic appeal, he meets all her pleas with with-
ering scorn and sweeping negation. Shakespeare might have
depicted Adonis as experiencing a common adolescent conflict between newly felt desire and fear of sexual inadequacy
due to inexperience. But though Adonis claims he is too
young to love, what he conveys in deeds as well as in words is
that he *will not* love. What lies behind this adamant refusal?

In Ovid's tale of Venus and Adonis, Adonis is characterized merely as a handsome youth. He is Venus's lover, and
no point is made of his attitude toward her. He merely ignores
her fond warning against the boar hunt; there is no conflict
between them about it.[17] In Shakespeare's poem that conflict
is the main issue, and in a striking reversal of roles that parallels the stories of Narcissus and of Hermaphroditus, the hero
is courted by the heroine and strenuously rejects her advances.

Though Shakespeare directly likens Adonis to Narcissus
only once (lines 161–162), Ovid's conception of the cold,
withdrawn, beautiful youth and his self-destructive resistance
to love permeates the poem. The frequent comparison of
Adonis to a flower, for instance, is more than a merely conventional compliment because it refers unconventionally to a
man, and thus recalls Narcissus, who was changed into a
flower. Insofar as Adonis's beauty is fresh, delicate, and richly
hued, the flower metaphor daintily suggests his physical qualities. It furnishes arguments for Venus's urgency ("For flowers that are not gathered in their prime / Rot, and consume
themselves in little time" [131–132]), but also for Adonis's
stubbornness ("Who plucks the bud before one leaf put
forth?" [416]). Poignantly, it hints at an early mortality for the
youth but also foreshadows his transformation to a flower
after death.

Most significantly, the flower image comments on Adonis's attitude toward himself and others. Flowers grow and

17. See *Metamorphoses,* Book X, 585–863 (Golding's translation).

die heedless of human existence; they blush unseen on the desert air, sublimely indifferent to admiration or its absence. Capable of inspiring the tenderest feelings, they themselves feel nothing. Such flowerlike self-regard and self-sufficiency typify a number of Ovidian heroes and heroines: Daphne, Syrinx, the nameless heroines of the tales of Jove in Arcady and of the raven, Arethusa, and most notably, Hermaphroditus and Narcissus. All are young and surpassingly beautiful; all flee sexual encounter, perceiving it as an ultimate danger, and find their escape in metamorphosis.

In some stories, the youth's transformation into a natural object represents the power of art to sublimate sexuality: Daphne becomes the laurel, symbol of poetic achievement; Syrinx, the reed through which Pan pipes his songs. But in other stories, the children of earth who begged to be relieved of their bodies as a way of escaping from sex ironically become images for the imprisonment of human consciousness in mere physicality. Whether or not they themselves feel alien to their new nonhuman forms, Ovid makes us feel their transformations as a pathetic loss of human identity. For instance, the daughter of Coroneus flees Neptune's embraces only to be turned into a raven:

> Then called I out on God and man. But (as it did appeare)
> There was no man so neare at hand that could my crying
> heare.
> A Virgin Goddesse pitied me bicause I was a mayde;
> And at the utter plunge and pinche did send me present ayde.
> I cast mine armes to heaven, mine armes waxit light with
> fethers black,
> I went to cast in hast my garments from my back,
> And all was fethers. In my skinne the rooted fethers stack.
> I was about with violent hand to strike my naked breast,
> But nether had I hand nor breast that naked more did reast.
> I ran, but of my feete as erst remained not the print,
> Me thought I glided on the ground. Anon with sodaine dint,
> I rose and hovered in the Ayre. And from that instant time
> Did wait on Pallas faithfully without offence or crime.
> But what availes all this to me. . . .
>
> (II, 728–741)

The flower-children who unconditionally refuse love are trying to assert their separateness from eros, an impossibility in the Ovidian world. They flee the personal imperatives of their own natures, only to end up immured in the terrifyingly impersonal natural world. Though they retain their minds, without their bodies they no longer have human identities and are cut off forever from love and community.

These Ovidian stories provided Shakespeare with a broad sense of the role of the body and sexuality in the formation of identity. More specifically, he found the major elements of Adonis's character in Ovid's account of Narcissus, which begins,

> For when yeares three times five and one he fully lyved had,
> So that he seemde to stande beetwene the state of man and Lad,
> The hearts of divers trim yong men his beautie gan to move,
> And many a Ladie fresh and faire was taken in his love.
> But in that grace of Natures gift such passing pride did raigne,
> That to be toucht of man or Mayde he wholy did disdaine.
> (III, 437–442)

Rarely does Ovid give the precise age of his characters. Here and in the story of Hermaphroditus he notes that the hero is an adolescent, implying a connection between his age and his rejection of love. Significantly, Narcissus is "betweene the state of man and Lad"; since he is already sexually attractive to others, he can define himself as a man if he wishes to. But he would like to remain a boy forever, and repels attempts at sexual intimacy so strenuously that "no one can touch him," hinting at a fear that sexual contact might damage him physically, as it damages Hermaphroditus, who loses his masculinity as a result of Salmacis's embrace.[18]

Ovid stresses Narcissus's self-protective autonomy by contrasting him with Echo, an image of the person wholly de-

---

18. Philip Slater, *The Glory of Hera: Greek Mythology and the Greek Family* (Boston: Beacon Press, 1968), notes:

> For individuals in whom narcissistic anxieties are severe, the sexual act shatters the body image of both male and female. The boundary between Me and Not-Me crumbles, since the female is penetrated and part of the male disappears inside of another. In addition, psychological boundaries are obliterated through orgasm. The ego dissolves, inundated with impulse, and this may be experienced as a kind of death—as complete submersion in unconsciousness. (p. 101)

pendent on others for the creation and maintenance of a self. Incapable of speaking first, but also unable to remain silent when others talk, she parrots their words but cannot say anything of her own. When Narcissus fails to respond to her ardent wooing, she literally wastes away, becoming only a voice. His stout resistance to bodily contact with her emphasizes his precious dedication to his own body as an object:

> Upon these wordes she left the Wood, and forth she yeedeth
> streit,
> To coll the lovely necke for which she longed has so much.
> He runnes his way, and will not be imbraced of no such.
> And sayth: I first will die ere thou shalt take of me thy plea-
> sure.
>
> (III, 484–487)

Shakespeare's Adonis reveals a similar attitude toward his body in the famous "divedapper" passage, when he offers his lips to Venus, then "winks" and turns away. Venus, of course, is the counterpart of Echo, and though she easily manages to do more than get her arms around Adonis, he stalwartly maintains his emotional distance from her: "Still is he sullen, still he lours and frets," despite her tenderest embraces.

Narcissus's rejection of Echo stands for his rejection of all proffered love, and Ovid portrays his death as resulting directly from this rejection. One of his despairing suitors prays that the youth may actually fall in love with himself so that he too will suffer unrequited love, and Nemesis, goddess of vengeance, answers the prayer. Even though Narcissus realizes that his self-love is destroying him, he is helpless to stop it. Burning with love of his own body, he prays to escape from it in order to possess it; but death brings only the ironic retribution of transformation into the object he most resembled in life, a flower.

Shakespeare, following Ovid's tale of Narcissus, centers his poem on a conflict between the ardent pursuing female and the retreating, rejecting male. In both heroes, the preference for the self is revealed only by pressure to give the self to another. While the exceptional beauty of both heroes leads others to love them, that is not why they love themselves. Their primary need is to defend against sexual involvement in order to protect the fragile inner self. This defense is ironically self-destructive, as Narcissus's death (in Ovid's version, he wastes away gradually, literally consumed by love of himself) and Adonis's in the boar hunt, as I shall show, make clear. Shakespeare suggests that Adonis's fate will resemble Narcissus's, because he is similarly unable to nourish and develop the self by intimacy. In the striking phrase

> Narcissus so himself himself forsook,
> And died to kiss his shadow in the brook
> (III, 161–162)

the repetition of *himself* imitates Narcissus's intense need to fasten on himself as an object to the exclusion of others. To forsake oneself means to lose consciousness of oneself in relation to others and to external reality, as in the expression "to forget oneself"; in the context of the legend, it means to die, symbolizing the utter annihilation of self. When Venus reproaches Adonis with failing a duty to reproduce his kind, she calls his body "a swallowing grave" that buries his posterity, and phrases the idea much as in the earlier passage, commenting, "So in thyself thyself art made away" (763). The second *thyself* means both Adonis's potential offspring and his sense of himself as a human being and specifically as a man, both of which he "makes away" or destroys by rejecting Venus. In Adonis, Shakespeare depicts not only a narcissistic character for whom eros is a threat to the self, but also a boy who regards woman as a threat to his masculinity. But the real threat is internal, and comes from his very urge to defend against eros.

II. VENUS

Adonis would be threatened by any kind of intimacy because it might force him to reveal his secret—that he has no core, nothing to offer from within, only an enormous need to be reassured. It is precisely Venus's kind of love, however, which mirrors this need Adonis would keep hidden.

First, both by virtue of traditional associations invoked in the poem and through Shakespeare's characterization of her,

Venus is something of a mother figure. When she bases her arguments for love on procreation as the law of nature, she is *Venus genetrix*, and she presides over a lush natural ambiance that suggests omnipresent fecundity, especially in the coupling of the horses and the rabbit hunt. Her oft-repeated plea for a kiss is an invitation to physical fusion that suggests a parallel with the infant's relation to the mother at the breast, before he has begun to differentiate between self and others— precisely the stage at which Adonis exists psychologically. In this sense, Venus offers the only kind of relationship with another that Adonis is capable of—one in which he is totally dependent on a nurturing maternal figure who offers him unending oral gratification.

But the kiss is also an act of sexual intimacy, so that to kiss willingly would in a crucial way define Adonis as a man. And Venus is the queen of love, the supreme object of desire for any man, whose manliness is defined by his desire for a woman; thus Venus asks,

> Art thou a woman's son and canst not feel
> What 'tis to love, how want of love tormenteth?
> (201–202)

Furthermore, at certain moments she embodies lust as a blind impersonal force in the Ovidian sense, desire for the opposite sex which overwhelms man or woman and momentarily obliterates self-consciousness. It is this aspect of her that mirrors the narcissist's basic fear: that he who has such a slender sense of self will lose it all if he allows himself to be loved.

All these aspects of Venus—mother, woman, eros itself— are depicted in oral imagery, the imagery of kissing or eating. At the crises of her passion, the two kinds of imagery merge, in the kiss that devours its object. Thus Venus bears a highly ambivalent quality; union with her would both confer manly identity and obliterate the self. The kiss she pleads for evokes conflicting reactions from the reader, in effect putting us in Adonis's place. The oral contact she seeks bears, despite her good intentions and the naturalness of her desire, an aggressive and even murderous quality. As she begins, trying to be gently seductive, she unwittingly conveys an insatiable eagerness:

> Here come and sit, where never serpent hisses,
> And being set, I'll smother thee with kisses.
> And yet not cloy thy lips with loathed satiety,
> But rather famish them amid their plenty. . . .
>   (16–19)

After she "plucks" Adonis from his horse and pushes him to the ground, she "stops his lips" with kisses to keep him from speaking, and when he protests, "what follows more, she murders with a kiss" (42–54).

That kiss is described through the comparison of Venus to an eagle devouring its prey, a simile that both repels and awes the reader:

> Even as an empty eagle, sharp by fast,
> Tires with her beak on feathers, flesh and bone,
> Shaking her wings, devouring all in haste,
> Till either gorge be stuffed or prey be gone:
> Even so she kiss'd his brow, his cheek, his chin,
> And where she ends she doth anew begin.
>   (55–60)

This all-consuming, never-ending kiss becomes rapaciously impersonal. Yet the stanza also suggests an Ovidian perspective on it as a natural urge. We learn in the first line that the eagle is "empty" and "sharp by fast"; therefore, her ferocious appetite gains a certain legitimacy. In the next stanza, when the panting Adonis breathes in Venus's face,

> She feedeth on the steam as on a prey,
> And calls it heavenly moisture, air of grace. . . .
>   (63–64)

The imagery of preying is softened and prettied into a joke; Venus may act like a hungry eagle, but she is forced to content herself with conceits. Finally, in a third stanza, Adonis is no longer being devoured; he is merely "a bird . . . tangled in a net," captured in Venus's loving embrace.

Shakespeare orchestrates this dominant oral motif in various keys. In the following lines, for example, Venus's devouring qualities are balanced by the erotic appeal of her coy pre-occupation with lips:

> "Touch but my lips with those fair lips of thine—
> Though mine be not so fair, yet are they red—
> The kiss shall be thine own as well as mine.
> What see'st thou in the ground? Hold up thy head,
>   Look in mine eyeballs, there thy beauty lies:
>   Then why not lips on lips, since eyes in eyes?"
>   (115–120)

The description of the kiss begins as a touch in the first line, and the fusion it involves is pictured as a gain to Adonis in the third line ("The kiss shall be thine own . . ."). But by the fifth line, Adonis, his image reflected in Venus's eyes, has become part of her, and the last line suggests a blurring of boundaries, an anonymous merging of eyes and lips that echoes the narcissistic fear of losing the self. In the famous passage in which Venus compares her body to a park (229–240), inviting Adonis to "feed where thou wilt," her devouring aspect gives way to her nurturing side. Yet later, when Adonis offers her a goodnight kiss (only in order to make his escape), her voracious drive returns, again in the imagery of an animal devouring its food:

> Now quick desire hath caught the yielding prey,
> And glutton-like she feeds, yet never filleth.
> Her lips are conquerors, his lips obey,
> Paying what ransom the insulter willeth;
>   Whose vulture thought doth pitch the price so high
>   That she will draw his lips' rich treasure dry.
>
> And having felt the sweetness of the spoil,
> With blindfold fury she begins to forage;
> Her face doth reek and smoke, her blood doth boil,
> And careless lust stirs up a desperate courage,
>   Planting oblivion, beating reason back,
>   Forgetting shame's pure blush and honour's wrack.
>   (547–558)

In contrast to the earlier eagle image, these lines convey a cruel lust for conquest, rather than hunger. In the first stanza, gluttony has replaced fast; the eagle is now a vulture, and the kiss a kind of rape in which eros seems heartless fury rather than pleasure. These stanzas, in fact, use imagery strikingly similar to that describing Tarquin when he is about to rape Lucrece; in both situations, lust becomes a tyranny of force, likened both to the animal world and the battlefield.[19] In the first stanza, Venus's lips are "conquerors," and the kisses she takes "ransom," and then (in the first line of the second stanza) "spoil." The dehumanization of Venus is stressed more strongly than that of Adonis, for the reeking, smoking, and boiling of the third line personify in her the turmoil and destruction of battle itself.

This frightening depersonalization strongly recalls Ovid's tale of Hermaphroditus, in which the amorous woman destroys the sexual and thus the human identities of herself and her reluctant lover. Venus's style of wooing is, in general, inspired by that of Salmacis, who first offers herself to Hermaphroditus boldly, but in carefully controlled rhetoric. Later, her desire inflamed by the sight of his naked body, she cries in the language of conquest, "Vicimus, et meus est" ("I win, and he is mine"), as she struggles to clasp him to her. When he resists, she struggles the harder, and her embraces are compared to a snake coiling itself around the eagle that has caught it, to ivy twining itself around tree trunks, and to an octopus's tentacles grasping its prey on every side. When she prays that she and Hermaphroditus may never be separated, the prayer is granted with ironic literalness:

> The members of them mingled were and fastned both
>   together,
> They were not any longer two: but (as it were) a toy
> Of double shape. Ye could not say it was a perfect boy,
> Nor perfect wench; it seemed both and none of both to beene.
>   (IV, 367–370)

Had Hermaphroditus yielded to her, the actual intimacy would have been less injurious than the metamorphosis he suffers. Like Narcissus and Adonis, he is punished for his resistance by being robbed of his individuality, and in his case, of his manhood. While Salmacis obtains the eternal union she desires, he suffers a loss and becomes "but halfe a man." The

19. See *Lucrece,* 421–427, 554–560, in the Arden edition.

defense brings worse results than the fear threatens; the attempt to protect the masculine self ends in the loss of masculinity.

We know Venus as a character only through the demands she makes on Adonis; the overwhelming impression we have of her is of a mouth, pressing insistently on or toward him.[20] Most of the poem's twelve hundred lines are hers, in the form of direct speech; in contrast, Adonis speaks only eighty-eight lines. Venus pours forth a flood of words at Adonis and at us. This volubility contributes to the comic situation, of course; the queen of love can only assuage "love's fire" through words, and her oral aggressiveness is humorously at variance with the conventional female role of silent auditor receiving poetic tribute from a male poet-speaker. Adonis's passive silence also becomes a joke when, after speaking only two curt sentences in the first four hundred lines, he opens up with three stanzas of high-pressured argument against love. Venus remarks in mock surprise, "What, canst thou talk?" (427) and then, true to form, launches into another amorous sermon. The more stubbornly a silent Adonis "winks, and turns his lips another way," the thirstier Venus grows for a taste of those lips. For each character, a fundamental need is at stake. The struggle of the open heart against the closed heart and of the male against the female is imaged in an oral war.

III. THE BOAR AND THE FLOWER

The needs that impel Adonis to reject Venus are now clear, I hope, and we are ready to ask why he should choose to hunt the boar *instead* of loving her. I propose two kinds of explanation for his strange choice: a general one, in which hunting serves as a defense against eros; and a specific one, in which the boar, though it is inimical to all Venus stands for, serves as a projection of Adonis's fears of her.

20. The words *kiss, kiss'd, kisses,* and *kissing* are used more often in *Venus and Adonis* than in any other Shakespearean work. *The Harvard Concordance to Shakespeare,* by Martin Spevack (Cambridge, Mass.: Harvard University Press, 1973), lists thirty-two instances of them, compared with the next highest number of twenty, in *Troilus and Cressida.*

If Shakespeare had intended hunting to be understood as an acceptable alternative to Venus and a viable mode of releasing Adonis's closed self, he might have presented it as an activity suitable to young men of good birth, valuable in teaching skills and forming character, pleasant in the male camaraderie it offers.[21] He might have sketched a scene of hairbreadth 'scapes and heroic challenge in the hunt. But the hunt appears only in terms of its object, the boar—a powerful creature wholly and blindly destructive. We see it only through Venus's jealous and fearful eye. Adonis himself makes no arguments for hunting *per se;* in opposition to Venus, he holds only that he is too young to love, without saying why boar hunting is a better pursuit for one of his age.

In fact, hunting serves Adonis's deepest unconscious need, which is to keep eros out of his life. He acts as though hunting *is* his life; the action begins when Venus accosts him even as he "hies him to the chase," and their encounter consists of her resourceful (but ultimately futile) attempts to stop him from mounting his horse to resume that chase. In his first major speech, Adonis states his opposition to love in a strangely turned phrase that puts the boar in the place of the love object:

> "I know not love," quoth he, "nor will not know it,
> Unless it be a boar, and then I chase it.
> 'Tis much to borrow, and I will not owe it;
> My love to love is love but to disgrace it,
>   For I have heard, it is a life in death,
>   That laughs and weeps, and all but with a breath."
>   (409–414)

The alliterated double negatives of the first line, *not, nor,* and *not,* stress the intensity of his aversion. After its first use, the word *love* is suppressed into the unaccented pronoun *it* and the contraction *'tis* in lines one through three, minimizing its

---

21. See Don Cameron Allen, "On *Venus and Adonis,"* cited in note 4, for a discussion of the traditional distinction between the soft hunt of love and the hard hunt, "the honest training of those who would be heroes." Streitberger (cited in note 14) argues for the importance of Venus's attempt to persuade Adonis to hunt animals other than the boar, and sees Adonis's dedication to hunting as part of his concern with "proper preparation which will lead him to the ideal of noble manhood" (p. 286).

importance. In the fourth line it is the repetition of *love* that
serves a similar purpose—to mock it; here Adonis comes
close to saying he hates love. In the last two lines, he seems to
ridicule love as it appears in Petrarchan poetry, making its
paradoxes and oxymorons sound absurd. But the phrase "life
in death" alludes ironically to the boar hunt as well, since it is
quite easily a fatal sport, and one to which he devotes his life.

Adonis's use of *know* in the first line provides a clue to the
nature of his defense against love. In this context, knowing
suggests carnal knowledge, and the verb hints at a criticism of
the youth on his own grounds. How can he reject something
of which he "knows" nothing? Later he plays on *know* again
in the sense of carnal knowledge: "Before I know myself seek
not to know me" (525), he warns Venus, and again unintentionally raises the question of how he can know what his self
is by isolating it from experiences that help to form it. The
playful suggestion in the second line that he would rather
"know" or love the boar seems a kind of risqué joke at first, a
glance at sodomy. But it carries the serious undertone that he
is deeply alienated from his own kind, determined not to love
even at the expense of being perverse. The boar, as Elizabethans knew, is an ugly creature, and the effect of identifying it with love is to make love not only repulsive but impossible; one could never love a boar. All the poetic devices
employed in this stanza combine to reveal Adonis's unconscious intention: to make love nonexistent by denying its existence for him. Clearly, he is using denial as a defense against
love, and hunting as a defense of his masculine self.

His conscious objection to love elsewhere is that he is too
young for it. He compares himself to an unfinished garment, a
leafless bud, an unbroken colt, an undersized fish, and a green
plum, with an air of narcissistic pride in his very insufficiency
(415–420, 526–528). By arguing that he is too young, he uses
defenselessness as a defense and dares Venus to be so heartless
as to hurt him.

In a similar sense, it is not hunting that Adonis uses as a
defense, but his very self, precarious and incomplete though it
is. This is revealed in the imagery of the following stanzas,

imagery that is so strongly oriented toward outer threat and resistance from an inner stronghold:

> "If love have lent you twenty thousand tongues,
> And every tongue more moving than your own,
> Bewitching like the wanton mermaid's songs,
> Yet from my heart the tempting tune is blown;
>   For know, my heart stands armed in mine ear,
>   And will not let a false sound enter there;
>
> Lest the deceiving harmony should run
> Into the quiet closure of my breast,
> And then my little heart were quite undone,
> In his bedchamber to be barr'd of rest.
>   No, lady, no; my heart longs not to groan,
>   But soundly sleep, while now it sleeps alone.
>   (775–786)

Adonis begins by hyperbolically evoking Venus's amorous rhetoric ("twenty thousand tongues") as an oral threat against which his heart "stands armed," oddly perched outside the body, in the ear. But then in the second stanza, the heart turns out to be not only protector and defender but also the thing being protected that ordinarily dwells inside, in a "quiet closure" like the womb. The contradictions in this metaphor are psychological truths. If "heart" is the inmost self and the capacity for loving, it is Adonis's inmost self that keeps him from loving, in order to protect him from a threatening seductive female (the "wanton mermaid" in the first stanza) who, like the sirens singing to Ulysses, deceptively lures him not to love but to death. The conception of the heart as a static realm of pure rest, dwelling in the solitude and quiet of a bedchamber, is rather preciously emphasized in the repetition of *my* before *heart* and *breast* in both stanzas. That his heart is *his* matters to Adonis, and so long as it is his he can remain in a regressive, unchanging state of utter calm.

Edward Hubler's remarks on "the closed heart" of the young man in the sonnets are highly appropriate to Adonis. Commenting on sonnet 94, he says,

> The closed heart may be poor, but it is at ease. Those men are most content who, though they inspire affection in others,

have no need of it themselves. . . . They are the owners of themselves, whereas throughout Shakespeare's works self-possession in the sense of living without regard for others is intolerable.[22]

Shakespeare's great heroes are men who finally appreciate the supreme value of love and human bonds, no matter how blindly they may have denied it before: Lear, Othello, Macbeth. His great villains are solitary individualists who hate love and also, incidentally, demean women: Iago, Edmund, Richard III. In *Venus and Adonis* Shakespeare is saying that the life apart from eros is death, and that for a man, sexual love of woman is vital to masculinity.

Specifically, the boar reflects Adonis's fear of Venus. Though from the first stanza hunting is opposed to love, curiously it is Venus who describes the boar at some length, who actually sees it, and who supplies our only vision of the boar killing Adonis. Even more curiously, Shakespeare suggests through imagery associated with these two opposed figures a similarity in their meanings for Adonis. The hero's insistence on an absolute boundary between hunting and love actually masks how by chasing the boar, he acts out his deeper feelings toward Venus.

What Venus stresses most in her account of the boar is, not surprisingly, his destructiveness; in particular, his tusks. Those are his mortal weapons, and make him, like Venus, the personification of an oral threat:

> O be advis'd, thou know'st not what it is,
> With javelin's point a churlish swine to gore,
> Whose tushes never sheath'd he whetteth still,
> Like to a mortal butcher, bent to kill.
> (615–618)

The phrase "bent to kill" refers to the placement of his tusks, pointing downward, and his natural habit of foraging by "rooting the mead" with his snout to earth. Driven by instinct, he seeks food and unintentionally "digs sepulchres,"

22. Edward Hubler, *The Sense of Shakespeare's Sonnets* (Princeton: Princeton University Press, 1952), p. 103.

"killing whate'er is in his way." Just as Venus at the height of
her desire turns into an eagle or a vulture blindly seeking the
gratification of natural needs she is denied, and thus seems to
murder what she would enjoy, so does the boar. Both are
capable of a purely natural, unreflective, and impersonal kind
of aggression. The boar personifies the aspect of Venus most
threatening to Adonis: her seemingly insatiable desire. The
more he resists her, the more her ardor increases, and causes
him to resist her all the more. In a supremely revealing speech
delivered as she gazes at the dead Adonis, the fondly grieving
goddess imagines that the boar was as taken with his beauty as
she was. The boar becomes the very image of Venus:

> "If he did see his face, why then I know,
> He thought to kiss him, and hath kill'd him so. . . ."
>
> (1109–1110)

Then why does Adonis prefer the boar to Venus, when both
bear a fatal oral quality in his eyes? We can look at the hunt as
Adonis's attempt to regain mastery over the inner danger of
losing his sense of self by mastering an external representative
of that danger. In short, he projects onto the boar his anxiety
about being devoured by Venus, and attempts to destroy the
boar so that Venus will not destroy him.

The danger emanating from the boar hunt is physical, and
that emanating from Venus is emotional. But insofar as
Adonis is narcissistically oriented toward his own body, the
physical act of love carries a threat of castration, and thus of
losing masculine identity, which is pointedly suggested in the
goddess's vision of the boar emasculating Adonis:

> And nuzzling in his flank, the loving swine
> Sheath'd unaware the tusk in his soft groin.
>
> "Had I been tooth'd like him, I must confess,
> With kissing him I should have kill'd him first. . . ."
>
> (1115–1118)

The irony of his death parallels the irony of narcissism suggested throughout the poem. Adonis flees Venus to avoid becoming a man at the cost of losing his manhood, just as the

44   MAN'S ESTATE

narcissist withdraws into the self at the cost of killing it. The
emasculation of Adonis recalls that of Hermaphroditus in this
respect.

But in a deeper sense, projecting Venus onto the boar allows him to establish a rudimentary, provisional kind of
"negative identity," a total identification with what he is least
supposed to be.[23] Venus argues that a lover "follows the law
of nature" (171) and feels desire like every man of woman
bred (214–216); it would be only normal, she makes us feel,
for the youth to love her. The boar, on the other hand, embodies all that is inimical to life, beauty, and love. Adonis
scornfully rejects the easier, more overtly pleasurable and
normal course for the fatal one. He takes the boar as his object
because, like her, it is blindly destructive in an oral way and
thus most dangerous and most real to him. Yet it also provides a way of defending his inner self against her; it gives him
a substitute self as a hunter, as one who loves a boar instead of
a woman. His readiness to face danger or death in the manly
boar hunt conceals his inability to be more than a boy—
"not-quite-somebody"—in the love hunt. He would rather
pursue death in seeking the boar, than risk the annihilation of
self which loving Venus threatens.

Adonis's metamorphosis is the symbolic resolution of his
struggle against eros. His transformation to a purple (from
Lat. *purpureus,* a variety of red) and white flower represents
the ending of the war of white and red mentioned so often.[24]
Adonis's pale coldness opposes Venus's fiery ardor; in death,
his red blood stains the perfect whiteness of his skin. Now, as
a flower, he can "grow unto himself" as he wanted to in life,
and Venus can possess him totally and forever as she could

23. Erikson, "The Problem of Ego Identity," in his *Identity and the Life
Cycle: Selected Papers* (New York: International Universities Press, 1959),
shows this to be a characteristic defense against identity confusion in adolescents.
    24. Hereward T. Price (cited in note 4) notes that, in Ovid, Adonis is
turned into a red flower, while in Bion's elegy for Adonis, two separate flowers, red and white, spring up after Adonis's death. Shakespeare seems to have
conflated these two sources in making the single flower both red and white,
intending a unification of opposites for which the Tudor rose gave him ample
precedent. See also Hulse (cited in note 4) on the flower, p. 101.

not before. But in order to do so, she must pick the flower—
that is, she must kill him.

Thus in one sense, the ending recapitulates the fear of eros
that dominated Adonis in life. When Venus picks the flower
and puts it in her bosom, sexual fusion is equated with death
and envisioned as her total possession of him, obliterating his
identity. But the terms of union are no longer sexual: they are
infantile. Venus calls Adonis the father of this flower, and puts
the baby in the father's place, at the breast:

> "Here was thy father's bed, here in my breast;
> Thou art the next of blood, and 'tis my right.
> Lo in this hollow cradle take thy rest;
> My throbbing heart shall rock thee day and night:
> There shall not be one minute in an hour
> Wherein I will not kiss my sweet love's flower."
> (1183–1188)

The devouring mother whose oral demands constitute a
threat to Adonis's very identity has now become the nurturant mother on whom he depends as an infant for survival.
Several previous mentions of Adonis as an infant and Venus
as a mother have hinted at this relationship. Taunting him for
his coldness, Venus asks, "Art thou a woman's son? . . ."
(201) and later describes him as "a son that sucked an earthly
mother" (863). When she searches anxiously for him in the
hunt, she is compared to "a milch doe, whose swelling dugs
do ache, / Hasting to feed her fawn" (874–875). In the stanza
quoted above, the fierce oral qualities of Venus's desire are
transmuted to an omnipotent maternal tenderness that
nevertheless carries disturbing overtones of Adonis's anxieties
about sexual fusion: "It is as good / To wither in my breast as
in his blood," says Venus to the flower. Here Shakespeare
suggests that this resolution of Adonis's dilemma is but
another kind of death, parallel to the murder of the self
through narcissistic withdrawal. Venus's apostrophe to the
flower concludes with the image that dominates the poem, a
kiss—the kind of perpetual oral gratification she sought in the
poem. No longer able to deny her, Adonis is now but a
gratifying object, lacking mind and will.

The metamorphosis, however, can just as fittingly be seen as the fulfillment of his deepest narcissistic wish: to regress to the state in which he has no separate identity—nothing to fight for and nothing to lose. Paradoxically, though in this state he is wholly dependent on Venus, he also dominates her totally; he is always with her and she kisses him every minute. The metamorphosis is undeniably tender and moving: it appeals to a desire present to some degree in all of us. But it also implies the desperation underlying the narcissist's dominance. Adonis has finally allowed Venus to get close to him, on the only terms he can tolerate: her total subservience to his need for constant reassurance.

Thus the poem's ending is as ambivalent as any narcissist or any boy who fears woman sexually but desires her nurturance could wish. Venus loses her lover to the boar, but wins symbolic possession of him as a flower. Adonis successfully fights off Venus's sexual demands, but surrenders to her all-embracing love after death. In his total passivity, he dominates Venus, but she also dominates him. *Venus and Adonis* has long been seen as a young man's poem for relatively superficial reasons: its erotic subject matter and sensuous playfulness. But Shakespeare deserves more credit than he has been given for his understanding of youth's deeper conflicts, of how eros shapes the growing masculine self.

CHAPTER THREE

"The Shadow of the Male": Masculine Identity in the History Plays

Thy mother's son! Like enough, and thy
father's shadow. So the son of the female is the
shadow of the male; it is often so, indeed—but
much of the father's substance!
2 Henry IV, 3.2.128–130

T he patriarchal world of Shakespeare's history plays is
emphatically masculine. Its few women are relatively
insignificant, and a man's identity is determined by
his relationship to his father, son, or brother. The two
tetralogies are a continuous meditation on the role of
the father in a man's self-definition. In *Venus and
Adonis*, the maternal image dominated the separation
crisis with which that self-definition began. In these
plays, it is the father from whom men strive to
separate themselves or with whom they merge.

The shift from mother to father can be explained
both in psychoanalytic and in historical terms. In
Freud's developmental scheme, the father looms
mainly as the castrating forbidder of the oedipal
phase. But Mahler and others posit an earlier, more
supportive role for him. The child's awareness of the
father, they hold, begins at about the same time
(eighteen months of age) he becomes decisively
conscious that he and his mother are distinct entities.
Concurrently, the child learns to walk, and if he is a
boy, discovers he has a penis.[1] These several
discoveries—of his separateness from his mother, the
existence of his father, his possession of a penis, and

---

1. See *The Psychological Birth of the Human Infant: Symbiosis
and Individuation*, by Margaret S. Mahler, Fred Pine, and Anni
Bergman (New York: Basic Books, 1975), on the third subphase
of separation individuation, especially pp. 91, 102–106.

his ability to stand upright and move freely—coincide, with important ramifications. Associating phallic consciousness with upright mobility, the boy is strongly motivated to turn away from his mother and toward his father. Furthermore, he feels profoundly ambivalent toward his mother, because he wants both to regress into symbiotic union with her and to move away from her into realistic interaction with the world. His father, associated with this newly perceived world of objects to be manipulated, places to be explored, and people to know, can help the child resist reengulfment with the mother.[2] In the history plays, the intensity of the son's identification with the father measures the strength of the pull toward such reengulfment, and the son's difficulty in separating from the mother.

In historical terms, Shakespeare makes late medieval society a mirror of his own by stressing its obsession with paternal authority and power. He shows families destroying themselves, in the first tetralogy, by their rigid insistence on paternal priority; in the second, he shows a dynasty growing to power by creatively molding that principle to personal need. Shakespeare uses history to test the lineal principle of patriarchy—that the son inherits his identity (the name and role by which he is known in society, and his inner sense of self) from his father. What Roland Barthes says of the father in Racine is also true of the father in the history plays:

> . . . his being is his anteriority; what comes after him is descended from him, ineluctably committed to a problematics of loyalty. The Father is the past . . . he is a primordial, irreversible fact: what has been *is*, that is the code of Racinian time. . . . Thus Blood is literally a law, which means a bond and a legality. The only movement permitted to the son is to break, not to detach himself.[3]

2. See Ernest L. Abelin, "The Role of the Father in the Separation-Individuation Process," in *Separation-Individuation: Essays in Honor of Margaret S. Mahler,* ed. J. B. McDevitt and C. F. Settlage (New York: International Universities Press, 1971), pp. 229–252.

3. Roland Barthes, *On Racine,* tr. Richard Howard (New York: Hill and Wang, 1964), pp. 37–38. Sir Robert Filmer's *Patriarcha* (in *Patriarcha and Other Political Works,* ed. Peter Laslett [Oxford: Basil Blackwell, 1949]) in effect translates Barthes's Racinian paradigm into a comprehensive justification of the father's absolute and eternal supremacy as the source of all social order.

As historical event and psychological experience, the history plays present the problematics of loyalty to the father. The first tetralogy, the three parts of *Henry VI* and *Richard III*, traces the decline of the father-son bond, from the son's emulation of his father in a feudal context, then to the son as his father's avenger, and finally to the breakdown of all filial bonds in *Richard III*. The second tetralogy, *Richard II*, the two parts of *Henry IV*, and *Henry V*, begins with the civil havoc caused when Richard fails to respect the fathers, flaunting the "fair sequence and succession" governing both Bolingbroke's inheritance and his own right to rule. In the dramatic *bildungsroman* of the next three plays, Shakespeare recasts the traditional notion behind masculine identity in the first tetralogy, that the son's identity is the imprint of the father's, in two ways. First, he gives Hal the chance to rebel against his inherited identity, but the will to check that rebellion before it threatens lineal succession. Second, he portrays identity not as a vertical transmission downward from father to son, but as a horizontal process in which Henry and Hal reaffirm their political identities reciprocally.[4]

In both sets of plays, the means of masculine self-definition is aggression, in the French campaigns or the English civil wars—aggression in defense of fathers or in emulation of fathers or on behalf of the king as the national father. The

He holds that all men are subjected to their fathers because they were created after them in time, and that their subjection even as adults ends only when they themselves become fathers and, at the will of the king as supreme father, transfer their allegiance to him. (See note 28, chapter 1.)

4. I am of course indebted to those critics who have written inclusively on the history plays as a genre—their literary and dramatic origins, their relation to the historical thinking of Shakespeare's times, and their artistry, especially E. M. W. Tillyard, *Shakespeare's History Plays* (London: Chatto and Windus, 1944); Irving Ribner, *The English History Play in the Age of Shakespeare* (Princeton: Princeton University Press, 1957); M. M. Reese, *The Cease of Majesty: A Study of Shakespeare's History Plays* (London: Edward Arnold, 1961). The only critics who have specifically addressed father-son relationships in the history plays are Ronald S. Berman, "Fathers and Sons in the Henry VI Plays," *Shakespeare Quarterly* 13 (1962): 487–497; Robert B. Pierce, *Shakespeare's History Plays: The Family and the State* (Columbus, Ohio: Ohio State University Press, 1971); and Edward I. Berry, *Patterns of Decay: Shakespeare's Early Histories* (Charlottesville, Va.: University of Virginia Press, 1975), chapter 3, "*3 Henry VI*: Kinship."

father's role is to maintain, mostly by martial valor in the first tetralogy, mostly by wise government in the second, the inheritance of family honor left to him by his father, and to pass it on to his son, who is expected to follow his father's example and find a ready-made identity in it. So long as aggression is mediated into martial valor by loyalty to the king, fathers can successfully pass on their identities to their sons, though not without certain difficulties.

One problem is the perennial conflict between the father's "anteriority," as Barthes calls it, and the son's individuality. A son was expected to emulate his father, in the sense of following his example and carrying on what he had begun. But in Shakespeare, emulation in this sense (the first meaning of the word listed by the OED) almost always shades into ambitious rivalry for power or honors (the second meaning), which is frequently contaminated by envy or "the grudging dislike of those who are superior" (the third).[5] In these plays, the political and social structure rests on the expectation that the sons will emulate their fathers in the first sense, by following the paternal precedent. But this inevitably leads, in the heat of competition, to fratricidal rivalry that cannot be contained by that precedent. The first tetralogy is significantly framed by the outstanding and contrasting characters of Talbot, who receives the selfless loyalty of his son, and Richard III, the unscrupulous younger son who exterminates his family to get the crown his father sought in vain. Freud sums up the ambivalence inherent in emulating the father thus: "It seems as though the essence of success were to have gotten farther than

---

5. See particularly *Troilus and Cressida,* which contains the most instances (eight) of emulation and its variants, e.g., Ulysses' advice to Achilles:

> Take the instant way,
> For honor travels in a strait so narrow,
> Where one but goes abreast. Keep then the path,
> For emulation hath a thousand sons
> That one by one pursue.
>
> (3.3.155–157)

Particularly in this play, but throughout Shakespeare, emulation is not the disinterested pursuit of excellence for its own sake, but competition against others for first place, which only one can occupy.

one's father, and as though to excel one's father were forbidden."[6]

Another problem of masculine self-definition in the Henry VI plays is created by the particular historical circumstance of Henry's birth and character. He never comes close to emulating his father; he never attains the paternal authority he needs to keep order and inspire loyalty. And without a strong father to control them, the sons of England collectively fall into the second kind of emulation, ambitious rivalry, which David Riggs calls "the chaos that ensues when the weakling son succeeds the all-conquering father."[7] A plangent note of longing for the lost father, Henry V, resonates throughout these plays. *1 Henry VI* opens with his funeral, and recollections of his glorious reign recur in all three plays. To control his squabbling nobles, instead of relying on his own sovereignty, Henry VI frequently evokes the memory of his father and the warriors united under him who won France:

> O, think upon the conquest of my father,
> My tender years, and let us not forgo
> That for a trifle that was bought with blood!
> (*1 Henry VI*, 4.1.148–150)

He defers to his surrogate fathers—Gloucester, Bedford, Winchester—but they are already elbowing each other for the power that should be his. In the terms of masculinity that prevail in his world, he never reaches full manhood or assumes rule firmly; he remains effeminate and typically weeps, prays, or entreats rather than commands. One of his characteristic responses is to discern the hand of God in events when

6. Sigmund Freud, "A Disturbance of Memory on the Acropolis," *Standard Edition* 22, p. 247.

7. In *Shakespeare's Heroical Histories* (Cambridge, Mass.: Harvard University Press, 1971), an excellent study of humanistic conceptions of history and dramatic conventions of heroism influencing Shakespeare's predecessors and Shakespeare himself, David Riggs remarks:

> These plays keep saying that the received ideals of heroic greatness may be admirable in themselves, but they invariably decay, engender destructive violence and deadly rivalries, and in the process, make chaos out of history . . . because the notions of "honor" that regulate the heroic life can never be securely realized within any stable historical form of national life. (p. 99)

he should be watching out for the wiles of men; for example, he piously accepts the miracle at St. Albans that Gloucester then exposes as fraud (2 *Henry VI*, 2.1.82–84). Passively venerating God the father, he fails to emulate his own father, in the sense of following his example and governing actively.

Talbot is the tetralogy's great exemplar of chivalric masculinity based on devotion to the father. A fiercely valiant warrior fiercely loyal to his sovereign, he rests his identity on his reputation for courage, but it is not his personally so much as it is a family possession and national asset; Shakespeare stresses, especially in the scene with the Countess of Auvergne (2.3), that Talbot's "substance" is England. When Talbot lays his numerous honors at the king's feet (in 3.4), what might have seemed heroic self-assertion becomes submission to the father. He and his fellow warriors fight to keep France because their "great progenitors" conquered it before them. Talbot's final battle and death (4.5, 6, 7) constitute the climax of the play, a last look at the nobly flawed ideal of chivalric masculinity based on identification with the father, an ideal no longer viable in this twilight of feudalism.[8]

Talbot and his son John are trapped and outnumbered, fighting for their lives. The issue they debate, reiterated in two successive scenes, is whether John should stay to face certain death with his father, or "fly" to seek his own safety and possible rescue for his father. If he leaves, John will survive to carry on the family name in his sons, but forfeit its essence: an unbroken reputation for courage handed on from father to son. On the other hand, if he stays to defend his father, he will surely die, and though the name of Talbot will remain unsullied, the line will literally die out—and of course, name and line are inseparable. Talbot urges his son to leave, but John passionately pleads to stay:

> Then talk no more of flight, it is no boot;
> If son to Talbot, die at Talbot's foot.
> (4.6.52–53)

---

8. Riggs's discussion of the Talbot incident perceptively illustrates the decline of chivalry with special reference to Talbot as representing a humanistic ideal of heroic virtue, and supports my reading of Talbot as exemplar of masculinity. Edward I. Berry (cited above, note 4) sees Talbot as the spokesman for the sacramental and ceremonious view of life central to feudalism, and as

There seems to be no way for John to keep his identity and live; identity as repetition is death. Surprisingly, he does not die as a consequence of staying to defend his father; when his father is safe, he rushes back into battle for no reason and is slaughtered.

Is John trying to imitate his father's courage, or to excel it? Or, in Barthes's terms, is he trying to "break" from his father's anteriority? The very ambiguity of the action perhaps expresses his ambivalence as a son. Significantly, his reckless dash takes place after he has saved his father; had it been successful, it would have redounded to his glory alone. Talbot's two references to his son as Icarus interpret his action as "pride" and his death as punishment for it:

> Then follow thou thy desperate sire of Crete,
> Thou Icarus; thy life to me is sweet:
> If thou wilt fight, fight by thy father's side,
> And, commendable prov'd, let's die in pride.
> (4.6.54–57)

> Dizzy-ey'd fury and great rage of heart
> Suddenly made him from my side to start,
> Into the clust'ring battle of the French;
> And in that sea of blood my son did drench
> His ever-mounting spirit; and there died
> My Icarus, my blossom, in his pride.
> (4.7.11–16)

In Ovid's *Metamorphoses,* the story of Icarus strongly resembles two similar cautionary tales, that of Phaeton and Apollo and that of Daedalus's nephew, who tries to surpass his uncle's work. The point of all three stories is that the son should not attempt to excel his father in striving to be worthy of him.[9] John at first identifies himself with his father, saying,

---

the casualty of feudalism's decline (chapter 1, "*1 Henry VI*: Chivalry and Ceremony," pp. 1–28).

9. See *Shakespeare's Ovid, Being Arthur Golding's Translation of the Metamorphoses,* ed. W. H. D. Rouse (Carbondale, Ill.: Southern Illinois University Press, 1961). In Golding's translation, Daedalus warns his son, "But ever have an eie / To keepe the race that I doe keepe, and I will guide thee right" (VIII, 279–280); when his nephew precociously outstrips him by inventing the saw and the drawing compass, he hurls him from a tower. But Pallas saves the boy by turning him into a partridge—significantly, though, "mounteth not this Bird aloft ne seemes to have a will / To build hir nests in tops of trees

"Stay, go, do what you will, the like do I" (4.5.50), but then like Icarus he attempts to emulate his father in the sense of rivaling him, and like Icarus crashes to earth because he flies too high. In Barthes's terms, any attempt to detach himself from his identification with his father and seek a separate identity is doomed.

A powerful image countervails the Icarus emblem in these scenes, however. Father and son are merged, verbally and visually onstage, in the perfect parity of death:

> Come, side by side together live and die;
> And soul with soul from France to heaven fly.
>
> (4.5.55–56)

> Come, come and lay him in his father's arms;
> My spirit can no longer bear these harms.
> Soldiers, adieu! I have what I would have
> Now my old arms are young John Talbot's grave.
>
> *Dies.*
>
> (4.7.29–32)

Shakespeare uses verse to stress the tie between father and son; their two debates on whether John should stay or fly and Talbot's elegy to him are entirely in couplets, unlike any other scenes in the play. John Talbot does not succeed his father and thereby achieve his own separate identity; rather, he remains identified with his father in death. This kind of same-sex warrior bonding recurs in all the history plays, indicating a strong regressive pull into an undifferentiated unity resembling the symbiotic union of mother and child in early infancy.[10] The

---

among the boughes on hie / But flecketh nere the ground . . ." (VIII, 338–340). Shakespeare's conception of the tension between the father's authority and precedence and the son's desire to break away from them in the Talbot incident was surely influenced by these tales. The tale of Phaeton puts the issue much more strongly, for Phaeton, provoked by taunts that Apollo isn't really his father, seeks out the sun god and demands "Some signe apparant . . . whereby I may be knowne thy Sonne" (II, 50). That sign is the privilege of driving the horses of the sun, and when Phaeton proves unfit for the task, the rampaging horses nearly destroy the earth and create chaos again, as do the civil wars under Henry VI's inept rule. The Phaeton image crops up in similar contexts of paternal domination and filial disobedience in *Two Gentlemen of Verona*, 1.3.78–79 and 3.1.153–156.

10. See my discussion of this symbiotic union in chapter 1.

son's difficult task is to mold his identity on his father's without threatening his father's superiority, and when the risks are too great, he recoils into merger without ever gaining autonomy.

No other relationship between men or between men and women in the tetralogy is so securely tied by bonds of love and duty as this one, however confining they may be. Liaisons with women are invariably disastrous because they subvert or destroy more valued alliances between men. In Part 1, as David Bevington has shown, all the female characters—Joan of Aire, the Countess of Auvergne, and Margaret of Anjou—seek mastery over men and all have some access to supernatural power.[11] Men are not depicted as drawn naturally to women; they must be enchanted or hoodwinked into an attachment. (In Part 2, Gloucester's Duchess Eleanor consorts with witches to gain the throne; only Lady Elizabeth Grey in Part 3 has no associations with the demonic, but nonetheless, Edward's marriage with her cracks open the Yorkist alliance.) As virgin prophetess, mannish amazon, and seductive courtesan, Joan is a composite portrait of the ways women are dangerous to men.[12] She emasculates the French in two ways: by usurping the masculine role of warrior and by using her sexual appeal to dominate them. Her English opposite is Talbot, defined by his loyalty to the fathers and his total identification with a masculine "substance," and this contrast is made explicit when she denies her own father—a form of suicide in Talbot's world—in a vain attempt to save herself from being burned. In general, the English are manly

11. David M. Bevington, "The Domineering Female in *1 Henry VI*," *Shakespeare Studies* 2 (1966): 51–59. He appears to accept the traditional categories of male and female roles at face value, whereas I see them as projections of male anxieties, consciously presented as such by Shakespeare.

12. Leslie Fiedler, *The Stranger in Shakespeare* (New York: Stein and Day, 1972), argues that the women of the first tetralogy are "antiwomen, subverters of the role assigned to them by men who seek to naturalize their strangeness in a patriarchal world" (p. 74). He holds, however, that Shakespeare shares the misogyny of his characters; I see Shakespeare, rather, as criticizing a patriarchal world that bases the social order and the masculine identity on a destructively narrow and brittle foundation of identification with the father to the exclusion or repression of identification with the mother.

when they band together as men, and the French are emasculated by their association with women.

Part 2 begins with the reading of Henry VI's marriage contract with Margaret of Anjou, a league called "shameful" not
merely because it entails the loss of French territory, but because it violates what is felt to be a perpetual contract to keep
what Henry V, the model father-king, once won:

> And shall these labours and these honours die?
> Shall Henry's conquest, Bedford's vigilance,
> Your deeds of war, and all our counsel die?
> O peers of England, shameful is this league,
> Fatal this marriage, cancelling your fame,
> Blotting your names from books of memory,
> Razing the characters of your renown,
> Defacing monuments of conquer'd France,
> Undoing all, as all had never been!
>
> (2 Henry VI, 1.1.95–103)

"Honours," "fame," "names," and "renown" make up the
collective identity of England's men, an identity welded to the
principle of succession. Also implicated in the principle of
succession is the idea of virility, the loss of French territory
indicating the loss of virility, for the English are not men if
they cannot hold on to what their fathers have won. Jack Cade
hits a tender nerve when he taunts Lord Say and his fellows
with the loss of Maine, which "hath gelded the common-
wealth and made it an eunuch" (2 Henry VI, 4.2.157–159).

Henry VI fails to emulate Henry V in virility, valor, or
leadership, and his failure is significantly expressed in an echo
of the Icarus emblem—the Phaeton imagery given to Clifford
at the height of the civil war:

> O Phoebus, hadst thou never given consent
> That Phaeton should check thy fiery steeds,
> Thy burning car never had scorched the earth.
>
> (3 Henry VI, 2.6.11–13)

The resemblance is not exact—unlike Phaeton, Henry did not
seek his father's power; rather, it was thrust upon him—but
the point is clear enough. Each is a son unfit to succeed his
father, to manage in his place. The image also points ahead to

Richard II, who comes "down, down, like glist'ring Phaeton" from the kingly height he cannot sustain.

As the rival houses of York and Lancaster fall to scrabbling for the crown, what comes to replace martial valor or honor as paternal inheritance and identity in Henry's realm is the vendetta. Nominally, it is based on the same principle as paternal succession: sons are bound to avenge their fathers (and fathers their sons). Actually, it amounts to a war of all against all, fueled by personal ambition or hatred, and finally of Richard III alone against all. The fortunes of the York family, Richard Plantagenet and his three sons, best illustrate this decline from paternally defined identity to monstrous individualism.

In the famous Temple Garden scene of Part 1 (2.4), at which the hostilities between York and Lancaster begin, Somerset insults Richard by recalling that his father was executed as a traitor under Henry IV. "His trespass yet lives guilty in thy blood," he charges; the father's crimes, as well as his honors, are passed on to the son. Warwick defends Richard and argues that his proper status be restored legally, and the blot on his nobility be wiped off, "in the next Parliament." But when the dying Mortimer delivers the first of several increasingly tedious genealogical arguments for the Yorkist right to the throne over the Lancastrian (2.5), Richard's claim escalates. As Richard's uncle, dying without issue, Mortimer makes Richard his heir—heir to the thwarted ambition built up during his long years of imprisonment under the Lancasters. Thus when Henry formally restores Richard not only to his father's honors and titles, termed his father's "blood," but to "the whole inheritance . . . that doth belong to the house of York" (3.1), making him Duke of York, he unwittingly fans the flames of his newly "inherited" ambition.

The rest of the tetralogy traces the rise and fall of Richard, who takes center stage as villain in Part 2, announcing his plan to gain "the golden circuit." As a descendant nearer to Edward III than Henry is, he has the right to succeed to the crown, but he uses it only as a legal pretext. Its legality is belied by the "fell tempest" he is determined to raise, using Jack Cade's resemblance to Mortimer as a way of testing popular acceptance of the Yorkist claim. Thus succession becomes rebellion, and rebellion a parody of succession and the reverence for fathers on which it is based. Mouthing his spurious descent from honorable houses, Cade ignites smoldering class resentment and panders to the infantile appetites of the mob. In the reign he envisions, "All the realm shall be in common," yet he will be king:

> . . . all shall eat and drink on my score, and I will apparel them all in one livery, that they may agree like brothers, and worship me their lord.
>
> (4.2.70–72)

When he takes possession of London, he commands that the pissing-conduit run claret wine, and declares "my mouth shall be the parliament of England." His comic confusion of omnipotence and bounty, of tyranny and universal oral gratification, bespeaks the breakdown of all order based on the father, on paternal authority and paternal succession, and regression to an impossible fantasy of personal grandeur and endless maternal provision. Fittingly, the starving Cade meets his end in Iden's garden, a symbol of fertility based on paternal order, at the hands of Iden, the only son in all the history plays who truly and merely succeeds his father:

> This small inheritance my father left me
> Contenteth me, and worth a monarchy.
> I seek not to wax great by others' waning,
> Or gather wealth I care not with what envy.
>
> (4.10.18–21)

When war between York and Lancaster finally breaks out, and Richard kills Clifford in battle, the basis of masculine identity undergoes another crucial shift: the paternal inheritance becomes a license to kill. In Young Clifford's vow to avenge his father, which justifies and sets the tone for the rigidly schematic series of father-son murders to follow, lineal succession becomes identified with vengeance and justifies slaughter:

My heart is turned to stone: and while 'tis mine
It shall be stony. York not our old men spares;
No more will I their babes: . . .
. . . .
Meet I an infant of the house of York,
Into as many gobbets will I cut it
As wild Medea young Absyrtus did:
In cruelty will I seek out my fame.

(5.2.50–52, 56–59)

Exiting with his dead father on his back and alluding to
Aeneas carrying Anchises from Troy, Young Clifford's an-
cestral piety travesties Virgil; reverence for the father now
sanctions not order but anarchy.

In Part 3, hereditary, lineal succession as the basic principle
of political order is, from the first moments of the play,
hopelessly compromised.[13] Both sides base their claims to the
throne on it, Henry even going so far as to cloak his grand-
father's seizure of the throne in terms of succession:

Suppose by right and equity thou be king,
Think'st thou that I will leave my kingly throne,
Wherein my grandsire and my father sat?

(1.1.127–129)

The truth is, of course, that though Richard of York may invoke the purer hereditary claim, he does so only as a pretext
to conceal his ruthless ambition. And Henry's title to the
throne is equally weak, for though he got it from his father,
that father's father got it by usurpation. Groping for a way to
invoke lineal succession as the basis for his rule, he then argues

13. Gertrude Catherine Reese, "The Question of Succession in Elizabethan Drama," *University of Texas Studies in English* 22 (1942): 59–85, shows
that treatment of succession in the drama was complicated by Mary Queen
of Scots and by Elizabeth's lack of an heir. Until Mary was executed (in 1587),
discussion of hereditary right to the succession, as opposed to a succession
settled by law, was inhibited by Catholic support of Mary's claim. Shakespeare, writing when Mary had ceased to be a threat, was free to explore the
ins and outs of the various criteria of succession: hereditary right, legal right,
right by possession, and right by will. Reese's conclusions support my argument: "Shakespeare's plays emphasize what was true of the history of the period; although hereditary right was not the only criterion for possession of a
Crown, the principle was so strongly embedded in the minds of the people
that adherence to it was the safest course" (p. 82).

the legal fiction that Richard II adopted Bolingbroke as his
heir (139–144). But it is Henry's most zealous defender who
voices the only principle of succession that actually does
motivate political action:

> King Henry, be thy title right or wrong,
> Lord Clifford vows to fight in thy defence:
> May that ground gape and swallow me alive,
> Where I shall kneel to him that slew my father!
> (1.1.163–166)

Finally, when the Yorkists show their force, all legal argument becomes superfluous, and the king who argued for succession resigns it, lacking the moral or personal force to uphold it. He hands it over to Richard of York, betraying his
son's birthright and in effect thus denying his own manhood
as well as his son's. Everyone perceives this act as profoundly
unnatural. Clifford boldly rebukes him for violating a principle as fundamental as the law of kind that even beasts follow:

> Unreasonable creatures feed their young;
> And though man's face be fearful to their eyes,
> Yet, in protection of their tender ones,
> . . . .
> Make war with him that climb'd unto their nest,
> Offering their own lives in their young's defence.
> For shame, my liege, make them your precedent!
> Were it not pity that this goodly boy
> Should lose his birthright by his father's fault,
> And long hereafter say unto his child,
> "What my great-grandfather and grandsire got
> My careless father fondly gave away"?
> (2.2.26–28, 31–38)

Henry has no rejoinder, save that he was "enforc'd," when
Prince Edward asks him, "If you be king, why should not I
succeed?" (1.1.234). He later tries to redefine succession as a
legacy of "virtuous deeds" left to the son by his father
(2.2.45–53), but he is really trying to make excuses for not
resisting the Yorkists. To the felt absence of Henry V as
father-king there now succeeds a cause, the virtual absence of
Henry VI, who has failed to fulfill his duty as father and to
uphold his rule as king. From this point on, it is Margaret

who takes charge of the Lancastrian cause, a woman stepping into the vacuum of authority left by a weak man.

At the same time, that cause becomes almost identical with Clifford's vendetta, and his vendetta escalates from mere *talion*—a son for a father—to the determination to "root out their accursed line / And leave not one alive" (1.3.32–33). He begins by murdering Rutland, Richard's youngest son, who pleads with ironically fitting logic that Clifford pity him for the sake of his own son, "Lest in revenge thereof, sith God is just, / He be as miserably slain as I." Clifford inexorably replies, "Thy father slew my father; therefore die" (1.3.41–42, 46), yet later argues on behalf of Prince Edward's right, "Who should succeed the father but the son?" (2.2.94). The climactic scene in which Clifford and Margaret join forces to torment Richard with the murder of Rutland, mocking his fatherly love with a napkin stained in his son's blood, marks the extent to which the bonds of love between father and son, so clearly delineated in the Talbots in Part 1, have become perverted into a means of aggression that denies all humanity (1.4).

The famous episodes in which a father mourns the son he has unwittingly killed, and a son his father (2.5), also show how the father-son relationship has turned against itself. Formerly that bond was absolute; now, in the chaos of civil war, it is obliterated. Significantly, this scene begins with Henry's most famous and moving speech, his fantasy of a pastoral life removed from the toils of rule. Then he watches helplessly as the father and the son enter in turn and lament their terrible deeds. The point is clear. Because he has failed to be a strong father to his people, the paternal order has dissolved. Slaughter takes the place of succession, yet ironically, the two originate in the same need to establish order and maintain identity on the basis of the son following the father, in vengeance no less than in inheritance. Both order and chaos are patriarchal. Revenge even provides a certain artistic order, in that the murder of Henry's son Edward near the end of the play symmetrically answers the murder of Richard's son Rutland at the beginning.

But of course any order based on revenge is certain to destroy itself. The kiss Edward IV gives his baby son at the end of *3 Henry VI* is the kiss of death, for as he enumerates the fathers and sons he has killed to gain the throne it is evident he has already jeopardized his own son's life. In fact, the code of vengeance is now firmly identified with the principle of succession, and any man as father or son (or brother) is now vulnerable.

The prophecy uttered by Bedford in the first scene of the entire tetralogy actually comes true in the world of its last play:

> Posterity, await for wretched years,
> When at their mothers' moistened eyes babes shall suck,
> Our isle be made a nourish of salt tears,
> And none but women left to wail the dead.
>
> (*1 Henry VI*, 1.1.48–51)

"None but women left" is the fear behind this fantasy, the fear that without the masculine principle of succession the race will become impotent and feminized. A striking contrast exists between the comedies, written at roughly the same time, and these histories, for in the comedies, daughters lead sons to contend successfully against paternal domination, their protest then being reintegrated into the social fabric through marriage. As Charles Frey suggests,

> For Shakespeare, the decision to write romantic comedy involves the implicit decision to loosen the burdens of a father's will and to forego the loyalty expected of children in the histories.[14]

The holiday world of comedy *can* loosen those burdens, partly by giving women a larger and more creative scope of action than is allowed them in the real world of history. In the first tetralogy, however, the father's will holds sway. The wailing and cursing queens, mothers, and wives of *Richard III*, whose primary purpose was to bear sons, are survivors of dynasties that have virtually eliminated each other in the name of lineal succession through the male line. What is pursued in

14. Charles Frey, "Marriage and the Family in Shakespeare: Some Themes and Some Problems," a paper delivered at the Special Session on Marriage and the Family in Shakespeare at a meeting of the Modern Language Association, Chicago, December 30, 1977.

the name of the filially defined masculine self—loyalty to the father, family honor, and personal honor—destroys both the collective self of the family line and the individual men who are part of it. This self-reflexive and self-destructive quality is the essence of masculine identity conceived as the son's emulation of the father. The men of the first tetralogy gaze backward into their families' pasts, seeking to repeat their fathers either in virtue or in vengeance, enmeshed in rivalries with other men, fearful of and easily entrapped by women, incapable of making new alliances that break with the past and transform the future.

Critics have often interpreted Richard III as the lump of chaos born of England's chaos, the incarnation of its untrammeled slaughter of sons, brothers, fathers. Wolfgang Clemen argues that, though Richard is never at a loss for an explanation, none of his explanations suffices for the monstrosities he commits; he is more a symbolic than a realistic character.[15] Free of guilt or inner conflict, the aloof though appreciative spectator of his own performances, he thus accomplishes what few men would be capable of. But finally he destroys himself. The dominant pattern of Richard's character is the pattern of the play and of the tetralogy, a ricochet pattern of self-reflexiveness and self-destruction. England and Richard swallow themselves. The curses that only turn back on those who hurl them, the several small and the one large nemesis action running through the play, and Richard himself who "preys on the issue of his mother's body" (4.4.57)—all are analogous to the backward-looking, self-swallowing process by which men have defined themselves in the tetralogy.

There is a realistic psychological dimension to Richard's character as well as the symbolic one, however. Richard III of all the history plays most strongly suggests the importance of the mother, rather than the father, in the formation of mas-

15. Wolfgang Clemen, A Commentary on Shakespeare's Richard III, tr. Jean Bonheim (London: Methuen, 1968), pp. 6–7. For the argument that Richard is plausibly motivated by "a perversion . . . of his frustrated will to sexual power," see Murray Krieger, "The Dark Generations of Richard III," in The Design Within: Psychoanalytic Approaches to Shakespeare, ed. Melvin Faber (New York: Science House, 1970), pp. 347–366.

culine identity—but negatively, by showing how alienation from the mother helps turn a physical monster into a moral one. Taking into account the extent to which theatrical convention inspires Richard's confessions of his villainy, we must also heed his insights into his condition, which are borne out by other characters as well. In the first of his two great soliloquies in *3 Henry VI*, he cries, "Why, love foreswore me in my mother's womb" (3.2.153), and goes on to describe the hideous deformity that makes him

> Like to a chaos, or an unlick'd bear whelp
> That carries no impression like the dam.
>
> (3.2.161–162)

As Michael Neill argues, these lines suggest the mirroring process discerned by Winnicott, in which the mother, by responding actively and lovingly to her child, gives him back an image of himself and the basis for an identity. Richard, Neill says, "cannot know himself because he cannot love himself, and he cannot love himself because he has never been loved."[16] Confronted with the lumpish whelp her womb had formed, Richard's mother failed to lick it into shape, to imprint on it the "impression" of being loved and accepted. The circumstances of Richard's entrance into the world are mentioned frequently enough to demand our consideration: a difficult labor, a breech birth, his limbs deformed but his teeth already in his head, as even the young Duke of York has heard somewhere.[17] His mother's remembrance tends to confirm his contention that he was never loved:

> Thou cam'st on earth to make the earth my hell.
> A grievous burden was thy birth to me,
> Tetchy and wayward was thy infancy. . . .
>
> (*Richard III*, 4.4.167–169)

16. Michael Neill, "Shakespeare's Halle of Mirrors: Play, Politics, and Psychology in *Richard III*," *Shakespeare Studies* 8 (1976): 99–129. In a brilliant analysis, Neill goes on to argue that Richard's well-known theatricalism emanates from his lack of a self. As "dramatist, producer, prologue, and star performer of his own rich comedy," he narcissistically creates his own roles and through them, the roles of others, in effect making up "a false self to be the object of his consuming need for love."

17. See *3 Henry VI*, 3.2.153–162; 5.6.69–79; *Richard III*, 1.3.227–231; 2.4.27–28; 4.1.53–55; 4.4.47–55, 167–175.

Lacking that crucial two-way exchange with the mother as the primary representative of the human community, he never feels he is part of it. Thus, as he says,

> I have no brother, I am like no brother;
> And this word "love," which greybeards call divine,
> Be resident in men like one another,
> And not in me: I am myself alone.
> (3 Henry VI, 5.6.80–83)

Deprived of love, he is filled with rage, and puts his untimely teeth to use: he bites, as we are often reminded by the stream of canine images figuring his murderous aggression.[18] Henry VI interprets Richard's teeth as the sign of what he was fated to be:

> Teeth hadst thou in thy head when thou wast born,
> To signify thou camst to bite the world.
> (3 Henry VI, 5.6.53–54)

But the play also supports the psychological reading suggested by another "dog," Shylock:

> Thou call'dst me dog before thou hadst a cause,
> But since I am a dog, beware my fangs.
> (The Merchant of Venice, 3.3.6–7)

and by Richard himself:

> Then since the heavens have shap'd my body so,
> Let hell make crook'd my mind to answer it.
> (3 Henry VI, 5.6.78–79)

Thus Richard stands out from the men of the Henry VI plays, who even when they murdered did so in the name of their fathers. Though Richard resembles his father in ruthless ambition, he cannot be said to emulate him, in either the sense of following his example or of competing with him. He travesties the examples of family loyalty preceding him. Having no brother in the sense of having no kinship with people who are lovable and who love, being himself alone emotionally, in his utter lack of pity, as well as physically, he pursues the crown for himself alone. He sets his brothers against each

18. See 3 Henry VI, 5.6.53–54; Richard III, 1.3.288–290; 2.4.27–34; 4.4.47–58, 78.

other, by mimicking a brotherly love he has never felt so as to deceive and entrap them and by killing off or otherwise disposing of their children as obstacles to his succession. Perhaps his most shameless parody of the principle of succession that dominated the previous three plays is to sow the rumor that his brother Edward is illegitimate and thus not the true heir to the throne, so that *he* can claim, in Buckingham's words, to restore to its proper purity "the lineal glory of your royal house," "successively, from blood to blood," even as he murders its children (3.7.117–140). What began in the first play as dedication to the continuity of the family through the succession from father to son ends in the destruction of the family, and in the dissolution of masculine identity paternally defined.[19]

Like Richard III, the three kings of the second tetralogy are player-kings, with a fine theatrical sense of political action, setting up their own scenes for an audience whose applause they court.[20] The two Richards, diametrically opposite in some ways as they are, resemble each other as actors in that they play to themselves as audience as much as to the court or the populace. Both are fascinated with their mirror images, Richard III descanting on his shadow, and calling attention to his deformity the better to appreciate his triumph over it, Richard II dramatizing his crisis of identity in a real mirror. In contrast, the two Henrys are pragmatically concerned with evoking the proper responses from their real audiences; they want to see themselves reflected in the glass of popular opinion.

Though Richard III is aggressive, cunning, and ruthless, while the other Richard is passive, naive, and impotent, both are narcissists unable to form or sustain bonds with others;

19. "The Family and the Yorkist Cycle," a talk given by Norman Rabkin at the Special Session on Marriage and the Family in Shakespeare at the Modern Language Association's annual meeting in Chicago, December 27, 1977, first suggested the idea of Richard's destruction of the family to me and provided the stimulus for this essay.
20. For a thorough treatment of this conception of these two characters and others, see James Winny, *The Player-King: A Theme of Shakespeare's Histories* (London: Chatto and Windus, 1968); also Neill, cited in note 16.

they are fundamentally alone with themselves.[21] Richard of Gloucester knows neither brother nor father, and Richard II, though he is Shakespeare's best-known spokesman for kingship, lacks the sense of self apart from his role which would enable him to keep his throne. *Richard II* can be seen as an *agon* between maternal and paternal images of the kingship, Richard identifying himself with England as an all-providing mother, Henry with the patriarchal principle of succession. Both heroes invoke the principle, both violate it, and both suffer for that violation, but Richard's tragedy is that he fails to comprehend its meaning for his kingship or his identity as a man.

Throughout the play England is imaged in the traditional *topos* as a maternal presence, nurturing its people as her babes. In the tournament scene (1.3), Richard deplores the enmity threatening to "wake our peace, which in our country's cradle / Draws the sweet infant breath of gentle sleep" (132–135), and Bolingbroke departs for exile saying,

> Then, England's ground, farewell: sweet soil, adieu,
> My mother and my nurse that bears me yet!
> (1.3.306–307)

Gaunt's famous death speech (2.1) combines a fantasy of boundless maternal provision—England as "Eden," "nurse," and "teeming womb of kings"—with the idea of England as fortress, "built by Nature for herself," a walled and moated "seat of Mars." Mother and child, land and people, constitute a self-contained defensive alliance against external threat. Gaunt reproaches Richard for using this communal refuge as his own preserve, but Richard never fully understands the distinction between himself and the realm as belonging to all. He

---

21. That is, the impression of total egotism and self-aggrandizement that each character gives is defensive and delusory because, in very different ways, neither maintains a coherent, stable, realistic image of himself; he cannot love others because he cannot love himself. See Neill, cited in note 16, with regard to Richard III as a narcissist. For a useful account of narcissism in myth and in post-Freudian psychoanalytic thought, see Grace Stuart, *Narcissism: A Psychological Study of Self-Love* (London: George Allen Unwin, 1956), and Karl Abenheimer, "On Narcissism," *British Journal of Medical Psychology* 20 (1944): 322–329.

uses his country as the nurturant source of his own grandeur, literally, when he "farms" the crown's revenues, and figuratively, when he lands at Barkloughy, kissing "my earth." Though he calls himself the "long-parted mother" reunited with her child the earth, as his speech unfolds it is the earth who mothers. As the good mother, she comforts Richard with flowers and sweets, while as the bad mother, she repulses his enemies with spiders, toads, nettles, and adders.

First Gaunt, then York, reminds Richard of his paternal heritage, with its strict responsibilities, its well-delineated hierarchy of fathers and sons:

> O, had thy grandsire with a prophet's eye
> Seen how his son's son should destroy his sons. . . .
> (2.1.104–105)

> Take Herford's rights away, and take from time
> His charters, and his customary rights;
> Let not tomorrow then ensue today:
> Be not thyself. For how art thou a king
> But by fair sequence and succession?
> (2.1.195–199)

But Richard seems not to hear them; he even makes York his deputy after York's stinging reproof of his conduct. Bolingbroke, on the other hand, identifies with his father from the first moments of the play; when Richard bids him throw back Mowbray's gage, he replies, "Shall I seem crest-fall'n in my father's sight?" (1.1.188), and in the tournament scene he addresses John of Gaunt, the noble embodiment of "the fathers" in every sense,

> O thou, the earthly author of my blood
> Whose youthful spirit in me regenerate
> Doth with a two-fold vigour lift me up. . . .
> (1.3.69–71)

When he returns from exile, Bolingbroke (like Richard Plantagenet in the first tetralogy) claims only his paternal rights. But he stresses to York, as York stressed to Richard, the analogy between them and Richard's right to rule, implying that denial of the first endangers the second:

You are my father, for methinks in you
I see old Gaunt alive. O then my father,
Will you permit that I shall stand condemned
A wandering vagabond, my rights and royalties
Pluck'd from my arms perforce, and given away
To upstart unthrifts? Wherefore was I born?
If that my cousin be King in England,
It must be granted I am Duke of Lancaster.
(2.3.116–123)

When Bolingbroke challenges Richard not only in principle but with men and arms, Richard collapses with curious
swiftness. The formerly nurturant earth quickly becomes an
image of the grave, of sterility and nothingness ("Let's talk of
graves, of worms, and epitaphs . . ."), and the hollow crown a
negative version of Richard's encircling union with England's
earth. When he cannot call upon his identification with
mother England, Richard becomes a hollow king, incapable
of mustering any force save that of words that prophesy, truly
enough, civil war as God's retribution for his deposition. For
him there is no mean between fullness and emptiness, omnipotence or total dejection, because he is emotionally dependent on a boundless supply of reassurance, maternal in origin
and quality, which the real world cannot supply.

Richard II portrays a loss of identity through a loss of
kingship; the Henry IV plays, an identity won through kingship. The story of how Henry and his son reciprocally validate each other as father and son, king and prince, begins in
the last act of Richard II, when Henry cries, "Can no man tell
me of my unthrifty son?" (5.3.1). Henry's anxiety about Hal
is complexly related to his two last actions in the play: par-
doning Aumerle's treason and arranging for the murder of
Richard. The two actions are depicted so as to present a spec-
trum of attitudes toward the father-son bond. Though York
at first defends Richard as the divinely appointed king who
rules by successive right, he finally opts for loyalty to Henry
as de facto king, but not without misgivings. In accusing his
own son of treason, he acts on this new loyalty but violates
the blood tie between himself and his son—the tie that, the
Duchess argues, far outweighs any other. Surprisingly, Henry

pardons Aumerle and goes against his own characteristic allegiance to patriarchal order by failing to punish a man who would betray both father and king. Henry gives no explanation for his action except to say, "I pardon him as God shall pardon me" (5.3.129). Since this scene is followed by the scene in which Exton pins the responsibility for Richard's murder on Henry, we may infer that Henry pardons Aumerle's treason because he already feels guilty for his own. In order to be king, he kills the king, his brother-cousin, and must suffer Cain's guilt. Henry regards Hal as his punishment long before he explicitly admits (in *2 Henry IV*) having committed any crime. He who righteously invoked the principle of succession even as his troops massed before Richard at Flint Castle, and claimed to seek only his "lineal royalties," is appropriately punished by his own son's seeming unfitness to inherit the crown.

In the course of the two *Henry IV* plays, Shakespeare presents a conception of the father-son bond and its part in the formation of a masculine identity vastly different from that in the first tetralogy. In place of the emphasis on repetition and the past there, with its taut emulation of the father and inflexible vendettas, Shakespeare conceives of a relationship with some give to it, literally some free play, some space for departure from paternal priority and for experiences fundamentally opposed to it. In place of the failures in transition from sonship to fatherhood represented by Henry VI, John Talbot, Young Clifford, and Richard III, he tries to portray a successful passage negotiated, paradoxically, as lawful rebellion and responsible play. He makes Hal the stage manager of his own growing up, the embodiment of a wish to let go—but to let go only so far, without real risks. In the end, Falstaff's regressive appeal is so dangerously strong for Shakespeare that he cannot afford to integrate it into Hal's character, and must, to Hal's loss, exclude it totally.[22] From the sonnets to *The Win-*

22. Interpreters of the Henry IV plays divide into two camps: those who find Hal's rejection of Falstaff a limitation of Hal's character and/or of Shakespeare's breadth of sympathy, and those who justify it in terms of a moral

ter's Tale, the idea of remaining "boy eternal" exerts a powerful pull on Shakespeare's imagination that he strenuously resists. At the same time, however, he discovers new dimensions in the lifelong process of becoming a man; he begins to see how the father's identity is shaped by his son, as well as the son's by his father. In Henry and Hal he uses the renewal of the principle of succession as a way to validate Henry's kingship as much as Hal's; identity becomes a reciprocal process between father and son.

The relationship between the two men has three focal points of overdetermined needs and signals at which crises are defined or resolved. The first is the Boar's Head and Hal's reign there as madcap prince under the tutelage of Falstaff, who is usually seen as anti-king and anti-father, standing for misrule as opposed to rule.[23] But he is also the opposite of the king in the sense of being his predecessor psychologically, the king of childhood and omnipotent wishes, as Henry is king in the adult world of rivalry and care. Franz Alexander describes

theme unifying the plays. I line up behind those in the first camp, including C. L. Barber, "Rule and Misrule in Henry IV," in his *Shakespeare's Festive Comedy: A Study of Dramatic Form and Its Relation to Social Custom* (Princeton: Princeton University Press, 1959), pp. 192–218; Jonas Barish, "The Turning Away of Prince Hal," *Shakespeare Studies* 1 (1965): 9–17; A. C. Bradley, "The Rejection of Falstaff," reprinted in *Shakespeare, Henry IV, Parts I and II: A Casebook*, ed. G. K. Hunter (London: Macmillan, 1970), pp. 55–72; J. A. Bryant, "Prince Hal and the Ephesians," *Sewanee Review* 67 (1959): 204–219. However, John Dover Wilson, *The Fortunes of Falstaff* (Cambridge: Cambridge University Press, 1943), argues that the morality structure, in which Falstaff is the Vice, necessitates his rejection; and Sherman Hawkins, "Virtue and Kingship in Shakespeare's *Henry IV*," *English Literary Renaissance* 5 (Autumn 1975): 313–342, holds that the tradition of the four kingly virtues also dictates the rejection. Both convincingly show that these doctrines are at work in the plays. I maintain, however, that Shakespeare's purpose is to show in Hal the tension between Falstaff's encompassing humanity and the moral and political imperatives of rule, not to justify the latter at the expense of the former.

23. Notably, by Ernst Kris, "Prince Hal's Conflict," in *The Design Within: Psychoanalytic Approaches to Shakespeare* (cited in note 15), pp. 389–407, who takes Hal's friendship with Falstaff as an outlet for and defense against his hostility toward his father. Kris's case depends too heavily on the hypothesis that Hal had a previous friendship with Richard II, and on reading a parricidal urge into Hal's taking of the crown, however evident it is that Falstaff is a father-figure.

Falstaff as the personification of "the primary self-centered narcissistic libido of the child," commenting that

> the child in us applauds, the child who knows only one principle and that is to live. . . . Since the child cannot actually overcome any external interferences, it takes refuge in fantastic, megalomaniac self deception.[24]

"Banish plump Jack, and banish all the world!" Falstaff cries. Because of his sophisticated adult wit, however, he makes social capital out of his megalomania; men love his gloriously ingenious lies better than their own truth. Falstaff is a world unto himself, shaped like the globe and containing multitudes of contradictions as the world itself does; fat and aging in body, but ever young in spirit and nimble in wit; a shape-shifter in poses and roles, yet always inimitably himself; a man with a curiously feminine sensual abundance.

A fat man can look like a pregnant woman, and Falstaff's fatness is fecund; it spawns symbols. In the context of Hal's growing up, its feminine meaning has particular importance.[25] As W. H. Auden says, it is "the expression of a psychological wish to withdraw from sexual competition and by combining mother and child in his own person, to become emotionally self-sufficient."[26] Falstaff is said to be fond of hot wenches and leaping-houses, but he is no Don Juan even in Part 2 when his sexual relations with Doll Tearsheet and Mistress Quickly are made more explicit. They are fond of him rather than erotically drawn to him. It is not only tactful regard for Hal's legendary dignity as the perfect king that keeps Shakespeare from compromising him by making Falstaff a lecher. Rather, Falstaff represents the wish to bypass women; he has grown old, but remains young, and yet in terms of

24. Franz Alexander, "A Note on Falstaff," *Psychoanalytic Quarterly* 2 (1933): 392–406.

25. Suggested subtly and convincingly by Sherman Hawkins in "Falstaff as Mom," a talk given at the Special Session on Marriage and the Family in Shakespeare, at a meeting of the Modern Language Association, Chicago, December 30, 1977.

26. W. H. Auden, "The Prince's Dog," in his *The Dyer's Hand* (New York: Random House), p. 196.

women has "detoured manhood," as Harold Goddard says.[27] In the first tetralogy Shakespeare avoided treating the woman's part in male development by making women witches or helpless victims. In the second tetralogy he again treats the feminine obliquely, through its absence, as Falstaff's avoidance of sexual maturity. The fat knight desires food and drink more than he desires women. And though women are devoted to him, he cheats and deceives them, giving his own deepest affections to a boy. No wonder that, for Hal, Falstaff incarnates his own rebellion against growing up into a problematic adult identity.

Hal himself is unaware that his affinity for the fat knight constitutes rebellion; he conceives it, rather, as part of his long-term strategy for assuming a proper identity as king. That strategy reveals his likeness to his father, his ability to think and act in the same terms of political image-building as his father, his fitness for the very role he seems to be rejecting. Many parallels between Hal's first soliloquy (1.2) and the king's long admonitory speech to him (3.2) reveal the essential similarities between father and son. Both speeches dwell on the proper management of one's political visibility and the importance of avoiding overexposure. Hal pictures himself as the sun obscured by clouds and therefore more "wonder'd at" when he reappears, while Henry compares himself to a comet "wonder'd at" because it is "seldom seen." He implies that his is that "sun-like majesty" that, when it "shines seldom," wins an "extraordinary gaze," and Hal says that his reformation "shall show more goodly, and attract more eyes" because of his fault. Both use clothing imagery to denote a kingliness they put on or off at will; Hal says he can "throw off this loose behaviour," and Henry says that he too dressed himself in humility, then donned his "presence like a robe pontifical." Hal's soliloquy implies that the Hal we have just seen with Falstaff is no more genuine and spontaneous than the self he

---

27. Harold C. Goddard, "Henry IV," in his The Meaning of Shakespeare, 2 vols. (Chicago: University of Chicago Press, 1951), vol. 1, p. 184.

will assume as king, and it is immediately followed by Henry
addressing the Percys in equally ambiguous terms:

> I will from henceforth rather by myself,
> Mighty and to be fear'd, than my condition. . . .[28]
>
> (1.3.5–6)

Neither man can freely express his true self, whatever that
is, because each has something to hide. For reasons to be explained shortly, Hal hides his sympathy with his father, while
Henry hides his guilt over the deposition and murder of
Richard. Nonetheless, that guilt is revealed in the way he
splits his son into two contending images: the bad son, Hal
the wastrel; and the good son, Hotspur the king of honor. For
Hal to become his father's son personally (to be loved) and
politically (to be trusted as fit to succeed his father), he must
restore his reputation as heir apparent, triumph over Hotspur,
and assume Hotspur's identity as the model of chivalric manhood in England. This he obediently promises and economi-
cally does, in the sum-zero terms of heroic combat:

> Percy is but my factor, good my lord,
> To engross up glorious deeds on my behalf
> And I will call him to so strict account
> That he shall render every glory up,
> Yea, even the slightest worship of his time,
> Or I will tear the reckoning from his heart.
>
> (3.2.147–152)

Thus Shrewsbury is the second focal point of the father-son
relationship, and constitutes Hal's and Henry's first mutual
reaffirmation of identity.

But it mainly restores their public images as loyal prince
and lawful king, while their private feelings toward each other
remain to be worked out and transformed. Henry's "buried
fear" rises again in the form of further rebellions nourished by
lingering resentments against him as the usurper of Richard.[29]

28. A. R. Humphreys, editor of the new Arden text, glosses *condition* as
"natural disposition."

29. The second tetralogy can be seen as the story of two dynasties, the
Bolingbrokes and the Percys. By the end of *2 Henry IV,* the Percys are extinct
and the Bolingbrokes have become the royal house. Like the house of York in

It also takes the form of the disease, aging, and death that pervade Part 2. The king is sick and dying; his sins are still upon his head, and spreading throughout his body and the kingdom's. At the same time, Hal hasn't quite given up Falstaff and the still attractive world he represents. The shadow of Hal's misbehavior falls on his father's throne, casting its legitimacy further in doubt, and the shadow of his father's suffering falls on Hal's revels. Succession as Hal's full acceptance of the crown his father has to give, and as the public legitimation of his father's reign by virtue of that acceptance, has yet to take place.

In the deathbed scenes of Part 2, succession comes about in the completion of a mythic pattern that has given form to the father-son relationship all along: the motif of the Prodigal Son. Several specific references to the parable of the Prodigal Son crop up in the Henry plays, but more prominently, the legend of the Wild Prince, one of Shakespeare's sources for the plays, parallels the story of the young man who flouts expectations, sows his wild oats, and then reforms himself.[30] In the parable, it is the younger son who demands his inheritance from his father, squanders it, and returns home contritely to receive not only his father's forgiveness but a royal welcome with dancing, rejoicing, and the fatted calf, while the

the earlier tetralogy, the Percys justify their rebellion on the technicalities of the succession, arguing that Richard II proclaimed Mortimer the "true" heir. But the scene in which they carve up England among themselves (*1 Henry IV*, 3.1) makes it clear that like the house of York they serve their own selfish interests, not the principle of succession. Shakespeare depicts the Percys throughout as an echo of the earlier tetralogy, giving Hotspur's ideal of honor a quaint chivalric tone and making him the last representative of feudalism's anarchic, individualist strain, as Talbot is the last representative of its communal, ceremonial strain. In terms of the father-son relationship, Northumberland betrays his son's cause by not showing up at Shrewsbury, while Hal redeems his father's cause by his valor in the same battle. In *2 Henry IV*, Northumberland dedicates himself to a futile, backward-looking vengeance like the Cliffords and the Yorks in the earlier tetralogy, while Hal tries creatively to redeem his tainted legacy by moving forward to the succession.

30. See discussions of the Wild Prince legend and *The Famous Victories of Henry V* (which has a similar structure) by A. R. Humphreys in his introduction to *1 Henry IV*, Arden Edition (London: Methuen, 1960), pp. xxix–xxxi, xxii–xxiv, and Geoffrey Bullough, *Narrative and Dramatic Sources of Shakespeare*, 7 vols. (New York: Columbia University Press, 1966), vol. 4, pp. 155–180, especially pp. 159–160.

dutiful elder son receives only his due. Hal is the first-born and heir-apparent, but he has scorned his status and acted like the prodigal second son who gets less wealth from his father. Hal's prodigal behavior seems more strongly motivated, though, by a need to differentiate himself violently from his father, concealing and denying his likeness to and sympathy with him. It is as though he must first create the impression that he is not his father's son, that he is of a different nature altogether, before he can admit his family resemblance and accept his paternal inheritance. In fact, Hal never even intends his father to know that he is his son in the spirit as well as in the letter. Had Hal not been tricked by the appearance of his father's death and taken the crown as his "lineal honour," his father would never have accused him of seizing it unlawfully and wishing his death, and Hal would never have made his moving confession of love and loyalty. In effect, Hal reverses John Talbot's pattern of initial submission to the father and subsequent break away from him; he breaks away first, by loitering in Eastcheap. But like the prodigal son, he breaks away only to make his eventual submission the more genuine.

In Hal's first scene in Part 2 (2.2), he confesses, "My heart bleeds inwardly that my father is so sick" (46), but it requires the mistaken belief that his father is actually dead for Hal to reveal just how much he shares with him. As in Part 1, dramatic irony is the means of this revelation, through parallels between the soliloquies of father and son: Henry's meditation on sleep (3.1) and Hal's apostrophe to the crown (4.4). Both elaborate the same pair of comparisons between kingly luxury, "the perfum'd chambers of the great" and the polished gold of the crown, and humble poverty, with its "homely biggen" and "smoky crib"; between the king's sleepless "perturbation" and "care," and the lowly subject's slumber.

When Hal takes the crown from his father's bedside, he takes it in exactly the spirit Henry expects will legitimate his shadowed reign. His words stress the blood tie between father and son, and the son's restoration of the principle of succession the father denied when he took the crown:

> My due from thee is this imperial crown,
> Which, as immediate from thy place and blood,

Derives itself to me. [*Putting it on his head*] Lo where it sits,
Which God shall guard; and put the world's whole strength
Into one giant arm, it shall not force
This lineal honour from me. This from thee
Will I to mine leave, as 'tis left to me.

(4.5.40–46)

Only when the king realizes that his son accepts the crown
not as a license to riot but as the legacy due him as "a true
inheritor" can he admit the "crook'd ways" by which he got
it, and feel himself and his kingship redeemed by the succession:

And now my death
Changes the mood, for what in me was purchas'd
Falls on thee in a more fairer sort;
So thou the garland wear'st successively.

(4.5.198–201)

Hal does wear the garland successively, his title clear, his
power assured. But he also succeeds to his father's guilt,
which takes the form of a persistent private anxiety, and
which actually inspires his French campaign—a strategem
suggested by his father's dying advice to "busy giddy minds
with foreign quarrels . . . to waste the memory of former
days" (*2 Henry IV*, 4.5.213–215). In the scene that takes place
on the eve of Agincourt, Shakespeare is at pains to compare
Henry and Hal as kings, showing how Hal has infused his
new role with qualities he could only have gained through his
regression and rebellion in Eastcheap, while at the same time
revealing what of the father lives on in the son.

Henry V mingling unrecognized with his common soldiers
just before a crucial battle is a far cry from Henry IV hiding
behind the many "counterfeit kings" marching in his coats at
Shrewsbury. The common humanity from which Hal seemed
to exclude himself by rejecting Falstaff with neither love nor
regret now inspires him to share both his fear and his courage
with his men. He does it by acting—not the image-building
his father used to get the crown, but the self-expressive role
playing that he and Falstaff indulged in when they pretended
to be king and each other (*1 Henry IV*, 2.4). Speaking as Harry
le Roy, Hal really speaks from his own heart as king:

> For, though I speak it to you, I think the king is but a man, as I
> am: the violet smells to him as it doth to me; the element
> shows to him as it doth to me; all his senses have but human
> conditions: his ceremonies laid by, in his nakedness he appears
> but a man; and though his affections are higher mounted than
> ours, yet when they stoop, they stoop with the like wing.
>   (4.1.100–108)

Intending to practice what he preaches, Hal declares he will
refuse ransom and face death like any common soldier—then
picks a quarrel with the soldier who doubts him. He perpe-
trates the same kind of creative, illuminating trickery as he
did in the Gadshill robbery. Williams, maintaining his honor
honestly as Henry knows he will, is not afraid to protest his
own innocence before the king, saying, "I beseech you, take
it for your own fault and not mine" (4.8.54–56). Hal contrives
the whole incident with a combination of insight, humor, and
sympathy he could only have gained in Eastcheap, pursuing
his own eccentric course of growth.

The topic of Henry's conversation with the soldiers is the
question of whether the king is morally responsible for the
deaths of those who fight in his wars. Hal's argument is earnest and his logic convincing when he says, "Every subject's
duty is the king's; but every subject's soul is his own"
(4.1.182–184). However, he might well add, "and every king's
soul is not just his own but his father's as well." When the
soldiers leave, Hal delivers a long soliloquy that recapitulates
and combines the major motifs from two great speeches in *2
Henry IV*: his father's mediation on sleep (3.1) and his own on
the crown (4.5). The theme of all three speeches can be stated
as the ironic disparity between the tangible majesties of
kingship and its emotional burdens. Hal's soliloquy might be
uttered by any of Shakespeare's kings: its truths are universal.
But its context makes it a telling comment on Hal's particular
identity as king. Not only does it refer backward to the troubled circumstances of Hal's succession to the throne, it leads
into the prayer in which he confesses his fear that God will
punish him for his father's crime by giving the victory to the
French:

> Not today, O Lord!
> O not today, think not upon the fault
> My father made in compassing the crown!.
> (4.1.298–300)

Despite his ability to succeed where his father failed, unifying his kingdom and winning the love of all his people; despite the originality of his kingship, his playfulness and *joie de vivre* in such marked contrast to his father's careworn formality, he has inherited his father's sense of guilt along with his father's crown.[31]

Plus ça change, plus c'est la même chose, it might be said. The same mixture of originality and repetition characterizes attitudes toward women, and relationships between men, in this final play of the two tetralogies. Henry bases his claim to the French crown on the Salic Law, which forbids inheritance through the female and thus expresses the principle underlying masculine identity in the two tetralogies: men are defined by other men, not by women. Yet while the play contains an episode of masculine friendship that strongly recalls the idyllic warrior bonding of the Talbots, and while it evokes powerfully the brotherhood of warriors under a strong father-king, it concludes with a marriage that blesses rather than subverts that brotherhood. Though Katherine is actually part of Henry's French spoils, the first article in a treaty her father can hardly refuse to sign, like the Kate of an earlier comedy she is a woman willing to submit, and *Henry V* is a comedy, resolving discord in a symbolic marriage. Thus Shakespeare attempts to round off happily the story of Prince Hal's troubled progress to manhood: he is a successful father-king and a lusty bridegroom. Shakespeare leaves it to us to decide whether the

---

31. In a paper forthcoming in *Modern Language Studies,* "The fault / My father made': The Anxious Pursuit of Heroic Fame in Shakespeare's *Henry V,*" Peter B. Erickson offers a searching interpretation of Henry as a son still burdened by his father's guilt, and hears in Henry's soliloquy on the eve of Agincourt, describing the penance he has performed for the murder of Richard, "a clear note of futility about the absolution which Henry V seeks for himself." He finds tension and ambivalence between a desire for epic fame and a fear of oblivion, and between anger and pity, in Henry's character throughout the play, because "Henry must surpass his father ... that is the prearranged means of atoning for and with him."

terms in which his kingship and manhood are won—the French campaign with its doubtful rationale, its cruelty and destruction, as well as its effective political unification of England—can win our full approval.

Before he sets off for France, Henry must contend with treachery at home: Scroop's betrayal. In the longest speech of the play, he lashes out passionately at his former friend, terming his crime "another fall of man." Scroop's treachery constitutes Hal's initiation into bitter experience after the innocence of his Eastcheap days, and is deliberately contrasted to them in the following scene when Falstaff's death is recounted. Partly out of political necessity, Henry rejected the man who truly loved him and in his place nurtured a viper. Love and trust have no place at court; it is only in battle that friendships between men can flourish even unto death, as does that between York and Suffolk. Their dual death scene (4.6) is a sharply etched cameo of homoerotic martial pathos: York kissing Suffolk's wounds and lips, and envisioning their souls flying into heaven together—a complete merging of one man with another as in the Talbots' death scene. It resembles that episode in evoking a desire for the peaceful dual unity of mother and child, a unity based on sameness, before self is differentiated from other or male from female, and it stands in high contrast to the infrequent, dangerous, and unbalanced liaisons with women in the history plays.

These loving pairs of warriors invite comparison with the common band of warriors. Henry's first speech before Harfleur (3.1) employs heavily sexual imagery to exhort his men to courage and strength. The analogies between besieging a walled city and rape are brought to the surface when Henry urges each man to make himself, in effect, a battering ram or erect phallus: stiffening his sinews, making his eye a cannon and his brow a rock, setting his teeth and holding his breath. In the second half of the speech, he makes this martial virility a test of legitimacy (they must emulate their fathers in this collective erection, or dishonor their mothers by seeming bastards) as well as of nationality (the virile English as opposed to the effete French). Several other speeches by Henry and Exeter threaten the French with sexual violence against their mothers, wives, and sweethearts. Thus until Henry's wooing of Katherine, love is felt only between men as a form of complete pregenital merger, and sexuality takes the form of men's collective violence against women.

In dramatic and literary artistry, *Henry V* stands high above the *Henry VI* plays, yet it harks back eerily to the same patterns of male identity. After exploring the richly shaded, complex relationship between father and son in the *Henry IV* plays, after showing how problematic, psychologically as well as politically, the principle of succession is, Shakespeare returns to the simple, idealized male comradeships he began with. Henry woos Kate as a soldier—that is at once the charm and the necessary condition of his courtship; it sets the distance between them on which his manhood depends.

CHAPTER FOUR

Coming of Age: Marriage and Manhood in *Romeo and Juliet* and *The Taming of the Shrew*

I may chance have some odd quirks and
remnants of wit broken on me because I have
railed so long against marriage; but doth not
the appetite alter? A man loves the meat in his
youth that he cannot endure in his age.
    Much Ado about Nothing,
    2.3.233–234

In reality or in art, passages from one stage of life to
another are likely to be troubled and hazardous.
Shakespearean men discussed in previous chapters
faced the dilemma of passage from boyhood to
manhood. They had to forsake their dreams or fears
of union with the mother, move to identification
with the father, and then to their own identities as
men, the fathers of the future. Adonis refused
initiation into sexuality and love that he feared as
psychological annihilation. The sons in the first
tetralogy, initiated into manhood through war rather
than through women, either struggled to compete
with their fathers or sank into a maelstrom of
vengeance to prove themselves loyal. Prince Hal, on
the other hand, finally compromised neither his filial
loyalty nor his individuality, and capped his victories
with a wedding, a seal of manhood complementary
to those he won on the battlefield.

In Shakespeare's world, marriage denotes full
entry into society; when a son marries, he becomes a
man. But as *Romeo and Juliet* attests, the marital bond
may tragically conflict with paternal allegiance.
Written after the first tetralogy of history plays and

before the second, like them this early masterpiece deals with "the problematics of loyalty to the father" and places marriage within the context of this loyalty. As in the history plays, it is phallic violence that ties men to their fathers, the violence of the feud. This violence also serves as a defense against women, love, and sex, as the hunt did for Adonis. In the ambiance of the feud, marriage subverts patriarchal loyalty, not only because Romeo and Juliet are children of enemy houses, but also because marriage weakens the fathers' hold over their sons and the ties between men as comrades in violence. *Romeo and Juliet* plays out a conflict between manhood as violence on behalf of the fathers and manhood as separation from the fathers and sexual union with women.

In contrast, *The Taming of the Shrew* portrays marriage itself as a test of manhood. Petruchio must strive to assume the patriarchal role of command over Kate. He succeeds, of course, but Shakespeare makes the taming mirror the threat to manhood hidden in marriage. When a husband takes legal dominion over his wife, he also becomes socially and emotionally vulnerable to her. If she refuses to obey him, she calls his manhood into doubt, and he must use force to establish his authority as husband. In *The Taming of the Shrew* as in *Romeo and Juliet,* Shakespeare explores the role of force in patriarchal society, the husband's force rather than the father's. He also distinguishes tellingly between women and the roles they assume, voluntarily or reluctantly, in patriarchal marriage.

I

Romeo and Juliet is about a pair of adolescents trying to grow up.[1] Growing up requires that they separate themselves from their parents by forming an intimate bond that supersedes filial bonds, a bond with a person of the opposite sex. This, broadly, is an essential task of adolescence, in Renaissance England or Italy as in America today, and the play is

1. This discussion of *Romeo and Juliet* appeared in a longer version titled "Coming of Age in Verona," in *Modern Language Studies* 8 (Winter 1977–78): 5–22, and in *The Woman's Part: Feminist Criticism of Shakespeare,* ed. Gayle Greene, Carolyn R. S. Lenz, and Carol Thomas Neely (Champaign: University of Illinois Press, 1980).

particularly concerned with the social milieu in which these
adolescent lovers grow up—a patriarchal milieu as English as
it is Italian. I shall argue that the feud in a realistic social sense
is the primary tragic force in the play—not the feud as agent
of fate,[2] but the feud as an extreme and peculiar expression of
patriarchal society, which Shakespeare shows to be tragically
self-destructive.[3] The feud is the deadly *rite de passage* that
promotes masculinity at the price of life. Undeniably, the
feud is bound up with a pervasive *sense* of fatedness, but that
sense finds its objective correlative in the dynamics of the feud
and of the society in which it is embedded. As Harold Goddard says,

> The fathers are the stars and the stars are the fathers in the
> sense that the fathers stand for the accumulated experience of
> the past, for tradition, for authority, and hence for the two
> most potent forces that mold and so impart 'destiny' to the
> child's life . . . heredity and training. The hatred of the hostile
> houses in *Romeo and Juliet* is an inheritance that every member
> of these families is born into as truly as he is born with the
> name Capulet or Montague.[4]

2. A long-standing interpretation of *Romeo and Juliet* holds that it is a
tragedy of fate. F. S. Boas, *Shakespeare and His Predecessors* (New York, 1896),
p. 214; E. K. Chambers, *Shakespeare: A Survey* (London: Sidgwick and
Jackson, 1929), pp. 70–71; E. E. Stoll, *Shakespeare's Young Lovers* (London:
Oxford University Press, 1937), pp. 4–5; and G. L. Kittredge, ed., *Sixteen
Plays of Shakespeare* (Boston: Ginn, 1948), p. 674, are the most prominent of
the many critics who have shared this view. Stopford Brooke, *On Ten Plays
of Shakespeare* (London: Constable and Co., 1905), pp. 36, 65, held the quarrel
between the houses to be the cause of the tragedy, but saw the quarrel in
moral rather than social terms as an expression of any "long-continued evil."
More recently, H. B. Charlton, "Shakespeare's Experimental Tragedy," in
his *Shakespearean Tragedy* (Cambridge, England: Cambridge University
Press, 1948), pp. 49–63, calls the feud the means by which fate acts, but objects to it as such on the grounds that it lacks convincing force and implacabil-
ity in the play. For an orthodox Freudian interpretation of the feud as a regressive intrafamilial, narcissistic force that prevents Romeo and Juliet from
seeking properly nonincestuous love objects, see M. D. Faber, "The Adolescent Suicides of Romeo and Juliet," *Psychoanalytic Review* 59 (1971): 169–
182.

3. As usual, Shakespeare portrays the milieu of his source in terms with
which he and his audience are familiar; he is not at pains to distinguish the
Italian family from the English. See Lawrence Stone's definition of the patriarchal family, quoted in chapter 1, p. 13.

4. Harold Goddard, *The Meaning of Shakespeare*, 2 vols. (Chicago: University of Chicago Press, 1951), vol. 1, p. 119.

That inheritance makes Romeo and Juliet tragic figures because it denies their natural needs and desires as adolescents. Of course, they also display the faults of youth: its self-absorption and reckless extremism, its headlong surrender to eros. But it is the feud that fosters the rash, choleric impulsiveness typical of youth by offering a permanent invitation to and outlet for violence. The feud is first referred to in the play as "their parents' strife and their parents' rage," and it is clear that the fathers, not their children, are responsible for its continuance. Instead of providing social channels and moral guidance by which the energies of youth can be rendered beneficial to themselves and society, the Montagues and the Capulets make weak gestures toward civil peace while participating emotionally in the feud as much as their children do. While they fail to exercise authority over the younger generation in the streets, they wield it selfishly and stubbornly in the home. Critics have found so many faults of character in Romeo and in Juliet shared by their parents that the play cannot be viewed as a tragedy of character in the Aristotelian sense, in which tragedy results because the hero and heroine fail to "love moderately."[5] Rather, the feud's ambiance of hot temper permeates age as well as youth; viewed from the standpoint of Prince Escalus, who embodies the law, it is Montague and Capulet who are childishly refractory.

In the course of the action, Romeo and Juliet create and try to preserve new identities as adults apart from the feud, but it blocks their every attempt. Metaphorically, it devours them in the "detestable maw" of the Capulets' monument, a symbol of the patriarchy's destructive power over its children. Thus both the structure and the texture of the play suggest a

5. This is a more recent critical tendency than that referred to in note 2, and is represented by Donald A. Stauffer, *Shakespeare's World of Images* (New York: Norton, 1949), pp. 55–57; Franklin M. Dickey, *Not Wisely But Too Well* (San Marino, Calif.: Huntington Library, 1957), pp. 63–117; and Roy W. Battenhouse, *Shakespearean Tragedy: Its Art and Christian Premises* (Bloomington and London: Indiana University Press, 1969), pp. 102–119. However, Dickey and Paul N. Siegel, "Christianity and the Religion of Love in *Romeo and Juliet,*" *Shakespeare Quarterly* 12 (1961): 383, see the lovers' passion, flawed though it is, as the means by which divine order based on love is restored to Verona.

critique of the patriarchal attitudes expressed through the feud, which makes "tragic scapegoats" of Romeo and Juliet.[6] For the sons and daughters of Verona, the feud constitutes socialization into patriarchal roles in two ways. First, it reinforces their identities as sons and daughters by allying them with their paternal household against another paternal household, thus polarizing all their social relations, particularly their marital choices, in terms of filial allegiance. They are constantly called upon to define themselves in terms of their families and to defend their families. Second, the feud provides a "psycho-sexual moratorium" for the sons,[7] in which they prove themselves men by phallic violence on behalf of their fathers, instead of by courtship and sexual experimentation that would lead toward marriage and separation from the paternal house. It leads them to scorn women and to associate them with effeminacy and emasculation, while it links sexual intercourse with aggression and violence against women, rather than with pleasure and love. Structurally, the play's design reflects the prominence of the feud. It erupts in three scenes at the beginning, middle, and end (1.1, 3.1, 5.3) that deliberately echo each other. The peripateia, at which Ro-

6. Paul N. Siegel (cited in note 5) uses this phrase, but in a moral rather than social context; he sees them as scapegoats through whom their parents expiate their sins of hate and vengefulness.
7. The term is Erik Erikson's, as used in "The Problem of Ego Identity," in *Identity and the Life Cycle: Selected Papers* (New York International Universities Press, 1959), pp. 103–105. He defines it partly through a description of George Bernard Shaw's self-imposed "prolongation of the interval between youth and adulthood" in his early twenties. His comments on "the social play of adolescents" further explain the purpose of such a moratorium, and raise the questions I am raising with regard to the social function of the feud:

> Children and adolescents in their presocieties provide for one another a sanctioned moratorium and joint support for free experimentation with inner and outer dangers (including those emanating from the adult world). Whether or not a given adolescent's newly acquired capacities are drawn back into infantile conflict depends to a significant extent on the quality of the opportunities and rewards available to him in his peer clique, as well as on the more formal ways in which society at large invites a transition from social play to work experimentation, and from rituals of transit to final commitments. . . . (p. 118)

meo's and Juliet's fortunes change decisively for the worse, occurs exactly in the middle when Romeo kills Tybalt. This murder poses the two conflicting definitions of manhood between which Romeo must make his tragic choice.

It has been noted that *Romeo and Juliet* is a domestic tragedy but not that its milieu is distinctly patriarchal as well as domestic. Much of it takes place within the Capulet household, and Capulet's role as *paterfamilias* is apparent from the first scene in which his servants behave as members of his extended family, as *famuli* rather than employees. That household is a charming place: protected and spacious, plentiful with servants, food, light, and heat, bustling with festivity, intimate and informal even on great occasions, with a cosy familiarity between master and servant. In nice contrast to it stands the play's other dominant milieu, the streets of Verona. It is there that those fighting the feud are defined as men, in contrast to those who would rather love than fight, who in terms of the feud are less than men. Gregory and Sampson ape the machismo of their masters, seeking insults on the slightest pretext so that they may prove their valor. In their blind adherence to a groundless "ancient grudge," they are parodies of the feuding gentry. But in Shakespeare's day, as servants they would be regarded as their master's "children" in more than a figurative sense, owing not just work but loyalty and obedience to their employers as legitimate members of the household ranking immediately below its children.[8] As male servants their position resembles that of sons bound by honor to fight for their families' names. Most importantly, their obvious phallic competitiveness in being quick to anger at an insult to their status or manhood and quick to draw their swords and fight shades into phallic competitiveness in sex as well:

> I strike quickly, being moved . . . A dog of the house of Montague moves me . . . Therefore I will push Montague's men

8. See Gordon Schochet, *Patriarchalism in Political Thought: The Authoritarian Family and Political Speculation and Attitudes Especially in Seventeenth-Century England* (New York: Basic Books, 1975), especially pp. 65–68.

from the wall and thrust his maids to the wall. . . . Me they
shall feel while I am able to stand.

(1.1.6, 9, 12–14, 18–20, 30)[9]

In this scene and elsewhere, the many puns on "stand" as
standing one's ground in fighting and as erection attest that
fighting in the feud demonstrates virility as well as valor.
Sampson and Gregory also imply that they consider it their
prerogative as men to take women by force to demonstrate
their superiority to the Montagues:

> women, being the weaker vessels, are ever thrust to the wall.
> Therefore I will push Montague's men from the wall and
> thrust his maids to the wall . . . When I have fought with the
> men, I will be civil with the maids—I will cut off their
> heads. . . . the heads of the maids or their maidenheads. Take it
> in what sense thou wilt.
>
> (1.1.16–20, 24–25, 27–28)

As the fighting escalates, finally Capulet and Montague themselves become involved, Capulet calling for a sword he is too
infirm to wield effectively, because Montague, he claims,
"flourishes his blade in spite of me." With the neat twist of
making masters parody men who have been parodying them,
the fighting ends with the arrival of the Prince. At the cost of
civil peace, all have asserted their claims to manhood through
the feud.

Tybalt makes a memorable entrance in this first scene. Refusing to believe Benvolio's assertion that his sword is drawn
only to separate the fighting servants, he immediately dares
him to defend himself. To Tybalt, a sword can only mean a
challenge to fight, and peace is just a word:

> What, drawn and talk of peace? I hate the word
> As I hate hell, all Montagues, and thee.
> Have at thee, coward!
>
> (1.1.72–74)

In the first two acts, Shakespeare contrasts Tybalt and Romeo
in terms of their responses to the feud so as to intensify the

9. This and all subsequent quotations are taken from *The Complete Signet
Classic Shakespeare,* ed. Sylvan Barnet (New York: Harcourt, Brace, Jovanovich, 1963; rpt. 1972). Where relevant I have noted variant readings.

conflict Romeo faces in act 3 when he must choose between being a man in the sanctioned public way, by drawing a sword upon an insult, or being a man in a novel and private way, by reposing confidence in his secret identity as Juliet's husband.

In act 3, the fight begins when Tybalt is effectively baited by Mercutio's punning insults; from Mercutio's opening badinage with Benvolio, it is evident that he too is spoiling for a fight, though he is content to let the weapons be words. But words on the hot midday streets of Verona are the same as blows that must be answered by drawing a sword. When Romeo arrives, Tybalt calls him "my man," "a villain," and "boy," all terms that simultaneously impugn his birth and honor as well as his manhood. Mercutio made words blows, but Romeo tries to do just the opposite, by oblique protestations of love to Tybalt, which must seem quite mysterious to Tybalt if he listens to them at all: "And so, good Capulet, whose name I tender / As dearly as mine own, be satisfied" (3.1.72–73). Romeo's puns of peacemaking fail where Mercutio's puns of hostility succeeded all too well. Only one kind of rigid, simple language, based on the stark polarities Capulet-Montague, man-boy, is understood in the feud. No wonder Mercutio terms Romeo's response a "calm, dishonorable, vile submission" and draws on Tybalt: Romeo has allowed a Capulet to insult his name, his paternal heritage, his manhood, without fighting for them. Like Tybalt, Romeo owes a duty to "the stock and honor of his kin." When Mercutio fights for him and dies, the shame of having allowed his friend to answer the challenge that according to the code of manly honor he should have answered overcomes Romeo. He momentarily turns against Juliet, the source of his new identity, and sees her as Mercutio sees all women:

> O sweet Juliet,
> Thy beauty hath made me effeminate,
> And in my temper softened valor's steel!
> (3.1.115–117)

In that moment, caught between his radically new identity as Juliet's husband, which has made him responsible (he

thinks) for his friend's death, and his previous traditional identity as the scion of the house of Montague, he resumes the
latter and murders Tybalt. As Ruth Nevo remarks,

> Romeo's challenge of Tybalt is not merely an instance . . . of a
> rashness which fatally flaws his character . . . on the contrary,
> it is an action first avoided, then deliberately undertaken, and it
> is entirely expected of him by his society's code.[10]

As much as we want the love of Romeo and Juliet to prosper,
we also want the volatile enmity of Tybalt punished and the
death of Mercutio, that spirit of vital gaiety, revenged, even at
the cost of continuing the feud. Romeo's hard choice is also
ours. Though the play is constantly critical of the feud as the
medium through which criteria of patriarchally oriented masculinity are voiced, it is just as constantly sensitive to the association of those criteria with more humane principles of
filial loyalty, loyalty to friends, courage, and personal integrity.

Among the young bloods serving as foils for Romeo, Benvolio represents the total sublimation of virile energy into
peacemaking, agapé instead of eros; Tybalt, such energy chan-
neled directly and exclusively into aggression; and Mercutio, its attempted sublimation into fancy and wit. (Romeo
and Paris seek manhood through love rather than through
fighting, but are finally impelled by the feud to fight each
other.) That Mercutio pursues the feud though he is neither
Montague nor Capulet suggests that feuding has become the
normal social pursuit for young men in Verona. Through his
abundant risqué wit, he suggests its psychological function
for them, as a definition of manhood. Love is only manly, he
hints, if it is aggressive and violent and consists of subjugat-
ing, rather than being subjugated by women:

> If love be rough with you, be rough with love;
> Prick love for pricking and you beat love down.
> (1.4.27–28)

10. Ruth Nevo, "Tragic Form in Romeo and Juliet," Studies in English Literature 9 (1969): 238–258.

Alas, poor Romeo, he is already dead: stabbed with a white
wench's black eye; run through the ear with a love-song: the
very pin of his heart cleft with the blind bow-boy's butt-shaft;
and is he a man to encounter Tybalt?

(2.4.14–18)

The conflict between Mercutio's conception of manhood and
the one Romeo learns is deftly and tellingly suggested in
Romeo's line, "He jests at scars that never felt a wound."
Juliet is a Capulet, and Romeo risks death to love her; the trite
metaphor of the wound of love has real significance for him.
Mercutio considers love mere folly unworthy of a real man
and respects only the wounds suffered in combat. Ironically,
Mercutio will die of a real wound occasioned partly by
Romeo's love, while Romeo, no less a man, will die not of a
wound but of the poison he voluntarily takes for love.

Like Adonis, Mercutio mocks not merely the futile, en-
feebling kind of love Romeo feels for Rosaline, but all love.
Moreover, his volley of sexual innuendo serves as the equivalent of both fighting and love. In its playful way, his speech is
as aggressive as fighting, and while speech establishes his
claim to virility, at the same time it marks his distance from
women. As Romeo says, Mercutio is "a gentleman . . . that
loves to hear himself talk and will speak more in a minute
than he will stand to in a month" (2.4.153–155). Mercutio
would rather fight than talk, but he would rather talk than
love, which brings us to his justly famed utterance, the Queen
Mab speech. Like so much in this play, it incorporates opposites. While it is surely a set piece set apart, it is also highly
characteristic of Mercutio, in its luxuriant repleteness of images and rippling mockery. While it purports to belittle
dreamers for the shallowness of the wishes their dreams
fulfill, it sketches the world of which the dreamers dream
with loving accuracy, sweetmeats, tithe pigs, horses' manes
and all. In service to the purest fancy, it portrays Mab's coach
and accoutrements with workmanlike precision. It pretends
to tell us dreams are "nothing but vain fantasy," but this pose
is belied by the speaker's intense awareness that real people do

dream of real things.[11] In short, Mercutio's defense against dreams gives evidence of his own urge to dream, but it also reveals his fear of giving in to the seething nighttime world of unconscious desires associated with the feminine; he prefers the broad daylight world of men fighting and jesting. Significantly, his catalogue of dreamers ends with a reference to the feminine mystery of birth and an implied analogy between the birth of children from the womb and the birth of dreams from "an idle brain." He would like to think that women's powers, and men's desires for women, are as bodiless and inconsequential as the dreams to which they give rise, and to make us think so too he concludes his whole speech with the mock-drama of a courtship between the winds. For him the perfect image of nothingness is unresponsive and inconstant love between two bodies of air. But Mercutio protests too much; the same defensiveness underlies his fancy as his bawdy. Puns and wordplay, the staple of his bawdy, figure prominently in dreams, as Freud so amply shows; relying on an accidental similarity of sound, they disguise a repressed impulse while giving voice to it.[12]

What Mercutio would deprecate through jests and dreams, the threat of being unmanned by love, Romeo struggles with in the aftermath of murdering Tybalt. Doomed to banishment, in tears he hurls himself to the floor of Friar Lawrence's cell and petulantly refuses to rise. The significance of this pos-

11. Robert O. Evans, *The Osier Cage: Rhetorical Devices in Romeo and Juliet* (Lexington, Ky.: University of Kentucky Press, 1966), argues that the Queen Mab speech deals with the real subjects of the play—money and place, the main reasons for marriage—and in the extended treatment of the soldier that concludes its catalogue of Mab's victims, "presents what in the milieu of Romeo and Juliet was a principal destructive force—violence" (p. 79).

12. Norman Holland, "Mercutio, Mine Own Son the Dentist," in *Essays on Shakespeare,* ed. Gordon Ross Smith (University Park, Pa.: Pennsylvania State University Press, 1965), pp. 3–14, comments suggestively on the contrast between Mercutio and Romeo in this respect:

He jests at scars that fears to feel a wound—a certain kind of wound, the kind that comes from real love that would lay him low, make him undergo a submission like Romeo's. Mercutio's bawdry serves to keep him a non-combatant in the wars of love. . . . Not for Mercutio is that entrance into the tomb or womb or maw which is Romeo's dark, sexual fate. (p. 12)

ture is emphasized by the Nurse's exclamation, "O, he is even in my mistress' case, / Just in her case!" (3.3.84–85). Passive abandonment to grief is normal in a woman, but effeminate in a man. Echoing the sexual innuendo of the play's first scene in a significantly different context, the Nurse urges him vigorously,

> Stand up, stand up! Stand, and you be a man.
> For Juliet's sake, for her sake, rise and stand!
> Why should you fall into so deep an O?
>
> (3.3.88–90)

Friar Lawrence's ensuing philosophical speech is really only an elaboration of the Nurse's simple, earthy rebuke. The well-meaning friar reminds Romeo that he must now base his sense of himself as a man not on his socially sanctioned identity as a son of Montague, but on his love for Juliet, in direct conflict with that identity—a situation the friar sees as only temporary. But this conflict between manhood as aggression on behalf of the father and manhood as loving a woman is at the bottom of the tragedy and not to be overcome.

In patriarchal Verona, men bear names and stand to fight for them; women, "the weaker vessels," bear children and "fall backward" to conceive them, as the Nurse's husband once told the young Juliet. It is appropriate that Juliet's growing up is hastened and intensified by having to resist the marriage arranged for her by her father, while Romeo's is precipitated by having to fight for the honor of his father's house. Unlike its sons, Verona's daughters have, in effect, no adolescence, no sanctioned period of experiment with adult identities or activities. Lady Capulet regards motherhood as the proper termination of childhood for a girl, saying to Juliet,

> Younger than you,
> Here in Verona, ladies of esteem
> Are already made mothers
>
> (1.3.69–71)

and recalling that she herself was a mother when she was about her daughter's age. Capulet is more cautious at first: "Too soon marred are those so early made" (1.2.13), he says, perhaps meaning that pregnancies are more likely to be difficult for women in early adolescence than for those even slightly older. But the pun in the succeeding lines reveals another concern besides this one:

> Earth hath swallowed all my hopes but she;
> She is the hopeful lady of my earth.
>
> (1.2.14–15)

Fille de terre is the French term for heiress, and Capulet wants to be sure that his daughter will not only survive motherhood, but produce healthy heirs for him as well.

Capulet's sudden determination to marry Juliet to Paris comes partly from a heightened sense of mortality that, when it is introduced in the first act, mellows his character attractively:

> Welcome, gentlemen! I have seen the day
> That I have worn a visor and could tell
> A whispering tale in a fair lady's ear,
> Such as would please. 'Tis gone, 'tis gone, 'tis gone.
>
> (1.5.23–26)

But he cannot give up his claim on youth as easily as these words imply. When he meets with Paris again after Tybalt's death, it is he who calls the young man back, with a "desperate tender" inspired by the thought that he, no less than his young nephew, was "born to die." Better to insure the safe passage of his property to an heir now, while he lives, than in an uncertain future. Even though decorum suggests but "half a dozen friends" as wedding guests so hard upon a kinsman's death, he hires "twenty cunning cooks" to prepare a feast and stays up all night himself "to play the housewife for this once," insisting against his wife's better judgment that the wedding be celebrated not a day later. For him, the wedding offers a ´promise that his line will continue, though his own time end soon. Shakespeare depicts Capulet's motives for forcing the hasty marriage with broad sympathy in this regard, but withdraws that sympathy in the scene in which Juliet refuses to marry Paris.

In Shakespeare's source, Arthur Brooke's versification of an Italian novella, the idea of marriage with Paris isn't introduced until after Romeo's banishment. In the play, Paris broaches his suit (evidently not for the first time) in the second scene, and receives a temperate answer from Capulet, who at this point is a model of fatherly tenderness and concern:

> My child is yet a stranger in the world
> She hath not seen the change of fourteen years;
> Let two more summers wither in their pride
> Ere we may think her ripe to be a bride.
>
> . . . .
>
> But woo her, gentle Paris, get her heart;
> My will to her consent is but a part.
> And she agreed, within her scope of choice
> Lies my consent and fair according voice.
>
> (1.2.8–11, 16–19)

Significantly, though, this scene begins with Capulet acting not only as a father but also as the head of a clan; alluding to the recent eruption of the feud and the Prince's warning, he says lightly, " 'Tis not hard, I think, / For men so old as we to keep the peace." Only when his failure to exert authority effectively over the inflammatory Tybalt results in Tybalt's death, an insult to the clan, does Capulet decide to exert it over his daughter, with compensatory strictness. Thus Shakespeare, by introducing the arranged marriage at the beginning and by making Capulet change his mind about it, shows us how capricious patriarchal rule can be and how the feud changes fatherly mildness to what Hartley Coleridge called "paternal despotism."[13] After Tybalt's death, the marriage that before required her consent is now his "decree," and his anger at her opposition mounts steadily from an astonished testiness to brutal threats:

> And you be mine, I'll give you to my friend;
> And you be not, hang, beg, starve, die in the streets,
> For, by my soul, I'll ne'er acknowledge thee,
> Nor what is mine shall ever do thee good.
>
> (3.5.193–196)

---

13. *Romeo and Juliet: A New Variorum Edition,* ed. Horace Howard Furness (Philadelphia: Lippincott, 1871), p. 200.

Perhaps Shakespeare got the inspiration for these lines from Brooke's poem, where Capulet cites Roman law allowing fathers to "pledge, alienate, and sell" their children, and even to kill them if they rebel.[14] At any rate, it is clear that Capulet's anger is as violent and unreflective as Tybalt's though he draws no sword against Juliet, and that the emotional likeness between age and youth in this instance is fostered by different aspects of the same system of patriarchal order.

In Friar Lawrence, Romeo finds a surrogate father outside that system, and in fact he never appears onstage with his parents. Juliet, on the other hand, always appears within her father's household until the last scene in the tomb. Lodged in the bosom of the family, she has two mothers, the Nurse as well as her real mother. With regard to Juliet, the Nurse is the opposite of what the Friar is for Romeo—a surrogate mother within the patriarchal family, but one who is, finally, of little help in assisting Juliet in her passage from child to woman. She embodies the female self molded devotedly to the female's family role. The only history she knows is that of birth, suckling, weaning, and marriage; for her, earthquakes are less cataclysmic than these turning points of growth. She and Juliet enter the play simultaneously in a scene in which she has almost all the lines and Juliet less than ten, a disproportion that might represent the force of tradition weighing on the heroine.

The Nurse's longest speech ends with her telling an anecdote (35–48) she subsequently repeats twice. It is perfectly in character: trivial, conventional, full of good humor but lacking wit. And yet it masterfully epitomizes how woman's subjugation to her role as wife and mother, in the patriarchal setting, is made to seem integral with nature itself:

> And then my husband (God be with his soul!
> 'A was a merry man) took up the child.
> "Yea," quoth he, "dost fall upon thy face?

14. Arthur Brooke, *The Tragicall Historye of Romeus and Juliet,* / *Narrative and Dramatic Sources of Shakespeare,* ed. Geoffrey Bullough (London: Routledge and Kegan Paul, 1966), vol. 1, p. 336, lines 1951–1960.

Thou wilt fall backward when thou hast more wit;
Wilt thou not, Jule?" and by my holidam,
The pretty wretch left crying and said, "Ay."
                                              (1.3.39–44)

The story is placed between the Nurse's recollections of
Juliet's weaning and Lady Capulet's statements that girls
younger than Juliet are already mothers, as she herself was at
Juliet's age. This collocation gives the impression of an unin-
terrupted cycle of birth and nurturance carried on from
mother to daughter, under the approving eyes of fathers and
husbands. The Nurse's husband, harmlessly amusing himself
with a slightly risqué joke at Juliet's expense, gets more than
he bargains for in the child's innocent reply. The Nurse finds
the point of the story in the idea that even as a child, Juliet had
the "wit" to assent to her sexual "fall"; she takes her "Ay" as
confirmation of Juliet's precocious fitness for "falling" and
bearing. But in a larger sense than the Nurse is meant to see,
"falling" implies that it will be Juliet's fate to "bear" her
father's will and the tragic consequences of her attempt to cir-
cumvent it. And in a larger sense still, all women by virtue of
their powers of bearing are regarded as mysteriously close to
the Earth that, as Friar Lawrence says, is "Nature's mother,"
while men, lacking these powers, and intended to rule over
the earth, rule over women also. As the Nurse says, "Women
grow by men" (1.3.95).

   Against this conception of femininity, in which women are
married too young to understand their sexuality as anything
but passive participation in a vast biological cycle through
childbearing, Shakespeare places Juliet's unconventional, fully
conscious and willed giving of herself to Romeo. As she
awaits their consummation, the terms in which she envisions
losing her virginity parody the terms of male competition, the
sense of love as a contest in which men must beat down
women or be beaten by them:

      Come, civil night,
   Thou sober-suited matron all in black,
   And learn me how to lose a winning match,
   Play'd for a pair of stainless maidenhoods.
                                              (3.2.10–13)

She knows and values her "affections and warm youthful blood," but she has yet to learn the cost of such blithe individuality in the tradition-bound world of Verona. When the Nurse tells her that Romeo has killed Tybalt, she falls suddenly into a rant condemning him, in the same kind of trite oxymorons characteristic of Romeo's speech before they met (see especially 1.1.178–186); such language in this context reflects the automatic thinking of the feud, which puts everything in terms of a Capulet-Montague dichotomy. But she drops this theme when a word from the Nurse reminds her that she now owes her loyalty to Romeo rather than to the house of Capulet:

> *Nurse:* Will you speak well of him that killed your cousin?
> *Juliet:* Shall I speak ill of him that is my husband?
> Ah, poor my lord, what tongue shall smooth thy name,
> When I, thy three-hours' wife, have mangled it?
> (3.2.96–99)

Romeo's "name" in the sense of his identity as well as his reputation now rests not on his loyalty to the Montagues but on Juliet's loyalty to him and their reciprocal identities as husband and wife apart from either house.

The lovers want to live in union; the death-dealing feud opposes their desire. In this play ordered by antitheses on so many levels, the all-embracing opposition of eros and thanatos seems to drive the plot along.[15] The tragic conclusion, however, effects a complete turnabout in this clear-cut opposition between love and death, for in the lovers' suicides love and death merge. Romeo and Juliet die as an act of love,

---

15. This view is Harry Levin's, in "Form and Formality in *Romeo and Juliet*," reprinted in *Twentieth Century Interpretations of Romeo and Juliet,* ed. Douglas Cole (Englewood Cliffs, N.J.: Prentice-Hall, 1970), p. 90. He does not develop it, however. Norman Rabkin, in a richly illuminating chapter of *Shakespeare and the Common Understanding* (New York: Free Press, 1967), titled "Eros and Death," treats *Venus and Adonis, Romeo and Juliet,* and *Antony and Cleopatra* as works that link "love, the most intense manifestation of the urge to life" with "the self-destructive yearning for annihilation that we recognize as the death wish" (p. 151). Rabkin finds this death-wish inherent in the love of Romeo and Juliet itself. I find its source in the feud, seeing the lovers impelled to seek consummation in death only because the feud makes it impossible in life.

in a spiritualized acting out of the ancient pun. Furthermore, the final scene plays off against each other two opposing views of the lovers' deaths: that they are consumed and destroyed by the feud and that they rise above it, united in death. This ambivalent conclusion reflects the play's concern with the hazards in coming of age in the patriarchal family.

It cannot be denied that through the many references to fate Shakespeare wished to create a feeling of inevitability, of a mysterious force stronger than the individuals, shaping their courses even against their will and culminating in the lovers' deaths. Yet it is also true that, as Gordon Ross Smith says, the play employs fate not as an external power, but as a subjective feeling of the two lovers.[16] And this subjective feeling springs understandably from the objective social conditions of life in Verona. The first mention of fate, in the Prologue's phrase "fatal loins," punningly connects fate with feud and anticipates the rhyme uttered by Friar Lawrence, which might stand as a summary of the play's action:

> The Earth, that's Nature's mother, is her tomb;
> That which we call her burying grave, that is her womb.
>
> (2.3.9–10)

The loins of the Montagues and the Capulets are fatal because the two families have established a state of affairs whereby their children are bound, for the sake of family honor, to kill each other. It is hardly necessary to recall how Romeo's first sight of Juliet is accompanied by Tybalt's "fetch me my rapier, boy!", or how their very names denote the fatal risk they take in loving each other. Romeo's premonition, as he sets off for the Capulets' ball, that he will have "an untimely death," or Juliet's, as his banishment begins, that she will see him next in a tomb, are not hints from the beyond, but expressions of fear eminently realistic in the circumstances.

The setting and action of the final scene are meant to remind us of the hostile social climate in which the lovers have had to act. It begins on a bittersweet note as the dull and

16. Gordon Ross Smith, "The Balance of Themes in *Romeo and Juliet*," *Essays on Shakespeare,* ed. Gordon Ross Smith (University Park, Pa.: Pennsylvania State University Press, 1965), p. 39.

proper Paris approaches to perform his mangled rites, recapitulating wedding in funeral with the flowers so easily symbolic of a young and beautiful maiden, and reminiscent of her expected defloration in marriage. By paralleling the successive entrances of Paris and Romeo, one who has had no part in the feud, the other who has paid so much for resisting it, both of whom love Juliet, Shakespeare suggests the feud's indifferent power over youth. Each character comes in with the properties appropriate to his task, and enjoins the servant accompanying him to "stand aloof." Their ensuing swordfight is subtly designed to recall the previous eruptions of the feud and to suggest it is a man-made cycle of recurrent violence. Paris's challenge to Romeo,

> Stop thy unhallowed toil, vile Montague!
> Can vengeance be pursued farther than Death?
> Condemned villain, I do apprehend thee.
> Obey, and go with me; for thou must die,
>
> (5.3.54–57)

recalls Tybalt's behavior at the Capulets' ball, when he assumed Romeo's very presence to be an insult, and in act 3, when he deliberately sought Romeo out to get satisfaction for that insult. Romeo responds to Paris as he did to Tybalt, first by hinting cryptically at his true purpose in phrases echoing those he spoke in act 3:

> By heaven, I love thee better than myself,
> For I come hither armed against myself.
>
> (5.3.64–65)

Then once more he gives in to "fire-eyed fury" when Paris continues to provoke him, and in a gesture all too familiar by now, draws his sword.

Shakespeare prepares us well before this final scene for its grim variations on the Friar's association of womb and tomb. Juliet's moving soliloquy on her fears of waking alone in the family monument amplifies its fitness as a symbol of the power of the family, inheritance, and tradition over her and Romeo. She ponders "the terror of the place":

> . . . a vault, an ancient receptacle
> Where for many hundred years the bones
> Of all my buried ancestors are packed. . . .
>
> (4.3.38–41)

In a "dismal scene" indeed, she envisions herself first driven mad by fear, desecrating these bones by playing with them, and then using the bones against herself to dash her brains out. This waking dream, like all the dreams recounted in the play, holds psychological truth; it bespeaks Juliet's knowledge that in loving Romeo she has broken a taboo as forceful as that against harming the sacred relics of her ancestors, and her fear of being punished for the offense by the ancestors themselves—with their very bones.

When Romeo forces his way into the monument, he pictures it both as a monstrous mouth devouring Juliet and himself and as a womb:

> Thou detestable maw, thou womb of death,
> Gorged with the dearest morsel of the earth,
> Thus I enforce thy rotten jaws to open,
> And in despite I'll cram thee with more food.
>
> (5.3.45–48)

When the Friar hastens toward the monument a few minutes later, his exclamation further extends the meanings connected with it:

> Alack, alack, what blood is this, which stains
> The stony entrance to this sepulchre?
>
> (5.3.140–141)

The blood-spattered entrance to the tomb that has been figured as a womb recalls both a defloration or initiation into sexuality, and a birth. Juliet's wedding bed is her grave, as premonitions had warned her, and three young men, two of them her bridegrooms, all killed as a result of the feud, share it with her. The birth that takes place in this "womb" is perversely a birth into death, a stifling return to the tomb of the fathers, not the second birth of adolescence, the birth of an adult self, which the lovers strove for.

But in the second part of the scene, comprising Romeo's death speech, the Friar's entrance and hasty departure, and Juliet's death speech, imagery and action combine to assert that death is a transcendent form of sexual consummation and, further, that it is rebirth into a higher stage of existence—the counterpart of an adulthood never fully achieved in life. That Shakespeare will have it both ways at once is perfectly in keeping with a play about adolescence in that it reflects the typical conflict of that period, which Bruno Bettelheim describes as "the striving for independence and self-assertion, and the opposite tendency, to remain safely at home, tied to the parents."[17] This ambivalent ending is also similar to the ambivalent ending of *Venus and Adonis,* in which Venus's long-striven-for possession of Adonis takes the form of the total absorption of each person in the other, at the price of Adonis's death.

It might be argued that Romeo and Juliet will their love-deaths in simple error, caused by the mere chance of Brother John's failure to reach Romeo with the news of Juliet's feigned death, and that chance is fate's instrument. But the poetic consistency and force with which their belief in death as consummation is carried out, by means of the extended play of words and actions on dying as orgasm, outweighs the sense of chance or of fate.[18] When Romeo declares, the instant after he learns of Juliet's supposed death, "Is it e'en so? Then I defy you, stars!" (5.1.24),[19] the context in which we have been led to understand and expect the lovers' death is transformed. Ro-

17. Bruno Bettelheim, *The Uses of Enchantment: The Meaning and Importance of Fairy Tales* (New York: Alfred A. Knopf, 1976), p. 91.

18. The equation of loving with dying is introduced early, and most often dying is linked to the feud, for instance in Juliet's reference to grave and wedding bed in act 1, scene 5, restated in the wedding scene. Romeo's banishment produces an explosion of remarks linking wedding bed with tomb and Romeo as bridegroom with death: 3.2.136–137; 3.5.94–96, 141, 201–203. The Friar's potion inducing a simulated death on the day of Juliet's wedding with Paris titillates us further with ironic conjunctions of death and marriage.

19. The second quarto prints "then I denie you starres," which, though it offers a different shade of meaning, still expresses Romeo's belief that he acts independently from fate.

meo no longer believes his course of action to be a way of cir-
cumventing the feud, which now has no importance for him.
Rather, he wills his death as a means to permanent union with
Juliet. He says, in the same tone of desperate but unshakeable
resolve, "Well, Juliet, I will lie with thee tonight." As her
lover and bridegroom he assumes his role in the love-death so
amply foreshadowed, but that love-death is not merely fated;
it is willed. It is the lovers' triumphant assertion over the impoverished and destructive world that has kept them apart.
Romeo's ensuing conversation with the apothecary is full of
contempt for this merely material world, and his confidence
that he alone possesses Juliet in death is so serene that he indulges in the mordantly erotic fantasy that amorous Death
keeps Juliet in the tomb "to be his paramour" (5.3.102–105),
recalling and dismissing the earlier conception of death as
Juliet's bridegroom.

Shakespeare fills Romeo's last speech with the imagery of
life's richness: the gloomy vault is "a feasting presence full of
light," and Juliet's lips and cheeks are crimson with vitality.
His last lines, "O true apothecary! / Thy drugs are quick. Thus
with a kiss I die" (5.3.120), bring together the idea of death as
sexual consummation and as rebirth. Similarly, Juliet kisses
the poison on his lips and calls it "a restorative." They have
come of age by a different means than the rites of passage,
phallic violence and adolescent motherhood, typical for youth
in Verona. Romeo's death in the Capulets' (not his own
fathers') tomb reverses the traditional passage of the female
over to the male house in marriage and betokens his refusal to
follow the code of his fathers, while it is Juliet, not Romeo,
who boldly uses his dagger, against herself.[20]

20. In an interesting essay that stresses the importance of the family,
"Shakespeare's Earliest Tragedies: Titus Andronicus and Romeo and Juliet,"
Shakespeare Survey 27 (1974): 1–9, G. K. Hunter offers a different though
related interpretation:

It is entirely appropriate that the "public" wedding bed of Romeo and
Juliet (as against their private bedding) should be placed in the Capulet
family tomb, for it is there that Romeo may most effectively be seen to
have joined his wife's clan, where their corporate identity is most un-
equivocally established. (p. 8)

II

More than a difference of gender marks off Petruchio the
tamer from Kate the shrew.[21] He is a stereotype, animated
like a puppet by the *idée fixe* of male dominance, while she
is realistically and sympathetically portrayed as a woman
trapped in the self-destructive role of shrew by the limited
norms of behavior prescribed for men and women. Her form
of violence is a desperate response to the prevailing system of
female subjection; his represents the system itself, its basic
mechanisms displayed in exaggerated form. The taming
exaggerates ludicrously the reach and force of male dominance. Though it has long been recognized that Shakespeare
gives Kate's shrewishness a psychological and moral validity
lacking in all her literary predecessors, the corollary purpose
of the taming as a farce has not been noticed. Unlike other
misogynistic shrew literature, this play satirizes not woman
herself in the person of the shrew, but the male urge to control
woman.

Long before Petruchio enters, we are encouraged to doubt
the validity of male supremacy. First of all, the transformation
of Christopher Sly from drunken lout to noble lord, a transformation only temporary and skin-deep, suggests that Kate's
switch from independence to subjection may also be decep-
tive and prepares us for the irony of the denouement. More
pointedly, one of the most alluring perquisites of Sly's new
identity is a wife whose obedience he can demand. As scene 1
of the Induction begins, Sly suffers public humiliation at the
hands of a woman when the Hostess throws him out of her
alehouse for disorderly conduct. After he awakens from his
sleep in the second scene, it is the tale of his supposed wife's
beauty and Penelope-like devotion that finally tips the balance, convincing him that he really is the aristocrat of the servants' descriptions. He then glories in demanding and getting

21. This interpretation appeared in a different form in *Modern Language
Studies* 5 (Spring 1975): 88–102, as "*The Taming of the Shrew:* Shakespeare's
Mirror of Marriage," and was reprinted in *The Authority of Experience: Essays
in Feminist Criticism,* ed. Lee Edwards and Arlyn Diamond (Amherst: University of Massachusetts Press, 1976).

his "wife's" obsequious obedience (Ind.2.68–75, 102–107).
The humor lies in the fact that Sly's pretensions to authority
and grandeur, which he claims only on the basis of sex, not
merit, and indulges specifically with women, are contradicted
in his real identity, in which he is a woman's inferior. Similarly, Petruchio later seems to find in Kate the reflection of his
own superiority, while we know he is fooled by a role he has
assumed.

In the main play, the realistic bourgeois ambiance in which
Kate is placed leads us to question the definition of shrewishness the characters take for granted. In medieval mystery
plays and Tudor interludes, shrews were already married to
their pusillanimous husbands and were shown as domestic
tyrants. Male fears of female freedom were projected onto the
wife, who was truly a threatening figure because she treated
her husband as he normally would have treated her. When the
husband attempted rebellion, he usually lost.[22] Shakespeare
departs from this literary tradition in order to sketch Kate as a
victim of the marriage market, making her "the first shrew to
be given a father, to be shown as maid and bride."[23] At her
entrance, she is already, for her father's purpose, that piece of
goods Petruchio declares her to be after the wedding. Baptista
is determined not to marry the sought-after Bianca until he
gets an offer for the unpopular Kate, not for the sake of conforming to the hierarchy of age as his opening words imply,
but out of a merchant's desire to sell all the goods in his
warehouse. His marketing technique is clever: make the sale
of the less popular item the prerequisite of purchasing the de-

22. For a review of medieval shrew literature, see Katherine Rogers, *The
Troublesome Helpmate: A History of Misogyny in Literature* (Seattle: University
of Washington Press, 1966), pp. 88–93. Muriel Bradbrook, "Dramatic Role
as Social Image: A Study of *The Taming of the Shrew*," *Shakespeare Jahrbuch* 94
(1958): 132–150, discusses Tudor treatments of the shrew. For an example of
shrew literature contemporary with Shakespeare, see *Tom Tyler and his Wife*
(ca. 1578), ed. Felix E. Schelling, *PMLA* 15 (1900): 253–289. Strife, the hero's
wife, humiliates and tortures him, forcing him "to serve like a knave, and
live like a slave." His friend disguises himself as Tom and secures Strife's
surrender immediately by beating her. However, when Tyler confesses that
not he but another man did it, she turns on him again and resumes her
tyranny.
23. Bradbrook, "Dramatic Role," p. 139.

sirable one. As Tranio sympathetically remarks after Kate's marriage is arranged, " 'Twas a commodity that lay fretting by you" (2.1.321).

That money, not his daughter's happiness, is Baptista's real concern in matchmaking becomes evident when Petruchio brusquely makes his bid for Kate. Both Petruchio and Baptista pretend to make Kate's love the ultimate condition of the marriage, but then Petruchio simply lies in asserting that she has fallen in love with him at first sight. Her father, though he doubts this farfetched claim ("I know not what to say") claps up the match anyhow, for on it depends Bianca's match as well. Both marriages, we can assume, provide insurance against having to support his daughters in widowhood, promise grandsons to whom he may pass on the management and possession of his property, and impart to his household the prestige of "marrying well," for the wealth of the grooms advertises Baptista's own financial status. Petruchio's and Tranio/Lucentio's frequent references to their respective fathers' wealth and reputations remind us that wealth and reputation pass from father to son, with woman as mere accessory to the passing. As Simone de Beauvoir states in *The Second Sex,*

> The interests of property require among nobility and bourgeoisie that a single administrator take charge. This could be a single woman; her abilities were admitted; but from feudal times to our days the married woman has been deliberately sacrificed to private property. The richer the husband, the greater the dependence of the wife; the more powerful he feels socially and economically, the more authoritatively he plays the *paterfamilias*. [24]

Even the Bianca plot emphasizes heavily the venal aspects of marriage, though it is usually characterized as romantic, in contrast to the realism and farce of the taming. In act 2, scene 1, Baptista awards Bianca to Tranio/Lucentio solely because he offers more cash and property as "widowhood" (that is, claims to have more total wealth) than Gremio does. As

---

24. Simone de Beauvoir, *The Second Sex* (Paris: Librairie Gallimard, 1949; rpt. New York: Bantam-Knopf, 1953), pp. 93–94.

George Hibbard has shown, the scene satirizes the hardheaded commercial nature of marital arrangements.[25]

It is time to turn, with Kate, from the father to the husband. From the moment Petruchio commands his servant "knock, I say," he evokes and creates noise and violence. A hubbub of loud speech, beatings, and quarrelsomeness surrounds him. "The swelling Adriatic seas" and "thunder when the clouds in autumn crack" are a familiar part of his experience, which he easily masters with his own force of will or physical strength. Like Adam, he is lord over nature, and his own violence has been well legitimized by society, unlike Kate's, which has marked her as unnatural and abhorrent. But let us examine the nature of Petruchio's violence compared to Kate's.

The hallmark of a shrew is her scolding tongue and loud raucous voice—a verbal violence befitting woman, since her limbs are traditionally weak. It is interesting that Kate is given only twelve lines in her entrance scene, only five of which allude to physical violence:

> I' faith, sir, you shall never need to fear;
> Iwis it [marriage] is not halfway to her heart.
> But if it were, doubt not her care should be
> To comb your noddle with a three-legged stool
> And paint your face and use you like a fool.
>
> (1.1.61–65)

Here she threatens Hortensio in response to his greater threat, that no man will marry her. These lines have a distinctly defensive cast; Kate refers to herself in the third person and denies any interest in a mate because two prospective mates (Hortensio and Gremio) have just made it clear that they have no interest in her. Kate's vision of breaking furniture over a husband's head is hypothetically couched in the subjunctive. Yet later Tranio describes her speech in this scene as "such

25. George Hibbard, "*The Taming of the Shrew:* A Social Comedy," *Shakespearean Essays,* ed. Alwin Thaler and Norman Sanders, Special Number: 2, *Tennessee Studies in Literature* (Knoxville: University of Tennessee Press, 1964), pp. 16–30. Hibbard's remarks on the financial aspects of marriage in the play are most helpful. He is more sensitive to Kate's position as woman and as marriage-commodity than any critic I have read.

a storm that mortal ears might hardly endure the din" (1.1.172–173). Throughout the play, this kind of disparity between the extent and nature of Kate's "shrewish" behavior and the male characters' perceptions of it focuses our attention on masculine behavior and attitudes that stereotype women as either submissive and desirable or rebellious and shrewish. Kate is called devil, hell, curst, shrewd (shrewish), and wildcat and referred to in other insulting ways because, powerless to change her situation, she *talks* about it. That her speech is defensive rather than offensive in origin, and psychologically necessary for her survival, is eloquently conveyed by her own lines:

> My tongue will tell the anger of my heart,
> Or else my heart, concealing it, will break,
> And rather than it shall I will be free
> Even to the uttermost, as I please, in words.
>
> (4.3.77–80)

Though she commits four acts of physical violence onstage (binding and striking Bianca, breaking a lute over Hortensio's head, hitting Petruchio and then Grumio), in each instance the dramatic context suggests that she strikes out because of provocation or intimidation resulting from her status as a woman.[26] For example, the language in which her music lesson with Hortensio is described conveys the idea that it is but another masculine attempt to subjugate woman. "Why, then thou canst not break her to the lute?" asks Baptista. "I did but tell her she mistook her frets / And bowed her hand to teach

---

26. In her first manifestation of violence, she torments Bianca only in response to Bianca's more underhanded treatment of her in the first scene, when she subtly lorded it over Kate by acting as though she were a martyr to her elder sister's failure to attract suitors. Actually, Bianca's confinement is not Kate's fault; it is the whim of their father. When Kate declares, "Her silence flouts me," she means that Bianca intends her ostentatiously submissive attitude as a slap at her vocally rebellious sister. Kate responds to Bianca's slyness with blows, an "unfeminine" but understandable outlet.

After she breaks the lute on Hortensio's head, she strikes Petruchio, an outburst she could have avoided had she been able to think of an appropriately lewd rejoinder to his obscene remark, "What, with my tongue in your tail?" Invention fails her, as cunning later does when she fails to realize that Grumio, like his master, is only torturing her with the promise of food, and (in her last physical outburst) strikes him.

her fingering," replies Hortensio (2.1.147, 149–150). Later Petruchio explicitly attempts to "break" Kate to his will, and throughout the play men tell her that she "mistakes her frets"—that her anger is unjustified.

On the other hand, Petruchio's confident references to "great ordance in the field" and the "loud 'larums, neighing steeds, trumpets' clang" of battle bespeak a lifelong acquaintance with organized violence as a masculine vocation. The loud oaths with which he orders his servants about and startles the priest in the wedding service are thus farcical exaggerations of normal masculine behavior. In its volume and vigor, his speech also suggests a robust manliness that would make him attractive to the woman who desires a master (or who wants to identify with power in its most accessible form).

But if Petruchio were female, he would be known as a shrew and shunned accordingly by men. Behavior desirable in a male automatically prohibits similar behavior in a female, for woman must mold herself to be complementary to man, not competitive with him. When Petruchio declares, "I am as peremptory as she proud-minded," he seems to state that he and his bride-to-be are two of a kind. But that "kind," bold, independent, self-assertive, must only be male. Thus his image of himself and Kate as "two raging fires" ends on a predictable note:

> And where two raging fires meet together
> They do consume the thing that feeds their fury.
> Though little fire grows great with little wind,
> Yet extreme gusts will blow out fire and all.
> So I to her, *and so she yields to me,*
> For I am rough and woo not like a babe.
> (2.1.132–137; emphasis mine)

His force must necessarily triumph over Kate's because he is male and she is not. Those critics who maintain that his force is acceptable because it has only the limited, immediate purpose of making Kate reject an "unbecoming" mode of behavior miss the real point of the taming.[27] The overt force Petruchio wields over Kate by marrying her against her will in

27. For example, Richard Hosley argues that "more shrew than she, he 'kills her in her own humor' " ("Introduction," *The Taming of the Shrew, The*

the first place and then by denying her every wish and comfort, by stamping, shouting, reducing her to exhaustion, etc.,
is but a farcical representation of the psychological realities of
marriage in Elizabethan England, in which the husband's will
constantly, silently, and invisibly, through custom and conformity, suppressed the wife's.

In the wedding scene, when all the trappings are stripped
away (and they are, by Petruchio's design), the groom is simply completing the legal arrangements whereby he acquires
Kate as he would acquire a piece of property. Declaring he'll
"seal the title with a lovely kiss," he refers not just to Kate's
new title as his wife, but also to the title deed that, sealed with
wax, passed to the purchaser in a property transaction. In the
brutally plain statement Petruchio delivers at the conclusion
of the wedding scene, he bears down on this point:

> She is my goods, my chattels; she is my house,
> My household stuff, my field, my barn,
> My horse, my ox, my ass, my anything.
> (3.2.230–232)

His role as property owner is the model for his role as husband; Kate, for him, is a thing. Or at least she will become a
thing when he has wrenched unquestioning obedience from
her, when she no longer has mind or will of her own. It is
impossible that Shakespeare meant us to accept Petruchio's
speech uncritically: it is the most shamelessly blunt statement
of the relationship between men, women, and property to be
found in the literature of this period. After the simple declar-
ative statements of possession, quoted above, that deny humanity to Kate, the speech shifts to chivalric challenges of
imaginary "thieves" who would snatch her away. Is she
goods, in the following lines, or a medieval damsel?

Pelican Shakespeare [Baltimore: Penguin Books, 1964], p. 17); Muriel Bradbrook, "Dramatic Role as Social Image: A Study of *The Taming of the Shrew*"
(cited in note 22), agrees, stating, "The central knot, the point of the play is
here"; and Robert Heilman, "Introduction," *The Taming of the Shrew, The
Signet Classic Shakespeare* (New York: New American Library, 1966), p. xli,
says, "Kate's great victory is, with Petruchio's help, over herself." Certainly
Petruchio's method of taming is to mirror Kate's behavior to her as he sees it,
from his male viewpoint, but I argue that that is not Shakespeare's point in
the taming action as a whole.

Touch her whoever dare,
I'll bring mine action on the proudest he
That stops my way in Padua. Grumio,
Draw forth thy weapon, we are beset with thieves.
Rescue thy mistress, if thou be a man.

(3.2.233–237)

The point is that Petruchio wants to think of her in both kinds of terms. The speech concludes grandly with the metamorphosis of Petruchio into a knight-errant:

Fear not, sweet wench; they shall not touch thee, Kate.
I'll buckler thee against a million.

(3.2.233–239)

The modulation of simple ownership into spurious chivalry reveals the speaker's buried awareness that he cheapens himself by being merely Kate's proprietor; he must transform the role into something nobler.

Petruchio's thundering oaths and physical brutality reach a crescendo at his country house in act 4, when he beats his servants, throws food and dishes on the floor, stomps, roars, and bullies. These actions are directed not against his bride but at his servants, again in the name of chivalry, out of a fastidious devotion to his bride's supposed comfort. But his stance is rooted realistically in his status as lord of a manor and master of a household that is not Kate's but his. He ordered her wedding clothes, chose their style and paid for them. Kate wears them not at her pleasure but at his, as Grumio's jest succinctly indicates:

Petruchio: Well, sir, in brief, the gown is not for me.
Grumio: You are i' th' right, sir; 'tis for my mistress.

(4.3.152–154)

In the famous soliloquy which opens "Thus have I politicly begun my reign" (4.1.182–205), Petruchio reduces Kate to an animal capable of learning only through deprivation of food and rest, devoid of all sensitivity save the physical. The animal metaphor shocks us and I would suggest was meant to shock Shakespeare's audience, despite their respect for falconry as an art and that reverence for the great chain of being emphasized by E. M. W. Tillyard. The blandness of Petruchio's confidential tone, the sweep of his easy assumption that Kate is not merely an animal, but *his* animal, who lives or dies at his command, has a dramatic irony similar to that of his exit speech in the wedding scene. Both utterances unashamedly present the status of woman in marriage as degrading in the extreme, plainly declaring her a subhuman being who exists solely for the purposes of her husband. Yet both offer this vision of the wife as chattel or animal in a lordly, self-confident tone.

Shakespeare does not rest with showing that male supremacy in marriage denies woman's humanity. In the most brilliant comic scene of the play (4.5), he goes on to demonstrate how it defies reason. Petruchio demands that Kate agree that the sun is the moon in order to force a final showdown. Having exhausted and humiliated her to the limit of his invention, he now wants her to know that he would go to any extreme to get the obedience he craves. Shakespeare implies here that male supremacy is ultimately based on such absurdities, for it insists that whatever a man says is right because he is a man, even if he happens to be wrong.

Why does Kate submit to her husband's unreason? Or why does she *appear* to do so, and on what terms? On the most pragmatic level, she follows Hortensio's advice to "say as he says or we shall never go" only in order to achieve her immediate and most pressing needs: a bed, a dinner, some peace and quiet. Shakespeare never lets us think she believes it right, either morally or logically, to submit her judgment and the evidence of her senses to Petruchio's rule. In fact, the language of her capitulation makes it clear that she thinks him mad:

> Forward, I pray, since we have come so far,
> And be it moon or sun or what you please,
> *And if you please to call it a rush-candle,*
> Henceforth I vow it shall be so for me.
>
> . . . .
>
> But sun it is not when you say it is not,
> *And the moon changes even as your mind.*
> (4.5.12–15, 19–20; emphasis mine)

At this point, Hortensio concedes Petruchio's victory and applauds it; Petruchio henceforth behaves and speaks as though he has indeed tamed Kate. However, we must assume that since he previously donned the mask of the ardent lover, professing rapture at Kate's rudeness, he can see that she is doing the same thing here. At their first meeting he turned the tables on her, praising her for mildness and modesty after she gave insults and even injury. Now she pays him back, suddenly overturning his expectations and moreover mocking them at the same time. But he is not fooled and can take that mockery as the cue for compromise. It reassures him that she will give him obedience if that is what he must have, but it also warns him that she, in turn, must retain her intellectual freedom.

The scene then proceeds on this basis, each character accepting the other's assumed role. Kate responds to Petruchio's outrageous claim that the wrinkled Vincentio is a fair young maiden by pretending so wholeheartedly to accept it that we know she cannot be in earnest. She embroiders the fantasy in an exuberant declamatory style more appropriate to tragedy than comedy:

> Young budding virgin, fair and fresh and sweet,
> Whither away, or where is thy abode?
> Happy the parents of so fair a child!
> Happier the man whom favorable stars
> Allots thee for his lovely bedfellow!
>
> (4.5.36–41)

Her rhetoric expresses her realization that the power struggle she had entered into on Petruchio's terms is absurd. It also signals her emancipation from that struggle, in the terms she declared earlier: "I will be free / Even to the uttermost, as I please, in words."

Of course, a freedom that exists only in words is ultimately as limited as Petruchio's mastery. Though Kate is clever enough to use his verbal strategies against him, she is trapped in her own cleverness. Her only way of maintaining her inner freedom is by outwardly denying it, a psychologically perilous position. Furthermore, to hold that she maintains her freedom in words is to posit a distinction without a difference, for whether she remains spiritually independent of Petruchio or sincerely believes in his superiority, her outward behavior must be the same—that of the perfect Griselda, a model for all women. What complicates the situation even more is that Kate quite possibly has fallen in love with her tamer, whose vitality and bravado make him attractive, despite his professed aims. Her failure to pursue her rebellion after the wedding or in the country house supports this hypothesis, as does the tone of her mockery in act 4, scene 5, and thereafter, which is playful and joyous rather than bitter and angry as it was in the first three acts.

Finally, we must remember that Shakespearean comedy celebrates love; love through any contrivance of plot or character. Here Shakespeare parts company with sterner moralists like Jonson or more relentless social critics like Ibsen. As Northrop Frye states, "In comedy and in romance, the story seeks its own end instead of holding the mirror up to nature."[28] Though Shakespeare quite astutely mirrors aspects of the human condition in this as in other comedies, that is not his only purpose. He also aims to present an idealized vision of love triumphant in marriage. The match between Kate and Petruchio bespeaks a comic renewal of society, the materialism and egotism of the old order transformed or at least softened by the ardor and mutual tolerance of the young lovers. Shakespeare wants to make us feel that Kate has not been bought or sold, but has given herself out of love. Thus he makes her walk a tightrope of affirming her husband's superiority through outward conformity while questioning it ironically through words.

In the last scene, Shakespeare finally allows Petruchio that lordship over Kate and superiority to other husbands for which he has striven so mightily. He just makes it clear to us, through the contextual irony of Kate's last speech, that his mastery is an illusion. As a contest between males in which

28. Northrop Frye, *A Natural Perspective: The Development of Shakespearean Comedy and Romance* (New York: Columbia University Press, 1965; rpt. New York: Harcourt, Brace & World, 1965), p. 8.

woman is the prize, the closing scene is analogous to the entire play. It was partly Petruchio's desire to show his peers that he was more of a man than they which spurred him to take on the shrew in the first place. Gremio refers to him as a Hercules and compares the subduing of Kate to a "labor . . . more than Alcides' twelve" (1.2.256–257). Hortensio longs but fails to emulate his friend's supposed success in taming. Lucentio, winner in the other wooing contest, fails in the final test of marital authority. Petruchio stands alone in the last scene, the center of male admiration.

As critics have noted, the wager scene is punctuated by reversals: quiet Bianca talks back and shrewish Kate seems to become an obedient wife. In a further reversal, Kate steals the scene from her husband, who has held the stage throughout the play, and reveals that he has failed to tame her in the sense he set out to. He has gained her outward compliance in the form of a public display, while her spirit remains mischievously free. Though she pretends to speak earnestly on behalf of her own inferiority, she actually treats us to a pompous, wordy, holier-than-thou sermon that delicately mocks the sermons her husband has delivered to her and about her. It is significant that Kate's speech is both her longest utterance and the longest in the play. Previously, Petruchio dominated the play verbally,[29] and his longest speech totaled twenty-four lines, while Kate's came to fifteen. Moreover, everything Kate said was a protest against her situation or those who put her in it, and as such was deemed unwomanly, or shrewish. Petruchio's impressive rhetoric, on the other hand, asserted his masculinity in the form of command over women and servants and of moral authority. Now Kate apes this verbal dominance and moralistic stance for satirical effect.

In content, the speech is thoroughly orthodox. Its sentiments, the platitudes of male dominance, can be found in a

---

29. Space does not allow me to compare the style and dramatic impact of Kate's and Petruchio's speech respectively. In quantitative terms, however, Petruchio speaks 564 lines in the play, Kate 207, less than half as many. In several scenes, notably 4.1, Kate is conspicuously silent while her husband utters a volley of commands, oaths, and admonitory remarks.

dozen treatises on marriage written in the sixteenth century.[30] Its irony emanates primarily from the dramatic context. First, it follows upon and resembles Kate's rhetorical performance on the road back to Padua. It is a response to her husband's demand that she demonstrate her obedience before others, as she did then before Hortensio, and as such it exceeds expectations once more. It fairly shouts obedience, when a gentle murmur would suffice. Having heard her address Vincentio as "young, budding virgin," we know what she is up to in this instance. Second, though the speech pleads subordination, as a speech—a lengthy, ambitious verbal performance before an audience—it allows the speaker to dominate that audience. Though Kate purports to speak as a woman to women, she assumes the role of a preacher whose authority and wisdom are, in the terms of the play, thoroughly masculine. Third, the speech sets the seal on a complete reversal of character, a push-button change from rebel to conformist that is part of the mechanism of farce. Here as elsewhere in the play, farce has two purposes: it completes the fantasy of male dominance, but also mocks it as mere fantasy. Kate's quick transformation perfectly fulfills Petruchio's wishes, but is transparently false to human nature. Toward the end of her lecture, Kate hints that she is dissembling in the line: "That seeming to be most which we indeed least are." Though she seems to be the most vocal apologist for male dominance, she is indeed its ablest critic.[31]

30. Carroll Camden lists and summarizes the contents of such works in his *The Elizabethan Woman* (Houston: University of Texas Press, 1952), pp. 61–75, 77–82. Katherine Rogers, *Troublesome Helpmate*, pp. 140–151, reviews Puritan treatises on marriage. Of the latter, two of the most easily obtainable are *A Preparative to Marriage* (1591) by Henry Smith, in his *Works*, ed. T. Fuller, 2 vols. (Edinburgh: J. Nichol, 1866), vol. 1, and "The Marriage Ring," by Jeremy Taylor, in *The Whole Works,* rev. ed., ed. R. Heber, 10 vols. (London: Longman, Green, Longman, Roberts, and Green, 1862–1865), vol. 4.
31. On this point I find myself in disagreement with Richard Henze, "Role Playing in *The Taming of the Shrew*," *Southern Humanities Review* 4 (1970): 231–240, who sees Kate as playing a succession of "complementary" roles at Petruchio's direction, culminating in the role of obedient wife that has by then become "natural" to her.

On one level, the denouement is the perfect climax of a masculine fantasy, for as Kate concludes she prepares to place her head beneath her husband's foot, an emblem of wifely obedience. On a deeper level, as I have tried to show, her words speak louder than her actions and mock that fantasy. But on the deepest level, because the play depicts its heroine as outwardly compliant but inwardly independent, it represents possibly the most cherished male fantasy of all—that woman remain *un*tamed, even in her subjection. Does Petruchio know he has been taken? Quite probably, since he himself has played the game of saying-the-thing-which-is-not. Would he enjoy being married to a woman as dull and proper as the Kate who delivers that marriage sermon? From all indications, no. Then can we conclude that Petruchio no less than Kate knowingly plays a false role in this marriage, the role of victorious tamer and complacent master? I think we can, but what does this tell us about him and about men in general?

It is Kate's submission to him that makes Petruchio a man, finally and indisputably. This is the action toward which the whole plot drives, and if we consider its significance for Petruchio and his fellows, we realize that the myth of feminine weakness, which prescribes that women ought to or must inevitably submit to man's superior authority, masks a contrary myth: that only a woman has the power to authenticate a man, by acknowledging him *her* master. Petruchio's mind may change even as the moon, but what is important is that Kate confirm those changes; moreover, that she do so willingly and consciously. Such voluntary surrender is, paradoxi-

---

Kate's pose of submissive wife is one of many instances in which characters assume roles or identities not their own. Christopher Sly, Tranio and Lucentio, Hortensio, and the Pedant all take on false identities, whereas Kate, Bianca, and the Widow behave so as to conceal their true natures. This common element of "supposes" (so named from one of Shakespeare's sources, Gascoigne's play *Supposes*) has long been recognized as a major source of meaning in the play. In the context of the play's treatment of marriage, the fact that not only Kate and Petruchio but also the other two couples assume sex-determined poses that their true personalities belie lends greater weight to my thesis that Shakespeare views traditional marital roles skeptically.

cally, part of the myth of female power, which assigns to woman the crucial responsibility for creating a mature and socially respectable man. In *The Taming of the Shrew*, Shake-speare reveals the dependency that underlies mastery, the strength behind submission. Truly, Petruchio is wedded to his Kate.

CHAPTER FIVE

"The Savage Yoke":
Cuckoldry and Marriage

O powerful love, that in some respects makes a
beast a man, in some other, a man a beast.
　　The Merry Wives of Windsor,
　　5.5.4–6

The Shakespearean comedies of courtship celebrate its
culmination in marriage. Women both witty and
beautiful mock their lovers' affectations and teach
them to love wisely and well; they lead them out of
the forests of desire and toward the altar of marriage.
Most of these comedies, though, stop short of
depicting married life. They merely leave us
confident that bride and groom will thrive as
husband and wife, for marriage in comedy represents
the ideal accommodation of eros and society. But
there also runs a vein, in these works as well as in the
other genres, of critical commentary on marriage as
tantamount to cuckoldry. In this vision of marriage,
women are betrayers and men their victims; wives
turn whore and men become monsters. Man's
vulnerability to woman in marriage is symbolized by
the cuckold, who skulks through Shakespeare's
works from early to late, his horns publishing his
shame: "a fixed figure, for the time of scorn, / To
point his slow unmoving fingers at." A man is
dishonored, his masculine identity is weakened, and
he acquires an indelible stigma when he becomes a

cuckold.[1] In this chapter I will explore the reasons for this stigma: first, by surveying the motifs associated with cuckoldry in Shakespeare—motifs he takes from the common stock used by his fellow dramatists; second, by examining in greater depth the particularly Shakespearean significance of cuckoldry as a masculine fantasy of feminine betrayal.

Before we can understand cuckoldry in Shakespeare's terms, we need to know its features as a literary and dramatic motif. OED defines *cuckold* as "a derisive name for the husband of an unfaithful wife," dating its earliest use ca. 1250, in *The Owl and the Nightingale*. The word is thought to derive from the cuckoo, the bird that lays its eggs in other birds' nests. In a linguistic turnabout, however, *cuckold* does not denote the male seducer who flits from one marital nest to another, but his victim, the husband who may be the unknowing father of another man's child. Significantly, the technical equivalent for the wife of an unfaithful husband, *cuckquean,* is little known and little used.[2] Cuckoldry is something that happens to husbands, not wives, and it happens to them because they are husbands. A man whose mistress is unfaithful does not become a cuckold, and a man who is un-

1. Puritan thought, of course, provides a vastly different perspective on marital infidelity than that which I find in Shakespeare's treatment of cuckoldry. In a flood of sermons and handbooks of domestic conduct, Puritan divines argue for reciprocity in all aspects of marriage, condemning the double standard and asserting the spiritual equality of women. See Louis B. Wright's review of the popular literature on marriage and on the status of women in his *Middle Class Culture in Elizabethan England* (Chapel Hill, N.C.: University of North Carolina Press, 1935) and William and Malleville Haller's "The Puritan Art of Love," *Huntington Library Quarterly* 5 (January 1942): 235–272, which explicates Puritan conceptions of marriage. More recently, Juliet Dusinberre, in her *Shakespeare and the Nature of Women* (New York: Barnes and Noble, 1975) holds that the drama from 1590 to 1625 is feminist in sympathy and motivated chiefly by a belief in chaste marriage. I believe, on the other hand, that while Shakespeare might give assent to Puritan ideals, he is mainly concerned to understand the psychological and social workings of cuckoldry as a powerful male fantasy; he is not arguing for or against any particular ideal of marriage when he deals with cuckoldry.

2. The OED defines *cuckquean* as a female cuckold, with instances dating from 1592, but the word does not appear in Shakespeare and, to my knowledge, is seldom found in his contemporaries. It has acquired neither the derisive force nor the cluster of motifs and corollary attitudes surrounding the cuckold.

faithful to his wife does not confer upon her the peculiarly galling identity the erring wife confers upon her husband.

The notion of cuckoldry results from the confluence of three mutually reinforcing phenomena. First, misogyny, in particular the belief that all women are lustful and fickle; second, the double standard, by which man's infidelity is tolerated, while woman's is an inexcusable fault; and third, patriarchal marriage, which makes a husband's honor depend on his wife's chastity. Typically, the injured husband first and most feelingly blames his wife, not her lover, and it is misogyny that fuels this response. No matter what the circumstances of the wife's infidelity, it only confirms what all men know—*così fan tutte*. The cuckold may take revenge against either his wife or her lover, or against both. According to the double standard, however, she has become a whore, irrevocably degraded by even one sexual transgression, while her lover's action invites disapproval but not the condemnation visited upon her.

Nor does he earn the scorn and ridicule that is the cuckold's lot. A puzzling disproportion exists between the everlasting shame of the cuckold as victim, and the mere disapproval directed at the cuckolder as perpetrator. The source of the cuckold's shame is patriarchal marriage, which determines "that men have property in woman, and that the value of this property is immeasurably diminished if the woman at any time has sexual relations with anyone other than her husband."[3] The nature of this property is hard to define, but it is closely allied to the status conferred by honor—the honor of having a chaste wife. Moreover, though the husband may be said to "own" his wife's sexual favors, while under the double standard she has no exclusive claim to his, he is under a certain obligation to keep her sexually satisfied. If she remains faithful, she in effect certifies his virility; if she strays, she calls it into question. A wife, like any property, can be "stolen" from her husband by another man if he sleeps with her. But the loss of a wife's chastity is more than a material loss to a

3. Keith Thomas, "The Double Standard," *Journal of the History of Ideas* 20 (1959): 195–216, especially 203–204.

husband. His dishonor and the scorn he endures are for him a loss of status in the community and particularly among his male peers that matters, in most cases, as much as the loss of his trust and her affection.

The cuckold's stigma is symbolized and imprinted on our visual imaginations by his horns—horns that produce the heartfelt or trivial, clever or tiresome flutters of quibbles, allusions, puns, and jokes that mark drama from Elizabethan times well into the eighteenth century. Dictionaries of slang list many expressions clearly implying that the horn is a phallic symbol, for it is colloquially "the physical sign of sexual excitement in the male" or "the male member" itself.[4] Virile animals, such as bulls, stags, and the traditionally lecherous goat have horns and are associated with cuckoldry. Horns would thus seem inappropriate for the cuckold who has not been able to keep his wife in his own bed; not he, but the sexually successful cuckolder should wear them. The cuckold's horns *are* his virility, however; or rather, as I will show, they are the mockery made of it by marriage. Regarded endopsychically, from the cuckold's point of view, horns are a defense formed through denial, compensation, and upward displacement. They say, "It's not that I can't keep my wife because I don't have enough of a penis. I have two of them, in fact, right up where everyone can see them."[5] But insofar as horns express society's understanding of the cuckold rather than his defense against being cuckolded, they indicate that a husband has allowed his virility to be yoked to a woman who leads him by the nose like an animal. The part of him that is at once his pride and his vulnerability, that makes him godlike in sexual power, but bestial in blind appetite, is exposed as his nemesis, his fatal flaw. Its power is mocked and its dumb bestiality confirmed in horns.

4. See Eric Partridge, *A Dictionary of Slang and Unconventional English* (New York: Macmillan, 1937), and John S. Farmer and W. E. Henley, eds., *Slang and Its Analogues Past and Present*, 7 vols. (London: Routledge, 1891–1904).

5. Sigmund Freud states in *The Interpretation of Dreams*, trans. and ed. James Strachey (New York: Avon, 1965), "If one of the ordinary symbols for a penis occurs in a dream doubled or multiplied, it is to be regarded as a warding-off of castration" (p. 392).

I

Cuckoldry is not central to the plot of any early or middle comedy, but insofar as these plays deal with courtship and marriage, it lurks in the wings, a potential threat to and mockery of marriage. In *Love's Labour's Lost*, the idea is voiced tellingly in the concluding song, which is built on the conventional *topos* of a debate between winter and spring. The chorus of the first two verses reads:

> The cuckoo then, on every tree,
> Mocks married men; for thus sings he,
>   Cuckoo!
> Cuckoo, Cuckoo: O word of fear,
> Unpleasing to a married ear!
>
> (5.2.888–892)

As spring suggests mating, and mating marriage, so marriage suggests cuckoldry; it must follow as the night the day, or as winter follows summer in the song itself. As the Clown in *All's Well That Ends Well* sings,

> For I the ballad will repeat
> Which men full true shall find:
> Your marriage comes by destiny,
> Your cuckoo sings by kind.
>
> (1.3.58–61)

Sometimes cuckoldry enters a comedy in association with hunting, the deer's horns suggesting the cuckold's.[6] *As You Like It* contains a gratuitous scene of some eighteen lines in which Jaques and other nobles, their hunt concluded, celebrate the hunter who killed the deer, planting its horns upon his head "for a branch of victory," and thus making him incidentally a cuckold figure:

> Take thou no scorn to wear the horn,
> It was a crest ere thou wast born;
> Thy father's father wore it,
> And thy father bore it.
> The horn, the horn, the lusty horn
> Is not a thing to laugh to scorn,
>
> (4.2.13–18)

6. See the elaborate banter between Boyet, Margaret, and Rosaline in *Love's Labour's Lost* (4.1.110–118).

they sing, voicing one of the most prominent motifs of cuckoldry: the brotherhood of all married men as potential if not
actual cuckolds. The horn is the "crest" of married manhood,
the sign of one's dubious or threatened honor as the possessor
of a wife's sexuality, just as a nobleman's crest is the sign of
his family honor. Touchstone, pondering his wedding in the
woods with "no assembly but horn-beasts," inevitably slides
into another ironic encomium:

> Courage! As horns are odious, they are necessary. It is said,
> "Many a man knows no end of his goods." Right! many a man
> has good horns, and knows no end of them. Well, that is the
> dowry of his wife, 'tis none of his own getting. Horns? even
> so. Poor men alone? No, no, the noblest deer hath them as
> huge as the rascal. Is the single man therefore bless'd? No, as a
> wall'd town is more worthier than a village, so is the forehead
> of a married man more honorable than the bare brow of a
> bachelor; and by how much defense is better than no skill, by
> so much is a horn more precious than to want.
>
> (3.3.52–63)

Turning shame to witty advantage by spurious logic, Touchstone touches on several prominent aspects of cuckoldry.
First, he notes the factor of obtuseness: the cuckold is frequently mocked for failing to see what is going on right under his nose, when it is obvious to others. Second, just as possession of a wife and founding a family with her increases a
man's honor, signifying his maturity and prestige within the
community, so a husband becomes more vulnerable to loss of
honor than a bachelor. The Clown in *All's Well That Ends
Well* also adopts the ironic mode of calling the cuckold's loss
his gain:

> He that ears my land spares my team, and gives me leave to in
> the crop; if I be his cuckold, he's my drudge. . . . If men could
> be contented to be what they are there were no fear in mar-
> riage; for young Charbon the puritan and old Poysam the
> papist, howsome'er their hearts are sever'd in religion, their
> heads are both one; they may jowl horns together like any deer
> i' th' herd.
>
> (1.3.42–54)

The Clown, like Touchstone, is about to take a wife, and he
shows himself a wise fool by recognizing and accepting the

folly that is inevitably his as a married man. "In time the savage bull doth bear the yoke," says Don Pedro, in *Much Ado about Nothing*. But Benedick the inveterate mocker of marriage, the free man, replies,

> If ever the sensible Benedick bear it, pluck off the bull's horns, and set them in my forehead, and let me be vildly painted . . .
>
> (1.1.255–257)

only to join the fools, when he prepares to marry Beatrice, in the familiar mock encomium, "There is no staff more reverend than one tipp'd with horn" (5.4.123).

Two strains of meaning run through these horn jokes. One is a kind of visual pun on the well-known emblem of marriage, the yoke; what joins husband and wife together is also what degrades the man to the level of a dumb, yoked beast— the destiny of being a cuckold.[7] The other also turns on the cuckold's resemblance to a beast; horned, he is "like any deer i' th' herd." Rather than being exceptional, a monster, he shares the common lot of men; if women are all whores, men are all cuckolds, and therein brothers. Thus though cuckoldry sets men against one another, cuckolder one-upping cuckold, it also creates a bond between men that, though it offsets rivalry to some degree, is based on shared humiliation.

Leontes, in *The Winter's Tale*, expresses most bitterly the tension of relations between men as defined by cuckoldry when he envisions a world in which each man preys on his neighbor by sleeping with his neighbor's wife. The paradisiacal union he knew with Polixenes in his youth has been superseded by an adult world in which men compete with other men for status through women—a smirking, hypocritical, vengeful contest:

> And many a man there is (even at this present,
> Now, while I speak this) holds his wife by th'arm,
> That little thinks she's been sluic'd in's absence
> And his pond fish'd by his next neighbour, by
> Sir Smile, his neighbour.
>
> (1.2.192–196)

7. See Cesare Ripa, *Iconologia* (1603), in which the figure representing Matrimony wears a yoke and a clog. The accompanying text reads, in part,

Faced with such a world, he takes the cuckold's cynical comfort, like Touchstone or Othello, in resignation to being one of the herd: "Many thousand on's / Have the disease, and feel't not" (1.2.206–207).

In the wager plot of *Cymbeline,* however, Shakespeare stresses rivalry, rather than brotherhood, in cuckoldry. When Iachimo draws Posthumus into betting on his wife's chastity, he compares that unseen essence to a jewel any thief can steal, thus reminding the hero that her chastity is valuable to him because his honor and his status depend on it. But for this very reason, it is also valuable to his rivals in the endless contest for status among men.

If one man can steal another's wife, he lowers the husband's status by besmirching his honor. And in the wager scene, it is Posthumus's superiority in the complete possession of his jewel that spurs Iachimo to challenge him: "I make my wager rather against your confidence than her reputation" (1.5.114–115), he declares. Posthumus boasts not of his wife's beauty—it is assumed—but of his exclusive right to enjoy it and control it; that is, her chastity, his property in her. Thus he innocently goads Iachimo into challenging him.

Posthumus never questions the terms Iachimo sets for the wager, which give the Italian the right to assail Imogen's virtue by any means he chooses. He unleashes his comrade on his wife and depends on her to defend her honor and in hers, his. When he is convinced she has fallen, he directs his fury and revenge against her rather than against the man who tempted, dared, and defeated him. He characterizes the inconstancy and hypocrisy of women as subversive action against men as husbands, fathers, and sons:

> Is there no way for men to be, but women
> Must be half-workers? We are all bastards,
> And that most venerable man, which I
> Did call my father, was I know not where
> When I was stamped.
>
> (2.4.153–157)

"The yoke shows that Matrimony tames the young man and renders him profitable to himself and to others" (my translation).

He dwells on "the woman's part" in making men; men are born of women, and all their faults derived from them, he claims. The irony is that all the "vice" he attributes to *them* lies in Iachimo, his real enemy: lying, flattering, deceiving, lust and rank thoughts, revenges, ambitions, covetings—it is these qualities, mediated by the perpetual contest to get or destroy honor, that led to the wager.

Horns make visible the emotional link between jealousy and cuckoldry, both of which make man a beast and thus a monster. In one breath Iago warns Othello against jealousy as "the green-ey'd monster, which doth mock / That meat it feeds on," and invokes the image of the horned beast, "that cuckold . . . certain of his fate" (3.3.174–176). With comparable swiftness, Othello is metamorphosed from jealous husband to convinced cuckold. Iago, with his genius for malice and his clever sexual imagination, just as effectively destroys his enemy with the mere idea of cuckoldry, by making him jealous, as he would by actually cuckolding him. Before Othello receives any proof at all, he confirms himself a cuckold, striking that ironic note of resignation heard before in the comedies:

> 'Tis destiny unshunnable, like death:
> Even then this forked plague is fated to us,
> When we do quicken.
>
> (3.3.279–281)

When Desdemona enters a few lines later, he tells her, "I have a pain upon my forehead, here" (288), beginning to visualize those horns that represent his new identity. The closest thing to actual "ocular proof" that Othello receives from Iago is the image of himself as the despised and outwitted husband refracted in Cassio's gestures and speech as (Othello is led to believe) he jokes about his affair with Desdemona (4.1.74–165). When Cassio leaves, Othello gives free rein to his rage and, morally speaking, is transformed from a man into "a monster and a beast," "the horned man" who would cut off Cassio's nose and throw it to a dog, and chop Desdemona into messes. As a cuckold, the "manly" recourse open to him is revenge, but in its ravenous cruelty it is bestial.

Othello is manipulated by means of jealousy into believing he is a cuckold; Leontes follows the same sequence but is self-deluded. The psychological causes of Leontes' jealousy are not relevant here; rather, what is important is how he manifests it in the imagery of the cuckold.[8] To put it simply, Leontes is obsessed with that imagery. Within ten lines of his first jealous suspicions, he alludes to horns: "O, that is entertainment / My bosom likes not, nor my brows" (1.2.119–120). His speech thereafter, until his mind clears, is thick with references to his horns, suggested at first by association with the deer, the calf, the steer. Then the horned image enters on its own account, in the "rough pash, and the shoots" he claims to have (128), giving visual form to "what's unreal," the "nothing" that his jealousy creates. What this obsessive imagery shows is that Leontes is as deeply concerned with how he appears to others as he is disturbed by Hermione's supposed infidelity; he sees himself as he thinks other people see him, not as a suffering husband but as a monster and object of ridicule, one who plays

> . . . so disgraced a part, whose issue
> Will hiss me to my grave; contempt and clamor
> Will be my knell.
>
> (1.2.188–190)

Here he puns on an aspect of the cuckold's fate that Shakespeare is little concerned with, outside of *Lucrece;* the expectation that he will nurture a bastard, another man's issue, another visible evidence of his disgrace.[9]

In *The Merry Wives of Windsor,* Ford is already an habitually jealous husband—as usual in Shakespeare, without foundation for his suspicions—when Pistol warns him that Falstaff intends to seduce his wife. Since in his jealousy he so fears the cuckold's fate of being mocked by other men as a dupe, Ford is eager to anticipate and avoid it, and thus is easily persuaded

8. For a discussion of Leontes' jealousy in the context of his desire to escape mature sexuality, see chapter 7, pp. 214–217.

9. Keith Thomas (see note 3, above) considers this justification for the double standard at some length, quoting Dr. Johnson's pronouncement from Boswell's *Life:* "Confusion of progeny constitutes the essence of the crime. . . . The man imposes no bastards upon his wife."

by Falstaff, without trying to corroborate his story or confront Mistress Ford herself, that his wife's assignation with the fat knight is tantamount to her literal infidelity. Ford compares himself favorably to Page, who is "an ass, a secure ass: he will trust his wife, he will not be jealous" (2.2.289–290), asses' ears being another emblem of the cuckold in addition to horns, and specifically denoting the stupidity of trusting a wife.[10] Ford, in contrast, is always on guard against being called cuckold, ass, or worse, "wittol," names that Falstaff, unaware that the "Master Brooke" he addresses was Ford in disguise, flings at him in their first interview. A wittol, according to the OED, is "a man who is aware of and complaisant about his wife's infidelity." The word thus singles out one aspect of the cuckold's situation for special ridicule; he who knows his wife untrue and doesn't take action against her and her lover is indeed less than a man. While Leontes is obsessed with his horns, Ford is obsessed with the names Falstaff calls him and the names he fears being called in the future, as his soliloquy reveals:

> See the hell of having a false woman: my bed shall be abused, my coffers ransacked, my reputation gnawn at, and I shall not only receive this villainous wrong, but stand under the adoption of abominable terms, and by him that does me this wrong. Terms! Names! Amaimon sounds well; Lucifer, well; Barbason, well: yet they are devils' additions, the names of fiends. But cuckold? Wittol? Cuckold! The devil himself hath not such a name. . . . Fie, fie, fie; cuckold, cuckold, cuckold!
> (2.2.280–289, 301–302)

Ford writhes more at the loss of name than at the loss of wife or wealth; more at the public shame of being *called* cuckold than at the reality. Better to be known as jealous than actually to be a cuckold, he thinks—but he is proven wrong.

---

10. The ass is known for his disproportionately large penis, as well as for his stupidity, which makes him an appropriate symbol for a man whose virility has been mocked, and in this context emphasizes the dumb, brutish aspect of sexuality. The Christian Feast of Fools is derived from the saturnalian Feast of Asses, an occasion for extreme licentiousness and priapic rites. See Beryl Rowland, *Animals with Human Faces: A Guide to Animal Symbolism* (Knoxville, Tenn.: University of Tennessee Press, 1973).

To be more of a man, he plans revenge immediately, and expects it to win back for him the respect lost in the public knowledge of his cuckoldry: "to these violent proceedings all my neighbours shall cry aim. . . . I shall be rather praised for this than mocked" (3.2.39–43). Unfortunately, the cost of revenge is perforce to be publicly revealed a cuckold. What he gains of manliness and honor with one hand, he gives away with the other. The equivalence of the jealous husband and the cuckold is neatly expressed in Ford's desperate assertion: "If I have horns to make one mad, let the proverb go with me—I'll be horn-mad" (3.5.140–142), the proverbial expression for a husband beside himself with jealousy or anger, "like a horned beast in the breeding season, ready to attack anything."[11] Whether he is jealous and vigilant of his wife, or a cuckold presumed careless of her, a husband is a horned man. The more Ford tries to extricate himself from humiliation as a cuckold, the more he lends himself to mockery for his jealousy.

Outwitted by his wife and her ally once in the buck basket episode, he comes in search of Falstaff a second time. Mistress Page describes how he "buffets himself on the forehead, crying, 'Peer out, peer out!'" (4.2.21–22) to the horns he actually has not incurred. When Falstaff tells Ford disguised as Master Brooke, "you shall cuckold Ford," he speaks more truly than he knows, for the jealous husband, anticipating what he fears, creates the image of it. The Merry Wives of Windsor moves nimbly between Ford's viewpoint and that of the loyal, witty, resourceful wives who cure him of his obsession by bringing it to a head, if not a horn. In its pastoral-comical world, women have the power through mockery to acknowledge and correct "men's propensities for folly, cuckoldry, promiscuity, and cruelty."[12]

---

11. See the new Arden edition of The Merry Wives of Windsor, for the note on "horn-mad" in 1.1.45.
12. Carol Thomas Neely describes the role of women in the comedies thus, in "Women and Men in Othello: 'What should such a fool / Do with so good a woman?,' " Shakespeare Studies 10 (1977): 133–158.

In the satirical-comical world of *Troilus and Cressida*, on the other hand, women *are* unfaithful as they never are in the comedies, and they are also powerless to temper the male rivalries that flourish in the wake of their betrayals. The play illustrates how honor, male rivalry, and cuckoldry are interwoven; as Thersites says, "All the argument is a whore and a cuckold" (2.3.72–73). By recurring frequently to the seizure of Helen as an act of cuckoldry, Shakespeare casts doubt on the value of honor, the play's great theme, and connects it with "sexual property in woman."

In *The Merry Wives of Windsor*, the comic action drives toward curing Ford of his obsession with reputation, as well as toward defeating Falstaff. When Ford is assured of his wife's fidelity, the name of cuckold and its stigma is wiped from his imagination and erased from public memory in Windsor. Then he becomes a man again, instead of a horn-mad beast. But there is no cure, no reprieve or salvation for the Greeks and Trojans of *Troilus and Cressida*. The Greeks argue themselves into fighting for the sake of valor and reputation; the Trojans do the same for the sake of chivalry and reputation. The military stalemate is echoed in the logical impasses of the council scenes, in which neither side can afford to admit the triviality of the war's precipitating incident because, on both sides, honor, reputation, and thus masculinity itself is at stake. The Greeks and the Trojans fight over the possession of a woman because for each of them, masculinity depends on retaining exclusive sexual property in women. Virility, honor, valor all are earned in defending one's right to that sort of property, and Shakespeare stresses evenly both the utter irrationality and the irreducible necessity of such a position. The war is folly, but essential to the identity of either side.

When Paris asks Diomede, "Who . . . deserves fair Helen best, / Myself, or Menelaus?" he replies, "Both alike":

> He like a puling cuckold would drink up
> The lees and dregs of a flat tamed piece;
> You like a lecher out of whorish loins
> Are pleas'd to breed out your inheritors.
> (4.2.55, 62–65)

Menelaus is a fool because, in fighting to get Helen back, he seems not to realize that as his sexual property, she is now tainted goods, her value nil because she can no longer belong only to him. Paris is a fool for not recognizing the same thing. Yet it is unthinkable for them *not* to fight. They, their armies, their culture, and Shakespeare's are trapped in defining masculinity as the retention of exclusive sexual property in woman, and under that definition, no man can rest secure. When a man steals a woman from another man, he enjoys the pleasure of dishonoring her husband, but by that very theft he destroys the value of the woman to himself. When a man is robbed of his wife, even if he wins her back, his manhood is tarnished; like Menelaus, "the primitive statue and oblique memorial of cuckolds" or "a herring without a roe" (5.1.53–66), he is socially emasculated. The real female equivalent of the cuckold is thus the raped woman, the Lucrece forever stained as the victim, not the agent, of a crime.

Madelon Gohlke outlines a paradigm of masculine identity in Shakespeare that illuminates this aspect of cuckoldry. For a Shakespearean hero, to be betrayed by a woman, she argues, is to be humiliated or dishonored, and thus placed in a position of vulnerability that makes him psychologically like a castrated man, and thus womanish. To defend against the fear of such castration, men anticipate it in fantasy, and turn it against women by calling them whores.[13] To be betrayed by a woman thus threatens a man's very masculinity—his identity as a man. Turning now to *Hamlet* and *Othello*, I will explore the implications of this psychosocial castration.

II

The Ghost in *Hamlet* is so poignantly powerful in his injured majesty that it seems ungracious to remember that he is

13. Madelon Gohlke, " 'I wooed thee with my sword': Shakespeare's Tragic Paradigms," in *Representing Shakespeare: New Psychoanalytic Essays,* ed. Coppélia Kahn and Murray Schwartz (Baltimore: Johns Hopkins University Press, 1980).

also a cuckold. He himself obliquely notes it when he calls Claudius "that incestuous, that adulterate beast," distinguishing incest, the fact of his brother's sexual liaison with Gertrude, from its timing, which made it adultery (1.5.42). Hamlet's awareness of this ignominious aspect of his father's grievance, though only indirectly revealed to us, shapes his attitude toward the great task of revenge by complicating his identification with his father.[14] A mighty wrong has been done to a noble king; as he is noble, so must his anger and his cause be great. But insofar as part of that wrong is cuckoldry, his nobility is diminished, his anger impotent, and his cause an embarrassment. Viewed in this context, Hamlet's well-known misogyny and preoccupation with Gertrude's faults are an outlet for the rage mingled with shame he feels at his father's situation. He must bury or disguise his awareness of it, because to admit it would damage severely his idealized image of that father. So long as he can blame a woman's frailty for the indignity his father suffers, as the conventions of cuckoldry enable him to do, that image can be saved. But at the same time, his concern with his mother's crime diverts him from revenge and inevitably reminds him of his father's weakness: King Hamlet, like the most ordinary cuckold, was hoodwinked by his own wife. Thus to the extent that Hamlet sees his father as a cuckold, his anxiety and propensity to delay revenge are increased by a paralyzing ambivalence.[15]

14. Cf. Avi Erlich's interesting argument in *Hamlet's Absent Father* (Princeton: Princeton University Press, 1978). He contends that Hamlet delays his revenge because he is waiting for his absent, ghostly father to prove his strength by returning to kill Claudius himself. The source of Hamlet's perception of his father as weak and absent, Erlich holds, is his unconscious fantasy that his father was castrated by Gertrude in a primal scene. I see evidence of a different kind of castration, in the fact rather than the fantasy of King Hamlet's cuckoldry.

15. Richard Flatter, in his *Hamlet's Father* (New Haven: Yale University Press, 1949), argues that Hamlet's delay is largely caused by the Ghost's prohibition against harming his mother, for Hamlet cannot properly revenge his father's murder until he discovers whether his mother was complicit in it. Flatter dismisses the question of Gertrude's adultery, saying that it has been

In the following discussion, I do not suggest that cuckoldry is a major issue in *Hamlet,* or for Hamlet himself. Rather, I merely wish to show that it is one aspect of Hamlet's dilemma, largely ignored by critics, and that if taken into account it deepens the tragic complications of his task. Much of the evidence I offer for the importance of cuckoldry has been presented before as evidence for the oedipal situation in the play.[16] In a longer study, it could be shown how cuckoldry participates in that situation, but here I am only concerned with isolating cuckoldry somewhat artificially from the play's other concerns so as to demonstrate its presence, and its importance.

The Ghost's "fair and warlike form" as he stalks before the sentries, Horatio's accounts of his "angry parle" with the Polacks and his victory over old Fortinbras, and his military dress cap-a-pe all create an impression of martial prowess; Hamlet's first soliloquy then introduces the question of his

---

partly absolved by time and her subsequent marriage, and stresses the problem of her complicity. But he does show, in a penetrating analysis of the closet scene, how obsessed Hamlet is with the connection between the adultery and the murder, and how the purposes of the father, to conceal this connection, and of the son, to discover it, diverge.

16. Ernest Jones's *Hamlet and Oedipus* (Garden City, N.Y.: Doubleday Anchor Books, 1955) remains the classic oedipal interpretation. For a useful review of similar interpretations from Freud to 1965, see Norman Holland, *Psychoanalysis and Shakespeare* (New York: McGraw-Hill, 1964), especially pp. 164–178 and pp. 180–184. In the oedipal situation, the son's feelings toward his mother are at least as complicated and ambivalent as those toward his father. Not only does he desire her, he also feels she has betrayed him, because he once thought her the virginal object solely of his affections—a feeling that would powerfully reinforce Hamlet's resentment at Gertrude's betrayal of his father. Incestuous desire also goes hand in hand with matricidal impulses, as Frederic C. Wertham believes, in "The Matricidal Impulse: Critique of Freud's Interpretation of *Hamlet,*" in *The Design Within: Psychoanalytic Approaches to Shakespeare,* ed. Melvin D. Faber (New York: Science House, 1970), pp. 113–120, arguing that "The basis of Hamlet's hostility against his mother is his overattachment to her," a reaction-formation sparked by fear of the castrating father. Hamlet's sexual disgust at Gertrude and women in general can be read both in oedipal terms and in terms of cuckoldry without conflict. In both contexts, Hamlet as son shares his father's sense of shame at having been sexually betrayed by a woman he loved.

father's prowess in the sexual realm. Clearly he intends the comparison of his father and his uncle "as an Hyperion to a satyr" to compliment his father, and it does; the sun god represents a summit of god-like perfections, beauty, and wisdom combined. In contrast, a satyr is hairy, horned, and lustful, a bestial creature of mere appetite. But he also traditionally has great phallic potency, by virtue of being half goat, an animal of whom Topsell says, "No beast is more prone and given to lust," and because satyrs are the companions of Pan, who is also half goat and has an enormous phallus.[17] Possibly to remedy the implication that Claudius excelled his brother in virility, Hamlet goes on to envision his father not as a father or a king, but as the perfect husband, so loving and so desirable to his wife that "she would hang on him / As if increase of appetite had grown / By what it fed on" (1.2.143–145). The unspoken question prompting the soliloquy is not only "How could my mother love Claudius after loving my father?" but also "If my father was really as sexually potent as I thought he was, how could he have lost my mother's affections to my uncle?" He comes up with cuckoldry's readiest answer: "Frailty, thy name is woman," regarding his father as the noble victim of Gertrude's inevitable falling off from virtue.

This vision of his father is confirmed by the Ghost's account of how Claudius, the "adulterate beast," murdered him and won Gertrude to his will. He depicts Claudius as a phallic serpent who poured poison into his victim's ear, an action that strongly suggests sexual penetration. The king, ignorantly "secure" and utterly passive and vulnerable in his sleep, is in the feminine position of being penetrated by the man who has already penetrated his wife.[18] The Ghost then interrupts his narrative of the murder to condemn, justifiably, both Claudius and Gertrude. Like Brabantio, he claims that Claudius

17. Rowland (cited in note 10), p. 80.
18. For another version of this point, see the comparison of Polonius, stabbed behind the arras, to the murdered King Hamlet, in Erlich (cited in note 14), pp. 76–77.

seduced Gertrude "with witchcraft of his wits," as though his personal attractions would not have been sufficient. We must surely agree with the Ghost that his brother's action was "wicked" and "traitorous" in the extreme. But do we not also feel that he is defensively trying to anticipate and forestall the usual mockery and condescending pity directed at the cuckold by calling attention to his own virtue as well as his "natural gifts," while disparaging his brother as "garbage"?

> O Hamlet, what a falling off was there,
> From me, whose love was of that dignity
> That it went hand in hand even with the vow
> I made to her in marriage, and to decline
> Upon a wretch whose natural gifts were poor
> To those of mine!
>
> But virtue, as it never will be moved,
> Though lewdness court it in a shape of heaven,
> So lust, though to a radiant angel linked,
> Will sate itself in a celestial bed
> And prey on garbage.
>
> (1.5.47–57)

Resuming his account of the murder, the Ghost stresses the physical action of the poison and its disfiguring effects on his "smooth body." He seems to take a notable pride in his appearance, as his son does in his first soliloquy and in the closet scene, and resents the "loathsome tetter" which spoils his looks. Concluding his appeal for vengeance, though, he strikes an official rather than personal note:

> Let not the royal bed of Denmark be
> A couch for luxury and damned incest.
>
> (1.5.82–83)

He makes his cuckoldry sound like a political crime rather than a personal injury, precluding his listeners' awareness of the doubt cast on his virility, the slur on his honor. The last words of his appeal specifically enjoin Hamlet from any action against his mother, hinting that her own sense of guilt might be punishment enough. But for him to encourage Hamlet to take revenge on Gertrude too would draw attention to the sexual as well as to the moral offense Claudius committed against him, lessening the dignity of his self-image and of the mission he enjoins his son to carry out for him. He seems no less anxious than his son to avoid the issue of cuckoldry.

Nevertheless, Hamlet remains aware of the sexual, as well as the moral injury done to his father. His scathing misogyny in the nunnery scene bespeaks it, especially his remarks on marriage:

> If thou wilt needs marry, marry a fool, for wise men know
> well enough what monsters you make of them.
>
> (3.1.134–136)

That is, women make cuckolds, horned monsters, of men. Surely some part of the murderous rage Hamlet feels toward his mother before and during the closet scene derives from his consciousness of the indignity she did his father by cuckolding him, and though he sharply reminds himself that he must speak daggers but use none, recalling his father's parting words, he follows the letter but not the spirit of them. He "contrives" nothing against Gertrude, but he certainly does not "leave her to heaven."

Their encounter begins with his rapier-sharp repartee, "Mother, you have my father much offended" (3.4.9), which alludes broadly to incest, adultery, "o'er-hasty marriage," or all three (though two subsequent lines stress incest). As the scene proceeds, after the killing of Polonius, Hamlet's description of Gertrude's crime as what "makes marriage-vows / As false as dicers' oaths" and "from the body of contraction plucks / The very soul" (3.4.45–46, 47–48) implies adultery more strongly than incest or simply female fickleness. He dwells again on the difference in appearance between his father and his uncle, idealizing his father by comparing him to Hyperion, Jove, Mars, and Mercury, concluding that in his father's face "every god did seem to set his seal, / To give the world assurance of a man" (3.4.63–64). In contrast, Claudius is again likened to garbage—"a mildewed ear, / Blasting his wholesome brother" (65–66). The speech echoes thought and imagery from Hamlet's first soliloquy and the Ghost's account of the murder; it restates defensively the sexual attractions of King Hamlet, frankly appealing to Gertrude's sexual appetite ("Could you on this fair mountain leave to feed, / And batten on this moor?" [67–68]) and her eyes more than to her moral judgment and conscience. Here Hamlet perceives her marriage as a sexual slight to his father and identifies with his father's presumable sense of being sexually rejected.

As his speech, one of the longest in the play, gathers emotional momentum, his denigrations of Gertrude become increasingly caustic and bitter, rising to a pitch of voyeuristic excitement in the lines,

> Nay, but to live
> In the rank sweat of an enseamed bed,
> Stewed in corruption, honeying and making love
> Over the nasty sty. . . .
>
> (3.4.92–95)

This vision resembles those concocted by Iago for Othello, and those Othello conjures up for himself, of Desdemona and Cassio in the blossoms of their sin; it is intended not only to excoriate the guilty couple, but to lacerate masochistically the one who suffers most—the cuckolded husband. Here it is Hamlet who unconsciously takes on that role for his father and thereby implicitly lowers his father's dignity, by dwelling on the adultery rather than on the murder.[19]

Thus it might be argued that the Ghost returns to his wife's bedroom to "whet," in a phallic phrase, his son's "almost blunted purpose" because his own phallic image as warlike

19. Frederic C. Wertham (cited in note 16) argues that the Ghost emanates from or expresses "that part of Hamlet's personality which identifies itself with the father . . . the self assertion within the son of the patriarchal father" who possesses "the patriarchal right and duty to guard the mother" (p. 114), but he does not see the conflict between that "patriarchal right and duty" and the other, of revenge for murder, that I see. For a highly original and persuasive account of Hamlet's responses to his mother and his father that takes issue with "patriarchal right and duty," see David Leverenz, "The Woman in Hamlet: An Interpersonal View," SIGNS, 4 (Winter 1978): 291–308. Leverenz finds Hamlet caught between the patriarchal order as represented by the Ghost and his demand for revenge, and feeling and the irrational as embodied, according to his society's code, in women. He argues that Hamlet delays revenge because, as stipulated by the Ghost, it precludes any expression of his heart's outrage at Gertrude.

majesty is beginning to suffer; his son is making him look too much like a mere cuckold. According to the stage direction in the First Quarto, he comes "in his night-gown" (3.4.103), not in military dress as he was on the battlements, but garbed informally as a husband might be garbed in his wife's chamber. He comes unarmed and defenseless, as he was before Gertrude's betrayal and during his "secure hour" in the orchard when Claudius violated his ear and his life, after violating his bed as well, and he comes to reiterate his desire that Hamlet take on the phallic role of avenger he cannot assume himself. However, of the six lines he speaks in the scene, four concern Gertrude, not revenge. His tone is full of tenderness and concern—he makes no angry accusations against her and calls her no names:

> But look, amazement on thy mother sits.
> O, step between her and her fighting soul!
> Conceit in weakest bodies strongest works.
> Speak to her, Hamlet.
>
> (3.4.114–117)

In demeanor, the Ghost is again, as in the first act, "pale," "more in sorrow than in anger" (1.2.230–232); "Look you how pale he glares," says Hamlet (3.4.127), fearing that the pity his father inspires in him will deprive his revenge of "true color . . . perchance for blood" (3.4.132). He wants an angry father, sure of himself, on whom to model himself as avenger. The Ghost's pallor and piteous demeanor indicate, I think, that he continues to love Gertrude though she has made him a cuckold and married his cuckolder and his murderer.[20] Against her his anger fails and his own purpose is blunted, not only by a loss of virility, but by a love he cannot help feeling. His father's tenderness makes it even more difficult for Hamlet as a son who identifies strongly with his father to fill the phallic role of avenger.

The word *cuckold* appears only once in *Hamlet,* but in a context that highlights the peculiar burden his father's cuck-

---

20. Thus King Hamlet differs from Shakespeare's other cuckolded heroes in not turning against his erring wife and accusing her of whoredom; his son performs this function for him.

oldry places on the hero. When Laertes storms into Elsinore with the rabble at his heels to demand redress for his father's death, he replies to Gertrude's restraining "calmly, good Laertes," with these words:

> That drop of blood that's calm proclaims me bastard,
> Cries cuckold to my father, brands the harlot
> Even here between the chaste unsmirched brow
> Of my true mother.
>
> (4.5.115–118)

In a hot-headed, simple-minded fashion impossible for Hamlet, Laertes defends his father's honor. He uses cuckoldry as a metaphor, to say that were he to regard his father's murder calmly, he would not be his father's son—he would be unworthy of him. Cuckoldry is for him the rhetoric of compliment, but for Hamlet it is a troubling, intractable reality added to the complications and anxieties of revenge.

In *Othello,* cuckoldry is a lie, but it convinces Othello because it confirms the fears he already has about women. At an unconscious level, the lie is believable to Iago, too, who made it up. He uses it to create a bond between himself and the Moor based on their mutual fantasy of women as betrayers and men as sexual rivals. Together they consummate this fantasy and give birth to themselves as monsters of jealousy. While Iago himself is a sick man, warped by hatred and envy, insofar as he uses the idea of cuckoldry to pursue his ends, he only takes to hand attitudes commonly held in his society, and in effect demonstrates their inner workings. Man's fear of cuckoldry is his primary weapon, and he always works indirectly, pitting another man against Othello as a sexual competitor, while at the same time he falsely binds himself to Othello as a brother.

He first attempts to discredit Othello with Brabantio, by portraying Desdemona's elopement as a sexual theft—which in a sense it is, since in patriarchal terms, a daughter belongs to her father as the guardian of her chastity. "Thieves, thieves, thieves!" he cries to Brabantio, "Look to your house, your daughter, and your bags" (1.1.79–80). When Roderigo, taking his cues from Iago, describes Desdemona's "gross revolt," he brings to light her father's unconscious fear that his daughter will be stolen.

> This accident is not unlike my dream,
> Belief of it oppresses me already,
>
> (1.1.142–143)

Brabantio says. Iago is not alone, here as elsewhere, in his imaginings; but he is unique in his ability to use men's fantasies against them.[21] After Desdemona and Othello foil this first attempt by eloquently defending their love before the Venetian council, Iago turns to a more threatening kind of sexual theft, cuckoldry. Again he works indirectly, this time with Roderigo as his instrument:

> I have told thee often, and I tell thee again, and again, I hate the Moor; my cause is hearted, thine has no less reason, let us be communicative in our revenge against him: if thou canst cuckold him, thou doest thyself a pleasure, and me a sport. There are many events in the womb of time, which will be delivered.
>
> (1.3.364–370)

If Iago can get Roderigo into Othello's bed, he will get back at his superior for the promotion denied him, and Roderigo will get even for the supposed "loss" of Desdemona. But in addition, Iago needs the emotional fuel of seeing *himself* as cuckolded by Othello. It makes him the Moor's equal in injury and in anger and "hearts" his cause even more strongly:

> I hate the Moor,
> And it is thought abroad that 'twixt my sheets
> He's done my office; I know not if't be true;
> Yet I, for mere suspicion in that kind,
> Will do, as if for surety.
>
> (1.3.384–388)

21. F. R. Leavis, "Diabolic Intellect and the Noble Hero," *Scrutiny* 6 (December 1937): 250–271, argues that Iago only taps feelings latent in Othello, but no one, to my knowledge, has focused on his use of cuckoldry in doing so.

But as usual, he refrains from revenging himself against Othello directly, and hits upon using Cassio instead of Roderigo as the cuckolder,

> To get his place, and to plume up my will,
> A double knavery.
>
> (1.3.391–392)

He is still interested in getting the promotion he was denied, and in revenging himself against Othello for denying it. But the phrase "to plume up my will" is at once vaguer and richer in meaning than these relatively clear motives. "Plume up" suggests a male bird showing himself off, and "will" indicates lust. Iago likes to imagine himself part of the only kind of community he enjoys: a community of men competing with each other, in this case, for women. At a deeper level, as the familiar psychoanalytic interpretation suggests, it may be argued that Iago uses this heterosexual competition as a way of getting closer to men, his real sexual objects.[22]

But what matters for an understanding of cuckoldry is Iago's vision of society as a network of cuckoldries, man against man, with women merely incidental to their contests. In its pathological extremity, this vision lays bare the vindictive and competitive aspects of cuckoldry:

> The Moor, howbe't that I endure him not,
> Is of a constant, noble, loving nature;
> And I dare think he'll prove to Desdemona
> A most dear husband: now I do love her too,
> Not out of absolute lust, (though peradventure
> I stand accountant for as great a sin)
> But partly led to diet my revenge,
> For that I do suspect the lustful Moor

---

22. See Norman Holland (cited in note 16), pp. 249–250, for a summary of this approach, and Martin Wangh, "*Othello:* The Tragedy of Iago," in *The Design Within: Psychoanalytic Approaches to Shakespeare,* ed. Melvin D. Faber (cited in note 16), pp. 155–168, for an interpretation of Iago as motivated by his homosexual attraction for Othello. I find this reading of Iago convincing, but prefer to focus on his ability to evoke typical male fantasies of cuckoldry rather than on his individual pathology as a homosexual. In line with a homosexual interpretation of Iago, however, cuckoldry provides the perfect means for Iago to separate Othello from Desdemona and draw closer to the Moor himself.

Hath leap'd into my seat, the thought whereof
Doth like a poisonous mineral gnaw my inwards,
And nothing can, nor shall content my soul,
Till I am even with him, wife for wife. . . .

(2.1.283–294)

Before, he consciously decided to act as if the rumor that
Othello had cuckolded him were true; here, the rumor has
become his own persistent fantasy and has led almost math-
ematically to a counterpart fantasy—that he should cuckold
Othello, to be "even with him, wife for wife." With striking
consistency he next produces the suspicion that Cassio has
cuckolded *him* ("For I fear Cassio with my nightcap too"
[302]). Thus in his fantasy he, Cassio, and Othello are bound
by an interlocking chain of sexual offenses and revenges that
makes each of them either cuckold, cuckolder, or both, each
one in sexual competition with another.

On the other hand, Iago's revenge depends on his gaining
the Moor's absolute trust, in order to destroy his trust in Desdemona; he must, in effect, take her place in Othello's heart.
As W. H. Auden remarks,

> Iago treats Othello as an analyst treats a patient, except that, of
> course, his intention is to kill, not to cure. Everything he says
> is designed to bring to Othello's consciousness what he has
> already guessed is there.[23]

Iago need only drop a few hints about the pranks his coun-
trywomen dare not show their husbands, only remind Othello that Desdemona deceived her father, and the "monster in
his thought" awakens the sleeping monster in Othello's mind,
"the green-ey'd monster" jealousy. I pointed earlier to the
rapidity with which that monster metamorphoses into the
horned beast of cuckoldry, as Othello begins to voice its
clichés:

'Tis destiny unshunnable, like death:
Even then this forked plague is fated to us,
When we do quicken.

(3.3.279–281)

23. W. H. Auden, "The Joker in the Pack," in *The Dyer's Hand* (New York: Random House, 1948; rpt. 1962), p. 266.

The "we" he assumes is all men; he flees from unbearable doubts about women to identify with men as the passive, fated victims of women, an identification coded into marriage through cuckoldry. Thus it is easy enough for Iago to make his bond with Othello seem a defensive alliance of men against women as betrayers, concealing, with a facade of brotherly sympathy, the fact that in cuckoldry, men are the real aggressors against each other:

> Good sir, be a man,
> Think every bearded fellow that's but yok'd
> May draw with you; there's millions now alive
> That nightly lie in those unproper beds
> Which they dare swear peculiar. . . .
>
>   (4.1.65–69)

He means, we men who bear the yoke of marriage are all horned; I am your brother, not your enemy. This idea later lends spurious weight to Othello's conception of murdering Desdemona as a just act, when he says, "Yet she must die, else she'll betray more men" (5.2.6).

Shakespeare stresses the bonding between Iago and Othello as the counterpart of marriage through a subtly forged chain of imagery involving conception, birth, and consummation that makes the two men one mind if not one flesh. Emilia remarks that jealousy is "a monster / Begot upon itself, born upon itself" (3.4.159–160), meaning that it is not produced by fact but by suspicions in the jealous mind itself. We might apply her notion of parthenogenesis to the dramatic circumstances of the birth of Othello's jealousy: it is not conceived by the union of male and female opposites, but by the union of like with like, a meeting of two male minds. When Iago first conceives the idea of making Othello jealous by telling him that Cassio is cuckolding him, he calls it a "monstrous birth" (1.3.402), and later the Moor, getting the drift of Iago's innuendoes, senses "some monster in his thought" (3.3.111). Iago inseminates Othello with his sexual fantasies verbally, through the ear:[24]

24. See Holland (cited in note 16), pp. 193–194, for a summary of psychoanalytic readings of the poisoning of King Hamlet through the ear as "some kind of insemination."

I'll pour this pestilence into his ear,
That she repeals him for her body's lust. . . .

(2.3.347–348)

He refers to his own fantasies as "a poisonous mineral" gnaw-
ing his inwards (2.1.291–292), then exults, "The Moor already changes with my poison" (3.3.330), when Othello refers to his cuckoldom as a fact, "destiny unshunnable." Actually, the exchange of vows between the two men, often
interpreted as a ritual marriage, is long preceded by the consummation of their thoughts when Othello says, "I am bound
to thee forever" (3.3.217), just after Iago first suggests that
Desdemona has slept with Cassio. It is Iago's word-picture
of Cassio's supposed erotic dream which directly precipitates
the formal vows. Like a microdrama of the whole play, it
confounds heterosexual intercourse, as Cassio dreams he is
making love to Desdemona, with homosexual intercourse,
as he suggestively embraces Iago at the same time (3.3.419–
432). And as Iago recounts this scene to Othello, he impreg-
nates him with the belief that he is a cuckold and thus
strengthens the bond between them as men.

If Othello is a cuckold, then Desdemona is a whore. As
certainty replaces doubt in Othello's mind, this simple change
of identities is accomplished there also. When Iago consoles
Othello with the idea that all men are cuckolds and that it is
better to know oneself as such than to writhe in jealous suspicion, he suggests the reciprocity of cuckold and whore:

O, 'tis the spite of hell, the fiend's arch-mock,
To lip a wanton in a secure couch,
And to suppose her chaste. No, let me know,
And knowing what I am, I know what she shall be.

(4.1.70–73)

No longer the sole possessor of his wife's sexuality, the cuckold knows what he is well enough: mocked with horns for his
deficient virility, deprived of honor, the butt of ridicule, he is
unmanned, a monster. But some redress is open to him,
though even revenge will never take away the stigma of his
horns; he can unwoman his wife by calling her whore, a
stigma she will find it hard to live down. Shakespeare shows
Othello bewhoring Desdemona by pretending that she enter-

tains him as a strumpet in a brothel (4.2). In this scene he plays
the moral tyrant, heaping shame upon her, his cuckoldry for-
gotten in his new pose. In the next scene, though, Shakespeare
radically shifts point of view to treat marital infidelity not
from the husband's side, as cuckoldry, but from the wife's.

Desdemona asks Emilia wonderingly if "there be women
do abuse their husbands / In such gross kind?" (61–62). Obviously, her naiveté, as well as her already-established innocence, is meant to show up the error of Othello's convictions
with a searing poignancy. But Emilia's more worldly comments have their own equally great force when taken in the
context of cuckoldry as a psychosocial phenomenon, for she
questions precisely those attitudes bolstering it: misogyny,
the double standard, and patriarchal authority in marriage:

> Let husbands know,
> Their wives have sense like them: they see, and smell,
> And have their palates both for sweet, and sour,
> As husbands have. What is it that they do,
> When they change us for others? Is it sport?
> I think it is: and doth affection breed it?
> I think it doth. Is't frailty that thus errs?
> It is so too. And have not we affections?
> Desires for sport? and frailty, as men have?
> Then let them use us well: else let them know,
> The ills we do, their ills instruct us so.
>
> (4.3.93–103)

Women, she argues, are neither the saints nor the whores that
men would have them be; in sense (desire), frailty, and affections they are like men. Thus their husbands cannot expect,
merely because they are men, to enjoy or to own women's
sexual fidelity by patriarchal right. If they are faithful and loving, they will inspire that fidelity. If they are not, women will
serve them in kind, whether the double standard punishes
them for it or not. The tone of the speech is tart, but its argument reasonable. Its common sense and fairness serve to stress
by contrast the anxieties and distortions underlying masculine
fantasies of betrayal by women, and their tragic cost, in cuckoldry.

III

To conclude this anatomy of Shakespearean cuckoldry, let me evoke the curious and comic figure of Falstaff in *The Merry Wives of Windsor*, lurking impatiently by the great oak in Windsor Park at midnight, a buck's head with spreading antlers planted on his shoulders. Tricked into an assignation with Mistress Ford, he is discovered according to plan, and conclusively exposed, mocked, and rejected as a would-be cuckolder. It might seem that Shakespeare violates convention here, by putting the despised horns on the cuckolder's head instead of the cuckold's. But a closer look reveals, I believe, that the poet has gathered up into the horned Falstaff all the ambivalence of cuckoldry as a product of misogyny, patriarchal marriage, and the double standard. Falstaff's antlers are richly multivalent.

They are associated first with virility as divine power. Falstaff's soliloquy puts forth this ancient idea in a comic vein because the fat, excited, sweating knight is so obviously human rather than divine as he would like to be:

Now, the hot-blooded gods assist me! Remember, Jove, thou wast a bull for thy Europa; love set on thy horns. O powerful love, that in some respects makes a beast a man; in some other, a man a beast. You were also, Jupiter, a swan for the love of Leda. O omnipotent love, how near the god drew to the complexion of a goose! . . . When gods have hot backs, what shall poor men do? For me, I am here a Windsor stag, and the fattest, I think, i' th' forest. Send me a cool rut-time, Jove, or who can blame me to piss my tallow?

(5.5.2–15)

The speech traces Jove's declension from bull (an animal worshipped almost universally from prehistoric times for its fertilizing power) to swan to goose, the emblem of folly, thus setting the keynote of grandeur mixed with folly, god with beast, love with lust, which resonates through the scene. In man's sexual behavior these distant opposites meet and clash.

Second, when Falstaff is "dis-horned" by Ford and Page, and publicly humiliated, he becomes the scapegoat in whom

the disruptive force of lust is embodied and symbolically rejected, whose sacrifice serves, as Jeanne Addison Roberts argues, "to draw the social group together and to create a new
harmony."[25] The play abounds in sexual rivalries, notably,
Falstaff against the wives and the husbands; the wives against
their husbands, particularly Mistress Ford against her jealous
mate; Caius, Slender, and Fenton all vying for Anne Page's
hand; and "Master Brooks" against Master Ford. The community of Windsor is based on marriage, and its domestic
tranquillity is threatened not only by Falstaff the opportunis-
tic outsider, but also by its own internal tensions; by making
him the scapegoat of lust and sexual competition, the community cleanses itself of them. In this context, Falstaff's
horns, which are specifically antlers, are most strongly associated with the deer as pathetic victim, that animal's typical
role in Shakespeare.[26] Falstaff is punished more than he deserves, for everyone's sexual license as well as his own, and
when in the final speech of the play Ford says to Falstaff that
"Master Brooke shall lie with Mistress Ford tonight," a transfer of potency and sexual rights is suggested, from the
would-be cuckolder to the rightful possessor of his wife's
sexual favors, her husband Master Ford alias Brooke. Thus
sexuality is returned to its proper well-ordered sphere within
marriage.

Finally, the stag-horned Falstaff in the forest recalls the
figure of Actaeon, the hunter turned into a stag as punishment
for inadvertently seeing Diana naked as she bathed. Actaeon is
a common cant term for cuckold; in fact, it crops up when
cuckoldry is first mentioned in the play. Pistol, warning Ford
that Falstaff intends to seduce his wife, says,

25. Jeanne Addison Roberts, "Falstaff in Windsor Forest: Villain or Victim?," *Shakespeare Quarterly* 26 (Winter 1975): 8–15, a perceptive article that
presents much interesting information about the horns imagery. See also
"The Merry Wives: Suitably Shallow, But Neither Simple Nor Slender,"
Shakespeare Studies 6 (1970): 109–123, by the same author; she argues that
Falstaff embodies the vices threatening "good marriage," primarily "uncon-
trolled sex," and reads the horns as symbols of sexual potency. In contrast, I
maintain that cuckoldry specifically, not lust, is at issue—cuckoldry as a system of rivalry between men which ultimately demeans their sexuality.
26. Roberts, "Falstaff in Windsor Forest" (cited in note 25), p. 14.

> Prevent,
> Or go like Sir Actaeon he,
> With Ringwood at thy heels!
> O, odious is the name!
>
> (2.1.115–117)

Why should Falstaff wear the cuckold's horns, then, when he is the cuckolder who conventionally goes scot-free? Poetic justice offers one answer, for Falstaff gets the horns he intended to give the husbands. This exchange of horns suggests an equality, and an identity, between the cuckolder and his victim that is reinforced when Falstaff says, "My horns I bequeath your husbands" (5.5.26–27) in the mistaken expectation of cuckolding them. The iconography of Actaeon as explicated by Renaissance mythographers also suggests a certain bond between cuckolder and cuckold: a common dilemma of desire as mediated by marriage. Whitney, following tradition, provides this interpretation of Actaeon as an emblem of the bestial transformation of man caused by the ravages of sexual desire:

> . . . those who do pursue
> Theire fancies fonde and thinges unlawful crave
> Like brutish beastes appeare unto the viewe . . .
> . . . . soe theire affections base
> Shall them devoure, and all theire deedes deface.[27]

As Actaeon was torn apart by his hounds, who mistook their master for their prey, so Falstaff is parodically pinched by fairies and deprived of his horns, his potency. This mockery of his desire, however, resembles the mockery of the cuckold's virility expressed *in* his horns, even though horns are removed in Falstaff's case and implanted in the cuckold's.

As the horned cuckolder, he embodies the plight of all men, which is corollary to the double standard and the sexual

27. John M. Steadman, "Falstaff as Actaeon: A Dramatic Emblem," *Shakespeare Quarterly* 24 (Summer 1963): 230–244, explicates the interpretations of Actaeon by Renaissance mythographers, and holds that their moral terms govern the depiction of Falstaff horned, punished for "unclean lechery." Again, I would argue that the horns express mockery or sexuality in marriage and cuckoldry rather than punishment for transgression *per se:* a psychological rather than moral reading.

property in women allotted to them by patriarchal marriage. The double standard grants free sexual activity to men only, but marriage, by making their honor and virility depend on their wives' chastity, turns that sexual freedom into a threat. It makes every husband a potential cuckold, and gives every man, married or not, the opportunity to "plume his will" by cuckolding his friend. Cuckoldry, like rape, is thus an affair between men, rather than between men and women or husbands and wives, though men blame women for betraying them. The horned Falstaff, then, is an emblem of Everyman as both cuckold and cuckolder, victim and offender; "the savage yoke" of marriage subjugates all men. Falstaff's horns as an emblem of virility are mocked as virility is mocked by the peculiar institution of marriage, which makes men monsters of jealousy and monsters as cuckolds, beasts in lust and beasts in that their wives and other men can lead them by the nose as easily as asses.

CHAPTER SIX

The Milking Babe
and the Bloody Man
in *Coriolanus* and *Macbeth*

Bring forth men-children only!
Macbeth, 1.7.73

A paradox of sexual confusion lies at the heart of these
two plays. Their virile warrior-heroes, supreme
in valor, are at the same time unfinished men—boys,
in a sense, who fight or murder because they have
been convinced by women that only through violence will they achieve manhood. Their manhood, displayed in the uncompromisingly masculine form of
bloodshed, is not their own, not self-determined nor
self-validated, but infused into them by women who
themselves are half men. These women, seeking to
transform themselves into men through the power
they have to mold men (the only power their cultures
allow them), root out of themselves and out of their
men those human qualities—tenderness, pity,
sympathy, vulnerability to feeling—that their
cultures have tended to associate with women. In the
intensity of their striving to deny their own
womanliness so as to achieve transcendence through
men, they create monsters: men like beasts or things,
insatiable in their need to dominate, anxiously
seeking security in their power and their identity, a
security they can never achieve because they do not

belong to themselves but to the women who made them.[1]

As he pursues the goal marked out for him by a woman, each of these heroes dedicates himself to an all-encompassing rivalry with another man, or men, a bloody antagonism as binding as any marriage. The rival is either a psychological synonym for the hero, sharing the same essential traits as he, an "enemy twin," or an ego ideal—the kind of man he would like to be, so that to triumph over him is to assimilate him, as Hal crops Hotspur's budding honors when he defeats him. In either case, "fratricidal violence exists to establish Difference" (as Joel Fineman argues): the difference between victor and vanquished that mirrors the difference between self and mother and between male and female.[2] It is through violence that the hero tries to individuate himself, and its bloodiness measures the instability that underlies not only his particular sexual identity, but the polarized definitions of sexual identity held by his culture. Furthermore, through their rivalries, Coriolanus and Macbeth reenact the basic ambivalence of their sexual identities; their efforts to surpass and destroy their antagonists and to be supreme among all men signify both their fusion with the stronger wills of women closest to them, their desire to be what those women want them to be, and

1. D. W. Harding, "Women's Fantasy of Manhood: A Shakespearean Theme," *Shakespeare Quarterly* 20 (Summer 1969): 245–253, also singles out this motif in Shakespeare, but reads *Macbeth, Lear, Antony and Cleopatra,* and *Coriolanus* as indictments of women for creating peculiar and unreal fantasies of manhood and forcing their men to act them out and suffer for them, while they (the women) collapse or withdraw. Once again, I distinguish between my conception of Shakespeare as a self-conscious (though also sympathetic) critic of ideals of masculinity emanating from patriarchal society, and the Shakespeare of Harding and others. The women Shakespeare portrays in these plays did not contrive their ideas of manliness out of whole cloth; they took them from a world managed by men.

2. In "Fratricide and Cuckoldry: Shakespeare and His Sense of Difference," *Psychoanalytic Review* 64 (Fall 1977): 409–453, Fineman applies to Shakespeare René Girard's idea that the purpose of fratricide myths is to reaffirm the binary structure of social order. According to Girard, brothers who are alike in blood fight to establish the crucial difference between victor and vanquished as a model of all other differences, which ward off the chaos of "no difference" (*Violence and the Sacred,* tr. Patrick Gregory [Baltimore: Johns Hopkins University Press, 1977]).

their need to differentiate themselves from those women, to be definitively separate from a significant other.[3]

In each play, the single striking image of a nursing babe defines this disrupted relationship between men and women. In *Macbeth*, the heroine voices it to her husband as an exemplum, an inspiration, to "be so much more the man," while she would be more than a woman:

> I have given suck, and know
> How tender 'tis to love the babe that milks me:
> I would, while it was smiling in my face,
> Have pluck'd my nipple from his boneless gums,
> And dash'd the brains out, had I so sworn
> As you have done to this.
>
> (1.7.54–59)

The mother loves her babe by nursing it, and it actively "milks" her; she gazes at it, and it smiles into her face. The babe's trust in the mother and the life-giving nourishment it receives from her give the mother her unique value as a mother, while she gives the babe not just milk, but the ontological reassurance of being seen and recognized.[4] But beyond this reciprocal exchange of identities, what the woman

3. Mahler *et al.* and Jacobson have noted that the child's definitive discovery of separateness from the mother coincides both with his discovery of the anatomical difference between the sexes and with his tendency to identify with the father, a person of the same sex, while his previous identification with the mother becomes subordinate. Jacobson holds that such same-sex identification with one who, at the same time, is beginning to be perceived as a rival for the mother's love promotes "testing of external objects and of his own self, helps him distinguish between fantasies about self and object, and real objects and his actual or potential self" (Edith Jacobson, *The Self and the Object World* [New York: International Universities Press, 1964], pp. 75–79). I regard the same-sex rivalries in *Coriolanus* and *Macbeth* as later versions of a similar attempt to differentiate oneself from a feminine matrix.

4. Murray Schwartz, in "Shakespeare Through Contemporary Psychoanalysis," *Hebrew University Studies in Literature* 5 (Autumn 1977): 182–198, calls this passage "the prototypical moment in Shakespeare's use of theatrical space in tragedy to enact the violent interruption of ceremonial order," and goes on to say,

> I feel this violent interruption of a nurturant, communal interplay as a source of Shakespeare's recurrent preoccupation with betrayal and with feminine powers to create and destroy *suddenly*, and in the repeated desire of his male characters both to be that all-powerful

wants is to transcend her femininity, to gain another identity through masculine action. In her fantasy, she does not murder the babe incidentally, as a way of showing her determination to act as a man; the murder of the babe represents the action she would take, and her conception of what masculine action is—murder. In *Coriolanus*, explaining to her daughter-in-law how blood "becomes a man," Volumnia says,

> The breasts of Hecuba
> When she did suckle Hector, look'd not lovelier
> Than Hector's forehead when it spit forth blood
> At Grecian sword contemning.
> (1.3.40–43)

As in the other passage, Shakespeare first evokes a traditional image of fulfilled womanhood, so as to strengthen the contrast between it and the masculine action the speaker envisions as its alternative. But this passage does more; as Janet Adelman argues, it pictures a masculine response to dependency on the mother—the child's adult transformation of feeding into warfare, vulnerability into attack, and incorporation into spitting out, which fends off dependency in a traditional masculine way, by aggression and violence.[5] In both passages, the women speakers identify completely with the masculine behavior they envision, unaware of how horrible it is. Proudly,

woman and to control the means of nurturance themselves, to the exclusion of the otherness of others. In Macbeth's response to Lady Macbeth's verbal violence—"If *we* should fail?" (1.7.59, italics mine)—I hear him identifying with the woman he fears would annihilate him. They are no longer separate psychologically: they have become a "we" who will murder Duncan, and live isolated from one another for the rest of the play. (p. 15)

Mahler *et al.* note that the human face in motion is the child's first meaningful percept, his or her first breakthrough from symbiotic fusion and focus on inner sensation to the outside world (p. 46). In Lady Macbeth's hyperbole, the mother murders her child at the very moment he first responds to her—his first step toward eventually establishing a self of his own.

5. See Janet Adelman, " 'Anger's My Meat': Feeding, Dependency, and Aggression in *Coriolanus*," in *Shakespeare: Pattern of Excelling Nature*, ed. David Bevington and Jay L. Halio (Newark: University of Delaware Press, 1978), pp. 108–124. She uses this passage as the starting point in her brilliant explication of the hero's phallic aggressive defense against dependency, and argues (as I do) that he has no self that is not Volumnia's creation. I am much indebted to her fine essay.

they exult in their affirmation of killing over nourishing. But their affirmations seem repulsive—in part because it is women who are making them, while in Coriolanus's Rome, Macbeth's Scotland, and to some extent our own culture, violent aggression, so long as it is sanctioned by the political order, is approved behavior only for men.

The aggression is figured verbally and dramatically in bloody men. In *Macbeth,* the bleeding captain of the second scene, who describes how Macbeth unseams the rebel from the nave to the chops, is followed by Duncan and his two grooms, Banquo's "blood-bolter'd" ghost, the armed man and bloody babe of the apparitions, Macduff untimely ripped from his mother's womb, and most of all, Macbeth—who says he wades in blood. The single image of Coriolanus himself "mantled in blood" dominates the other play, the blood an ambivalent metaphor for his supremacy as a warrior and his lack of human feeling. Both heroes begin their fatal courses in notably bloody actions—Macbeth fighting against the rebels, Coriolanus against the Volscians—that confer new names on them, names signifying and fixing definitively their preeminence as fighters and recognizing their maturity as men. Yet both are deeply dependent on the women who goad them on. When their honors lead them into new realms of political and moral experience, therefore, they are unable to cope, and undergo reversals in behavior, Coriolanus turning against the city whose paragon he has been, Macbeth becoming the hardened murderer he deplored. These tragic reversals reveal cracks in the armor of their manhood, places where ordinary humanity restricted to a feminine realm by their societies, humanity they so long repressed and split off from themselves, proves fatal to them. In actuality, the bloody encounters or exploits in which they sought a second, definitive birth into real manhood are abortive, ending in psychic collapse as well as death.

I

One need not fabricate a boyhood for Coriolanus, as Bradley did for Othello, growing up in the forests of Africa:

Shakespeare has brought it right into the play, by making both mother and son recall his upbringing. Volumnia's first speech is a straightforward account of how she made her son a man:

> I pray you, daughter, sing, or express yourself in a more comfortable sort. If my son were my husband I should freelier rejoice in that absence wherein he won honour, than in the embracements of his bed, wherein he would show most love. When yet he was but tender-bodied, and the only son of my womb; when youth with comeliness plucked all gaze his way; when for a day of kings' entreaties, a mother should not sell him an hour from her beholding; I, considering how honour would become such a person—that it was no better than picture-like to hang by th'wall, if renown made it not stir— was pleas'd to let him seek danger where he was like to find fame. To a cruel war I sent him, from whence he returned, his brows bound with oak. I tell thee, daughter, I sprang not more in joy at first hearing he was a man-child, than now in first seeing he had proved himself a man.
>
> (1.3.1–18)

This speech lays bare the extreme sexual polarization of Rome and reveals as much about how Volumnia came to be what she is as how she shaped her son. Every word of it echoes Cominius's simple summary of the Roman value system, "It is held that valour is the chiefest virtue" (2.2.83–84). This *virtus* is the property of *vir,* the male, while the *virtus* of women is to be chaste and to bear male children.[6] Philip Slater's paradigm of family structure in classical Greece applies to the family as we see it in this play. Woman, excluded from public life, is devalued save as the bearer of men-children; she must seek her primary emotional satisfaction through her son, who becomes a substitute for her absent husband, the vehicle through which she realizes herself, and a cure for the narcissistic wound of being a woman.[7]

6. Eugene M. Waith, "Manhood and Valor in Two Shakespearean Tragedies," *English Literary History* 17 (1950): 262–273, quotes Plutarch's "Coriolanus" to show that valor was called *virtus* in Latin and identified with virtue itself as "an all-inclusive virtue, the very emblem of manhood" (p. 262). Waith goes on to contrast this Roman ideal with the Renaissance ideal of manhood as moral virtue served by courage and fortitude.
7. Philip Slater, *The Glory of Hera: Greek Mythology and the Greek Family* (Boston: Beacon Press, 1968), pp. 23–30. Slater conceives the "oral-

Throughout the scene that begins with this speech, Volumnia's intense adherence to the masculine code of honor is
contrasted to Virgilia's feminine recoil from it. Virgilia fears
wounds, blood, and death because they may deprive her of
the husband she loves; Volumnia covets them as the signs and
seals of honor that make her son a man, and her a man, in
effect, through him. Coriolanus in himself does not exist for
her; he is only a means for her to realize her own masculine
ego ideal, a weapon she fashions for her own triumph. Virgilia, on the other hand, is the walking metaphor of her husband's inarticulate, unacknowledged, undeveloped other self:
pure love and utter vulnerability. In the extreme sexual polar-
ity of Rome, all she is must remain feminine, split off from
what is manly. She is the opposite of her husband without
being his complement. He brings noise and leaves tears, as his
mother boasts; Virgilia is "a gracious silence" shedding tears.[8]

Volumnia has succeeded all too well in making her son not
a person but a personification, a grotesque caricature of
Roman manhood. As the play unfolds, he seems to embody
Menenius's image of

> . . . the Roman state, whose course will on
> The way it takes, cracking ten thousand curbs . . .
> (1.1.68–69)

a huge impersonal mechanism that plows unseeingly through
men or nations, oblivious to their human needs, destroying
them on its progress toward some obscure and unchangeable
destination. In word and deed, Shakespeare's least sympathetic hero manifests a strangely mechanical quality of mind
and body in his pursuit of an heroic ideal dear to Roman soci-

---

narcissistic dilemma" in Greek males as resulting from the mother's treatment of her son. Because she sees him as an expression of and a cure for her
narcissistic wounds, she alternately belittles and exalts him, preventing him
from negotiating a normal transition from infantile narcissism and total dependence to individuation and an awareness of the separateness of others. I
find a similar pattern in Shakespeare's characterization of Coriolanus.

8. Philip Brockbank comments sensitively on the expressive power of
silence in the play, in his "Introduction" to the new Arden edition (London:
Methuen, 1976), particularly on how Coriolanus's silence as his mother
kneels before him in the climactic scene at Antium (5.3) is prefigured by
"other pleas, silences, intimacies, recognitions of kinship, and touches of nature" that were "compromised or contaminated" earlier.

ety. He cuts down enemies "like a harvest man that's task'd to mow / Or all or loss his hire" (1.3.36–37); "a thing of blood," he strikes Corioles like a planet, and runs "reeking over the lives of men" (2.2.105–122); he leads his soldiers "like a thing / Made by some other deity than Nature" (4.6.91–93); and "when he walks, he moves like an engine" (5.4.18–25). Obsessed with his supremacy as a warrior, happiest when bathed in the blood of his enemies, he is depicted as Mars himself. His feats of slaughter win him the adoration of the Roman public; the plebeians, despite their initial enmity, flock to his triumphal return from the Volscian wars, and his fellow patricians hasten uncritically to placate his rages.

Yet this god is but a boy, finally, a "boy of tears." Behind his superhuman courage and adamantine refusal to compromise, the play reveals an incomplete, psychologically immature half man who lacks the most basic skills for coping with change, opposition, frustration, duplicity, or his own needs to love or be loved. Coriolanus's warrior self resembles the "false-self system" that R. D. Laing describes as a component of the schizophrenic personality. This warrior self has arisen in compliance with his mother's conception of him, and has a false, automatic, inhuman quality, partly because it has been implanted in him rather than being allowed to develop from within, and partly because it is only half human in its exclusion of any emotional response to others save anger, scorn, and aggression.[9] Even these feelings, as I will argue when discussing Coriolanus's relations with the plebs, manifest his rebellion against the mother who has refused to allow him a self. His identity is based on an abstraction of Roman force and on his love for his mother, who makes her affection

9. R. D. Laing, *The Divided Self: An Existential Study in Sanity and Madness* (Harmondsworth, Eng.: Penguin, 1965). Laing shows how the false self system arises in response to a basic "ontological insecurity," in which "any and every relationship threatens the individual with loss of identity," thrusting him into isolation from others and into "a vision of reality as an antithesis between engulfment in another and complete isolation from any other" (p. 44). As a way of preserving himself from this dual threat, the individual assumes more and more of the characteristics of the person on whom his primary, crippling identification is based.

conditional on his fulfillment of her hopes. The more manly he is, in the exclusive and extreme terms of manliness Volumnia establishes, the more he is "bound to his mother," as she proclaims.

Volumnia's tendency to obliterate distinctions between herself and her son, to treat him as the embodiment of her own ego ideal, is reflected in the ways she and Coriolanus refer to each other, in terms that stress her role as bearer and nurturer so as to make her his creator. She calls him "the only son of my womb" (1.3.6) and tells him, "Thou art my warrior; / I holp to frame thee" (5.3.62–63) and more revealingly, "Thy valiantness was mine, thou suck'dst it from me" (3.2.129). He too finds his identity in her, calling himself "her blood" (1.9.13–14) and her "the honour'd mould / Wherein this trunk was fram'd" (5.3.22–23). At several points mother and son virtually echo each other. Volumnia envisions her son in battle, and acts out his fervor:

> Methinks I hear hither your husband's drum;
> See him pluck Aufidius down by th'hair,
> As children from a bear, the Volsces shunning him.
> Methinks I see him stamp thus, and call thus:
> "Come on you cowards, you were got in fear
> Though you were born in Rome."
>
> (1.3.29–34)

Then, in the next scene, he shouts to his soldiers, "He that retires, I'll take him for Volsce" (1.4.28). *Telle mère, tel fils;* Volumnia's curses against the plebs resemble her son's, as well they might, for he claims to have learned them from her. Compare, for instance, his

> What's the matter, you dissentious rogues
> That, rubbing the poor itch of your opinion,
> Make yourselves scabs?
>
> (1.1.163–165)

to her "Now the red pestilence strike all trades in Rome, / And occupations perish!" (4.1.13–14).[10]

---

10. The new Arden note states that the red pestilence is "probably typhus fever, which causes red skin eruptions."

The warrior self that Volumnia has created in Coriolanus isolates him from others and prevents him from developing the self still potential within him. Katherine Stockholder has perceptively remarked that

> Coriolanus devotes himself to creating the image of virile masculinity *qua* honour and then identifies his self with that image . . . a kind of murder of all parts of the self that do not fit into the preconceived image.[11]

His warrior self is "hard, isolate, stoic, and a killer" (to put D. H. Lawrence's description of the American hero in a different cultural context). Because it is also false, an artificially contrived image, he must constantly strive to maintain it, and Volumnia is always there to help him. This warrior self is separate from his humanity, which emerges only in the denouement and then with fatal effect, but identical with his manliness. Furthermore, because Volumnia's indoctrination of her son into the warrior mentality was identical with nourishing him, because he sucked "valiantness" and not milk, pleasing his mother is for him the same as serving Rome: Rome and Volumnia, mother country and mother, are equally ascendant in his inner world. Thus, paradoxically, his martial supremacy is actually an expression of his extreme dependency, but at the same time an attempt to defend against that very dependency, by achieving godlike superiority that marks him off from any other man.

In the heavily charged imagery of the battle scenes at Corioles, Shakespeare suggests this tragic paradox behind the hero's valor. There he reenacts the dilemma of his identity, of being bound to and striving to get away from his mother; of trying to be at once a man and her boy. He enters the gates of the city alone, his soldiers shrinking from what seems certain death; when he reappears, bleeding, the troops follow him and take Corioles. The city is traditionally a feminine enclosure, and Coriolanus's isolation within this hostile city is

11. Katherine Stockholder, "The Other Coriolanus," *PMLA* 85 (1970): 228–236.

stressed in the visual and dramatic action of act 1, scene 4, and verbally throughout the play:[12]

> . . . he is himself alone,
> To answer all the city.
>
> (1.4.51–52)

> Alone I fought in your Corioles walls . . .
>
> (1.8.8)

> Alone he enter'd
> The mortal gate of the city.
>
> (2.2.110–111)

> Alone I did it! Boy!
>
> (5.6.115)

At the same time that he is alone, he is also enclosed by the city walls and engulfed by a whole army. It is a perfect image for the two conflicting sides of his self: the determination his mother has planted in him to excel all others as Rome's unmatched warrior, which also means isolating himself from feeling and denying human bonds; and the underlying bond with his mother that makes his martial valor the means of her fulfillment rather than of his own. The duality of engulfment and isolation within the city walls also mirrors his ambivalent wish to separate himself as violently and bloodily from Volumnia as from his antagonists, and to fuse completely with her, even as he is surrounded by his enemies and masked in their blood.[13]

12. See William S. Heckscher, "Shakespeare in His Relationship to the Visual Arts: A Study in Paradox," *Research Opportunities in Renaissance Drama* 13–14 (1970–1971): 5–72, for a summary of the verbal and visual iconographic tradition of the city as woman.

13. The motif of simultaneous engulfment and isolation is strikingly repeated in act 1, scene 6. Those soldiers who wish to follow Coriolanus back into battle "shout and wave their swords," then "take him up in their arms,

In his behavior toward the plebeians, Coriolanus gives full rein to the first wish, for violent differentiation. The mob is depicted as a hydra with many mouths; dependent on the patricians for food, starved and clamoring for "corn gratis," it embodies his own dependency and impoverishment at his mother's breast, where he sucked "valiantness" but little else save the arrogance for which the people hate him. Its power is expressed orally, through "voices" or votes, as is its hungry presence, and in a similarly oral mode, Coriolanus attacks it with vicious, scornful abuse, using words as weapons. As Janet Adelman shows brilliantly, Volumnia has trained her son to despise dependency of any kind, and to turn his own into aggression.[14] Truly, he "leaves nothing undone that may fully discover him their opposite" (2.2.20–21), and that is the psychological function of his aggression toward the plebeians. Their faults are the opposite of his virtues, for the implicit standard by which he condemns them is his aristocratic one of stoic constancy and fortitude:

> He that trusts to you,
> Where he should find you lions, finds you hares;
> Where foxes, geese: you are no surer, no,
> Than is the coal of fire upon the ice,
> Or hailstone in the sun. Your virtue is,
> To make him worthy whose offense subdues him,
> And curse that justice did it. Who deserves greatness,
> Deserves your hate; and your affections are
> A sick man's appetite, who desires most that
> Which would increase his evil.
>
> (1.1.169–178)

The strong, repetitive rhetorical oppositions in which he characterizes the mob reflect his own need to split himself off

---

and cast up their caps," according to the Folio stage directions, as he shouts, "O me alone! Make you a sword of me!" (Some editors have assigned this line to the soldiers, as does Brockbank in the new Arden, but it is attributed to the hero in the Folio.) In his death scene, he is similarly isolated in a now hostile city, and surrounded by Aufidius's soldiers who swarm around him and kill him. Thus Shakespeare emphasizes visually and dramatically the hero's dominant ambivalence.

14. She argues that the crowd figures as a "multitude of demanding and feminized mouths," a dependent and castrated image of Coriolanus himself (p. 9). (See note 5, above.)

from their enveloping neediness. In battle they are cowards and he is a superhero; they drop their weapons to carry off the spoils while he fights without respite, careless of wounds; they complain of hunger and he scorns to eat. His attitude toward them is also congruent with his "zero-sum" hero's mentality: they are nothing, he is everything. If they are anything at all, he is nothing.[15]

While the wounds he hardly seems to feel are regarded by Rome as signs of his "service to the state," Coriolanus cannot bear to acknowledge them as such to the people, for that would be admitting a bond tantamount to his unconscious bond with the mother who is firmly identified with that state, its values, and its very existence. (He willingly acknowledges his bond to the senate when Menenius offers him the consulship, saying "I do owe them still / My life and services" [2.2.133–134], but cannot bear to show himself subservient to the plebeians.) Seeking wounds as he conspicuously does, he seems to court praise for them, yet when he receives it, he is driven to deny it and scorn those offering it. What he persistently seeks and finds, first in the mob and then in Aufidius, is an opposite with whom he can proclaim a negative bond, a bond of hate, the only kind he can afford to acknowledge and the kind that helps him maintain an identity that otherwise is too uncomfortably merged with his mother's.

As the plot unfolds, Volumnia and her son are trapped not only by the self-defeating emotional logic of their relationship, but also by historical circumstance. The play begins at a politically significant moment in the life of Rome—the creation of the tribuneship.[16] But this first recognition of the

15. Alvin Gouldner, *Enter Plato* (New York: Basic Books, 1965), shows how the Greek obsessions with fame and honor, competition, achievement, and envy combine with other salient traits in what he calls the Greek contest system, a zero-sum game, in which someone wins only if somebody else loses (pp. 41–74).

16. For a fascinating account of how the plebeians first separated themselves from the city as a group with separate interests, and then reintegrated themselves by means of the tribunes, see Numa Denis Fustel de Coulanges, *The Ancient City: A Study on the Religion, Laws, and Institutions of Greece and Rome* (New York: Doubleday, n.d.). He describes the plebeians and the patricians as "two people that did not even understand one another, not having, so

plebeians' political existence is purely formal. Menenius's fable presents a vision of Rome as a unified organic whole, but as Michael McCanles points out, according to this conception any single member of the body politic that does not cooperate is thus a faction at war with all the rest.[17] The organic model provides no means of solving conflicts by change and compromise. Coriolanus, on the other hand, sees the situation as one in which "two authorities are up, / Neither supreme" (3.1.109–110). Though his estimate is part and parcel of his defensive system that requires constant antagonism, it is nonetheless accurate. Each side uses the organic metaphor to refer to the other as extraneous to and destructive of the body politic. Coriolanus calls the people "scabs" and "measles" and curses them with boils and plagues, while the tribunes turn the metaphor against him: "He's a disease that must be cut away" (3.1.293), a metaphor made real when they banish him.

In this political context, election to the consulship is a kind of *rite de passage* that allows the patricians to reiterate ceremonially their adherence to the warrior ethic that defines them as an elite. To serve as consul is publicly regarded as "service to the state," and insofar as Coriolanus defends the city from the Volscians, he does serve the state. But in another sense, the external threat of war enables the patricians to validate their existence as an elite by creating and rewarding warriors, whose brave deeds make them worthy of civic office. The recent establishment of the tribunes makes it necessary, however, for the ritual of candidacy to reflect the new, supposedly representative government: the candidate must don humble garb and show his wounds to the people, to prove that his "service" makes him worthy of their votes. But since Coriolanus serves "to please his mother, and to be partly proud, which he is, even to the altitude of his virtue"

to speak, common ideas" (p. 297), which is surely the situation in *Coriolanus*. Leonard Tennenhouse, "*Coriolanus:* History and the Crisis of Semantic Order," *Comparative Drama* 10 (Winter 1976–1977): 328–346, shows how Shakespeare stresses the creation of the tribunes in contrast to his sources, and how they ramify the relationship between language and power.

17. Michael McCanles, "The Dialectic of Transcendence in *Coriolanus,*" *PMLA* 82 (1967): 44–55.

(1.1.38–39), and since he ultimately serves the interests of his own class more than those of the whole, the ceremony is a charade. In addition, it is hollow because the politically naive plebeians (whose intuitions about Coriolanus are devastatingly accurate) are at the mercy of their scheming self-interested tribunes. They faintly perceive the artificiality of the whole procedure but, schooled in habits of compliance, go along with it. Coriolanus's distaste for it is not merely defensive arrogance, but also an unblinking assessment of the situation from the patrician viewpoint, which he is the only one to press openly, as the last pure aristocrat of his class.

It is at this historical moment that the political terms in which Coriolanus is accustomed to maintain his warrior identity change and betray him. In this new political climate of accommodation and compromise, where gesture masks power, Coriolanus's rigid integrity is out of place and his aristocratic pride a liability. But his mother, who bred in him that integrity and pride, is determined that he shall "inherit the buildings of her fancy" and gain the consulship. Contradicting her own values for the sake of his success, she shows no understanding of his character when she urges him to humble himself to the people she has called "woollen vassals":

Cor: Would you have me be
         False to my nature? Rather say I play the man I am.
Vol: You might have been enough the man you are
         With striving less to be so.
                                                    (3.2.19–22)

What Coriolanus believes to be his authentic self is that self he has played all his life, with her prompting and for her applause. But now, having made him obstinate and cruel, Volumnia would have him false to himself—hypocritical and conciliatory. She has changed the script: now the word is "policy" instead of "valiantness," but she still relies on her power to make him play her part:

Cor: You have put me to such a part which never
         I shall discharge to the life.
Com: Come, come, we'll prompt you.

Vol: I prithee now, sweet son, as thou hast said
My praises made thee first a soldier, so,
To have my praise for this, perform a part
Thou hast not done before.

(3.2.105–110)

Even as he agrees to perform that part, he portrays it as emasculation. He will resemble, he says, a prostitute, a eunuch, a virgin, a schoolboy, or a beggar; he sees himself before the plebs as dependent, castrated, womanish. For perhaps the first time in his life, he defies her—but when she then withdraws her approval and proudly refuses to beg, he collapses in a flurry of reassurances. When he confronts the crowd in act 3, scene 1, however, to hear the charges brought against him, he reverts instantly to his warrior self—the intransigent, scornful, angry boy his mother has created.

When the tribunes call him traitor and rescind the consulship he has just won at such cost, they provoke him to reject Rome in what seems a startling transformation of his values. Their behavior toward him is really similar to Volumnia's in the previous scene. She enticed him with her approval, then refused it; they overlook his insults and reward him for his valor with the consulship, then rebuke him for his "power tyrannical" and dishonor him with banishment. Their actions provoke his ungovernable rage not merely because he suspects the tribunes have manipulated the people in order to keep their offices, or because of his scorn for plebeian malleability. The magnitude of his anger identifies it as the repressed rage he could not show against his mother. Like her, they gave him something and then took it back; they led him on and with a terrible power, deprived him, just as she made a man of him but deprived him of a self, even enough of a self to maintain a consistency she had abandoned.

"Like to a lonely dragon," Coriolanus stalks into exile. But isolated as he is, he cannot bear to be alone and immediately seeks the solace of antagonism. In a double reversal, he allies himself with his archrival and pits himself against Rome. This action exemplifies one of his most distinctive, oft-noted traits: his inability to temper his convictions or his anger, his absolute, univocal stance, his either-or, all-or-nothing mentality.

Thus his planned revenge against Rome is to be total and in-
discriminate, "as spacious as between / The young'st and old-
est thing" (4.6.68–69). Its intensity bespeaks the intensity of
the hurt he must hide. Rome was his mother and she has cast
him out, so he must cast her out. Coriolanus is Shakespeare's
least inward tragic hero. He has but one soliloquy, which,
significantly, charts his *volte-face* from Rome to Antium,
characteristically in terms of total fusion and violent antagonism:

> O world, thy slippery turns! Friends now fast sworn
> Whose double bosoms seems to wear one heart,
> Whose hours, whose bed, whose meal and exercise
> Are still together, who twin as 'twere, in love
> Unseparable, shall within this hour,
> On a dissension of a doit, break out
> To bitterest enmity; so fellest foes,
> Whose passions and whose plots have broke their sleep
> Some trick not worth an egg, shall grow dear friends
> And interjoin their issues. So with me:
> My birthplace hate I, and my love's upon
> This enemy town.
>
> (4.4.12–24)

The kind of twinning same-sex friendship he depicts resembles the narcissistic mirrorings of the comedies, enjoyed by
the Antipholi, Hermia and Helen, and Rosalind and Celia,
who abandon them from marriage.[18] But for Coriolanus and
for his fellow warrior Aufidius, these man-to-man relationships, whether based on love or hate, compete in passion with
their other marriages:

> *Cor:*   Oh! let me clip ye
> In arms as sound as when I woo'd; in heart
> As merry as when our nuptial day was done,
> And tapers burn'd to bedward.
>
> (1.6.29–32)

> *Auf:*   Know thou first,
> I lov'd the maid I married; never man

---

18. Marjorie Garber, "Coming of Age in Shakespeare," *Yale Review*
(Summer 1977): 517–533, describes these late adolescent friendships as bonds
normally limited by marriage and separation from the family.

> Sigh'd truer breath; but that I see thee here,
> Thou noble thing, more dances my rapt heart
> Than when I first my wedded mistress saw
> Bestride my threshold.
>
> (4.5.114–119)

Coriolanus's meditation on friendship ends with the fantasy that these loving male friends "interjoin their issues" and marry their children to each other—reflecting a wish for an actual marriage between men.

It is Aufidius who enlarges on this homoerotic theme quite startlingly when he welcomes Coriolanus as his ally. Aufidius last appeared early in the play, vowing eternal hate to his rival out of sheer envy at being defeated by him (1.10). His fall into craftiness, announced then, was contrasted with Coriolanus's steely integrity. Thus the Volscian's passionate reception of Coriolanus is a sudden and unmotivated reversal, one fire driving out another. But hate and love are really all one to him, for they both take the form of rivalrous combat, the dominant form of masculinity in Roman culture:

> Here I clip
> The anvil of my sword, and do contest
> As hotly and as nobly with thy love
> As ever in ambitious strength I did
> Contend against thy valour. . . .
> . . . .
> . . . Thou hast beat me out
> Twelve several times, and I have nightly since
> Dreamt of encounters 'twixt thyself and me—
> We have been down together in my sleep,
> Unbuckling helms, fisting each other's throat—
> And wak'd half-dead with nothing.
>
> (4.5.110–114, 123–127)

Aufidius cannot possibly sustain an alliance that even in his dreams can only dissolve into a fight. At the heart of his antagonism is envy. He is the second-rater who will stop at nothing to be first, while Coriolanus, obsessed by revenge, surpasses him in valor and popularity without even thinking about it. It is supremely fitting that aggressiveness and competitiveness unite to bring about the hero's downfall, for they

comprise the Roman warrior mentality: its extreme aggressiveness against enemies, which demands the suppression of
human sympathy, is embodied in Volumnia, and its extreme
competitiveness, which pits man against man in an incessant
contest for superiority, is embodied in Aufidius.

But on Coriolanus's side, this intense rivalry is another
reenactment of his ambivalent bond with Volumnia:

> I sin in envying his nobility;
> And were I anything but what I am,
> I would wish me only he. . . .
> Were half to half the world by th'ears, and he
> Upon my party, I'd revolt to make
> Only my wars with him.[19]
>
> (1.1.229–231, 232–234)

First he wishes to be Aufidius, his virtual double in all save
honesty, and then declares that he would join the enemy in
order to fight against him because only Aufidius is worthy to
be his rival. As in the battle at Corioles, the hero would both
fuse with another and also separate violently from him and
oppose him. He can only love someone who is the same as
himself, but then he must fight him. In the first half of the
play, the two men are more unified in their "violent'st contrariety" than they are in their alliance in the second half,
when Aufidius begins to plot against his partner. Both are
dedicated to achieving the kind of victory in which their opponent is reduced to absolute nothingness:

> *Mar:* I'll fight with none but thee, for I do hate thee
> Worse than a promise-breaker.
> *Auf:* We hate alike:
> Not Afric owns a serpent I abhor
> More than thy fame and envy. Fix thy foot.
> *Mar:* Let the first budger die the other's slave,
> And the gods doom him after.
>
> (1.8.1–6)

---

19. Judith Gray has pointed out to me that the wording of the last sentence
in the quoted passage ("I'd revolt to make / Only my wars with him") expresses the speaker's ambivalence in that "with" means both "together with"
and "against."

Shakespeare stresses the binding quality of their enmity throughout; in the first act, Aufidius declares, "He's mine, or I am his" (1.10.12), laying the foundation for the final confrontation in which "the fall of either makes the survivor heir of all" (5.6.18–19).

Coriolanus has behaved all his life so as "not to be other than one thing"—that perfect Roman his mother envisions him to be. When she pleads with him at Antium not to destroy Rome, that one thing splits in two, like a heart cracking. To pursue his revenge against Rome would indeed be, as he says, to "stand as if a man were author of himself / And knew no other kin," the most extreme denial of his bonds with his mother and with Rome, the cruelest and bloodiest separation from his emotional and social matrix. But it would also be completely congruent with the character she has instilled in him; to destroy Rome would demand that insulation from all human pity, that relentless, narrowly defined integrity she has taught him in the name of valor and honor.

On the other hand, to relent as he does means to feel pity and love, to admit and act upon "the bond and privilege of nature" that binds him not only to his mother, but to all that is human. Volumnia has always made her son's Roman valor the price of her affection. Now, as when she begged him to don the white robe and seek the consulship, she asks him to abandon valor and to act out of feelings she has done her best to kill in him. All his life, to be Roman has meant being inhuman, like a deity or a "thing." Now, to be Roman means to be human. Thus, though presumably he pleases Volumnia when he relents, he does not relent only to please her, but in answer to a tenderness within him that she has tried to eradicate and that she would not admire even if she could recognize it. Interestingly, Shakespeare gives us no hint of her responses to her son's climactic turnabout; she has not a word to say after he agrees not to march on Rome, and makes only a brief wordless appearance in act 5, scene 5, to be hailed as "our patroness, the life of Rome." That Coriolanus does yield bespeaks a transformation within him far deeper than his relatively superficial reversal of political affiliation. For the first time, he gives voice to the silence, the vacant emotional space within him. As a "boy of tears" he is more of a man—and paradoxically, less than ever Volumnia's son—than he was on the battlefield. It is appropriate, then, that when his silence finds voice she falls silent, unable to voice the sympathy, approval, or affection the moment naturally invites.

But there is no place for a man's tears in the Roman world of this play. Inevitably, Aufidius's taunts against Coriolanus's manhood send him reeling back into the anger and obtuse defiance that have always been the seal of his manliness:

> *Auf:* . . . at his nurse's tears
> He whin'd and roar'd away your victory,
> That pages blush'd at him, and men of heart
> Look'd wond'ring each at others.
> *Cor:* Hear'st thou, Mars?
> *Auf:* Name not the god, thou boy of tears!
> *Cor:* Ha!
>
> (5.6.97–100)

He cannot defend the peace he has made at his mother's urging because the man who made that peace is so newborn, so primitive and undeveloped, that he *is* like a boy, a helpless creature of tears and silence unable to stand up for himself. He vanishes at Aufidius's first insult, to be replaced by the cruel deity Mars, with whom Coriolanus has always been identified. And Coriolanus returns to being a warrior, "one thing" only, incapable of a temperate, rational response to any challenge. Though he briefly appeals to the "judgements" of the "grave lords" who (it is clear) might have kept Aufidius's minions from striking, he quickly falls into the warrior's mode of challenge, defiance, and boasting that plays into Aufidius's hands:

> Cut me to pieces, Volsces, men and lads,
> Stain all your edges on me. Boy! False hound!
> If you have writ your annals true, 'tis there,
> That like an eagle in a dove-cote, I
> Flutter'd your Volscians in Corioles.
> Alone I did it. Boy!
>
> (5.6.111–116)

In recalling his solitary entrance into Corioles, the hero re-creates his ideal self just before suffering the death that is the price of it—as Othello does when he remembers smiting the Turk, as Hamlet does when he asks Horatio to tell his story. His line "Alone I did it. Boy!" restates with a terrible irony the dilemma of his identity: his ambivalent attempt to sunder the maternal bond even as he fulfills its conditions, to be "alone" the warrior his mother wants him to be, and his fail-ure to do it, for in these last moments of his life he is more her "boy" than ever. He dies longing for another good fight against his supreme enemy, for a perpetuation of the "vio-lent'st contrariety" by which he has lived:

> O, that I had him,
> With six Aufidiuses, or more, his tribe,
> To use my lawful sword.
>
> (5.6.127–129)

II

By thrusting him from dependency and thrusting onto him a warrior self of her own devising, Volumnia effectively mur-dered the babe in Coriolanus—the loving and vulnerable self within him. He gains tragic stature in forsaking his revenge against Rome because he dares to revive that self and then dies because of the attempt. In contrast, Macbeth is more fully de-veloped emotionally, already enough of a man to feel the hor-ror of his cruel deeds—yet it is he who murders the babe of pity within himself as the play proceeds. The urges conflicting within him, the urges to kill and to nurture that infant self, are evenly matched and relentless. Though he gives in to the worse of the two, he is tragic because he lives each one out so fully, suffering for the good in his nature as well as for the evil.

But like Coriolanus, though he excels as a virile warrior, Macbeth has not fully separated himself from the feminine source of his identity. That he is destined to be defeated by a man "untimely ripp'd from his mother's womb" signifies, in Macbeth's sexually confused fantasy world, that only a violent and unnatural separation from woman can make a man whole, able both to feel and to fight, to be a father and to be valiant, as Macduff is.[20] The sources of his sexual confusion are the witches, who direct their mischief toward him, and Lady Macbeth, who seeks vicarious fulfillment through him. These female beings ally themselves with destruction, not creation (Lady Macduff, appearing in only one scene as an anxious and defenseless mother, is a foil to them). Macbeth's susceptibility to them, and his inability to maintain and defend his conceptions of manliness, emanate from his unconscious dependency on them as mentors. His kingship, gained by repeated murders that rob him of all content, might be symbolized by bloody men, himself and those he kills, and those men are in turn associated with the kind of action urged on him by his wife in the name of manliness. He sees her, in fact, as a kind of man, who should

> Bring forth men-children only!
> For thy undaunted mettle should compose
> Nothing but males.
>
> (1.7.73–75)

He speaks of her as though she were a sole godlike procreator, man and woman both. And she does have the terrible power to make him her kind of bloody man.[21]

20. David B. Barron shares my emphasis on Macbeth's domination by female influence in "The Babe That Milks: An Organic Study of Macbeth," in *The Design Within: Psychoanalytic Approaches to Shakespeare*, ed. Melvin D. Faber (New York: Science House, 1970), pp. 253–279. He wavers, however, between arguing that the hero "chooses to submit to female influence" and that he unconsciously identifies with his mother. While his essay illuminates the text at many points, he maintains that "Macbeth is desperate to unite sexually with a fertile woman," for which I find no evidence in the play, and sees his bloody deeds as an attempt to cut his way out of the confining female element, while I see them as a mode of conforming with it.

21. It might have been the following passage from *The Description of Scotland* by Hector Boece, included in Holinshed's *Chronicles* (the major source of *Macbeth*), which inspired Shakespeare's conception of Lady Macbeth's "undaunted mettle":

> Each woman would take intolerable paines to bring up and nourish hir owne children. They thought them furthermore not to be kindlie fostered, except they were so well nourished after their births with the milk of their brests, as they were before they were born with the bloud of their owne bellies, nay they feared least they should de-

Macbeth's dependency on women is closely related to a
second motif, the rivalries he pursues with men: his violent
agons with the rebels of the first act, and his equally violent
envy of Banquo and then of Macduff, each the kind of man
Macbeth could or would be. Like Coriolanus, Macbeth defines himself by fighting men who mirror him in some way,
but his antagonists are ego ideals, not carbon copies, as
Aufidius was of Coriolanus, for Macbeth's ego is more developed than Coriolanus's; he has greater self-awareness and a
wider range of feelings. As the play proceeds, Macbeth follows a pattern of first imbibing encouragement from female
sources, then attacking male antagonists. The first three
scenes reflect this pattern, with the witches (in scenes 1 and 3)
framing the accounts of Macbeth's valor (in scene 2). These
accounts are phrased as a succession of single combats, each of
which involves merger and then separation. Thus they constitute analogues to Macbeth's ambivalence: he merges his will
with the wishes of his female influences in order to ac-
complish bloody deeds, but through the deeds he differ-
entiates himself, to be singled out as a man and stand supreme.
The Captain's account of Macbeth's valor suggests that he
passes through a sort of initiation rite, to emerge fully vali-
dated as a man, warrior, and loyal subject. As the combat between Macdonwald and Macbeth begins, they merge in the
heat of the fight, equally matched in a hostile embrace "as two
spent swimmers, that do cling together / And choke their art"

generat and grow out of kind, except they gave them suck themselves,
and eschewed strange milke, therefore in labour and in painfulnesse
they were equall, and neither sex regarded the heat in summer or cold
in winter, but travelled barefooted. . . . In these daies also the women
of our countrie were of no lesse corage than the men, for all stout
maidens and wives (if they were not with child) marched well in the
field as did the men, and as soone as the armie did set forward, they
slue the first living creature that they found, in whose bloud they not
onelie bathed their swords, but also tasted thereof with their
mouthes. . . . (Geoffrey Bullough, ed., Narrative and Dramatic Sources of
Shakespeare, 7 vols. [London: Routledge and Kegan Paul, 1973], 7:
506–507)

These Scottish women showed as fierce a determination to nurse their children as to march beside their husbands in battle, and thus, in the terms their
culture offered, were men as well as women.

(1.2.7–8). But Macbeth triumphs with a vicious stroke, described so viscerally as to make us shudder, and at least momentarily question the value conferred on such brutality. When Norway enters the battle, Macbeth and Banquo are described as a pair, indistinguishable, both "bathe[d] in reeking wounds." And when Macbeth begins a third combat, with Cawdor, the equality of the match, and the likeness of the antagonists, is again stressed: Macbeth

> Confronted him with self-comparisons,
> Point against point, rebellious arm 'gainst arm,
>
> (1.2.56–57)

almost as though they are twins. As in the rivalry between Coriolanus and Aufidius, the combat seems like a marriage that confers manly identity. First the combatants merge as equals, and then one of them distinguishes himself as victor; Macbeth becomes "Bellona's bridegroom, lapp'd in proof," his manhood consummated, and acquires a new identity as Cawdor—an ominous one of rebel and hypocrite.

Finally, Macbeth's struggle toward manhood is refracted in a third motif: fatherhood, presented as the crown of manhood and, especially in his competition with Banquo, deeply entwined with male rivalry. His character and his career pivot on the crucial distinction made in the witches' prophecies between being a king and being a father. Macbeth, they declare, will be king hereafter, while Banquo will get kings but not be one. And Banquo, though lesser, will be happier than Macbeth. Fatherhood is based not on deeds of blood but on the mystery of procreation: the harmony of male with female powers, in step with the steady rhythms of the natural order. It might be symbolized by the apparition of the crowned babe, the ruler of that future forever beyond Macbeth's grasp. The men in the play are fruitful: Duncan, Banquo, Macduff, and Siward all have sons, for and through whom they act to perpetuate the natural and the social order. But the childless Macbeth's only "firstlings" are murders. The confusion of sexual identity pervading the play is offset by this contrast between the sterility of bloody deeds and the fruition of fatherhood.

Tracing Macbeth's progress from the properly sanctioned, morally clear manhood of martial valor in defense of Duncan, to his final delusion that "no man of woman born" can harm him, we begin with his experience of feminine powers represented by the witches. They create a murky atmosphere of blurred distinctions, mingled opposites, equivocations, and reversals. In their world, things "hover through the fog and filthy air" and "fair is foul and foul is fair." This murkiness extends through the play as Macbeth yields to them: in the darkness that entombs the living light of day after Duncan's murder; in the light that "thickens" as Macbeth's assassins prepare to kill Banquo; in the self-contradictory messages the apparitions give Macbeth; in Lady Macbeth's "thick-coming fancies." The feminine, as the play depicts it, is a chaos of physical as well as moral elements, deviously inviting men to their destruction by confusion rather than direct attack.

In imagery, the feminine takes the form of "spirits" ambiguously aerial, liquid, and solid. They are the opposite of that morally and physically nourishing "milk of human kindness" Lady Macbeth would deny her baby if it impeded her will and would drain out of her husband. As a thick liquid that stops up the passages of remorse, the feminine is most vividly imaged in the contents of the witches' cauldron, that "gruel thick and slab" well described by G. Wilson Knight:

> The ingredients are absurd bits of life like those of Othello's ravings (*Othello* 4.1.42), now jumbled together. . . . Though the bodies from which these are torn are often themselves, by association, evil, yet we must note the additional sense of chaos, bodily desecration, and irrationality in the use of the absurd members . . . a feast of death and essential disorder (because of the disjointed ingredients) giving birth to spirits suggesting life that is to come (the Apparitions and their prophecies).[22]

"Finger of birth-strangled babe, / Ditch-deliver'd by a drab" and "sow's blood, that hath eaten / Her nine farrow" point-

22. G. Wilson Knight, "The Milk of Concord: An Essay on Life-Themes in *Macbeth*," in *The Imperial Theme: Further Interpretations of Shakespeare's Tragedies Including the Roman Plays* (London: Methuen, 1951), 3rd ed., p. 139.

edly associate childbearing with murder and women with death, not in terms of legend or fantasy but as city and village realities. This hell-broth symbolizing chaos and destruction is a metaphor for the influence of the "spirits" who brew it; in a pervasive pun, "spirits" as devilish influences without and tendencies within man are like "spirits" or liquor, and they are feminine. Shakespeare establishes the connection between Lady Macbeth and the witches by having her invoke the spirits of evil and ask them to fill her with their spirits:

> Come, you Spirits,
> That tend on mortal thoughts, unsex me here,
> And fill me, from the crown to the toe, top-full
> Of direst cruelty! make thick my blood,
> Stop up th'access and passage to remorse;
> That no compunctious visitings of Nature
> Shake my fell purpose, nor keep peace between
> Th'effect and it!
>
> (1.5.40–47)

When she incites Macbeth to murder, she "pours" these same "spirits" into his ears, and like liquor, they make his will drunk, separating his eye from his hand and his reason from his actions. Similarly, Lady Macbeth drugs the grooms with wine and wassail that drench their memory and their reason, and prepares a drink for Macbeth before he goes to murder Duncan. While he awaits the drink, the vision of the dagger appears and plunges him into tortured ambivalence. To deny the reality of the feelings that gave rise to this vision, he evokes the same ritualistic, incantatory spirits of Witchcraft, Hecate, and Murder by which his wife originally persuaded him to the deed. Attaining the "rapt," spellbound state of blind readiness similar to that he experienced when the witches accosted him, as the scene closes he prepares to abandon himself to "the heat of deeds":

> I go, and it is done: the bell invites me—
>
> (2.1.62)

deeds he can perform only at the quasi-magical beckoning of the bell she rings and by quaffing the inebriating drink she serves him. The next scene begins with Lady Macbeth exulting in her "spirits," the possets she brews, and the powers of evil that possess her:

> That which hath made them drunk hath made me bold:
> What hath quench'd them hath given me fire.
>
> (2.2.1–2)

The kind of manly action to which she successfully incites her husband by taunting him with his failure to be as resolute as she is originates, then, in a profound passivity, a suffusion by a liquid feminine element that drowns whatever compunctions oppose it.

Inevitably, the action inspired by this surrender to feminine spirits must be as self-defeating and delusory as action inspired by drink. The Porter's wry, mordant comments on how liquor affects sexual desire and performance apply equally to the effect of Lady Macbeth's and the witches' "spirits" on Macbeth's performance as a man:

> Lechery, Sir, it provokes, and unprovokes; it provokes the desire, but it takes away the performance. Therefore, much drink may be said to be an equivocator with lechery: it makes him, and it mars him; it sets him on, and it takes him off; it persuades him, and disheartens him; makes him stand to, and not stand to: in conclusion, equivocates him in a sleep, and, giving him the lie, leaves him.[23]
>
> (2.3.29–37)

The spirits that seem to make him potent actually render him impotent.[24] For the more daringly, heartlessly, and blindly

23. A recent series of experiments explains the well-known capacity of alcohol to sharpen sexual desire in men but blunt its expression as a chain reaction that first drives down the production of testosterone, producing temporary impotency; concurrently, the lower testosterone level touches off the production of luteinizing hormone, which prompts sexual desire (Nils J. Bruzelius, "A Theory of Alcohol and Sex," *Boston Globe,* July 19, 1978).

24. Dennis Biggins, "Sexuality, Witchcraft, and Violence in *Macbeth,*" *Shakespeare Studies* 8 (1976): 255–277, demonstrates in fascinating detail that much of traditional witchcraft was believed to involve the sexual exploitation of men by the witches' insatiable lust, sexual perversion, and sexual domination of several kinds. He then shows how the language of the play sexualizes violence, suggesting both that Duncan's murder is a kind of rape and that the sexual act is, in turn, a kind of murder. This interpretation supplements my own, insofar as Macbeth's violence is his attempt to *become* a man in his wife's eyes and is thus a substitute for his full sexual possession of her. Furthermore,

Macbeth acts, the less he gains, the farther he places himself from the chimera of safety. The blatantly phallic reference of the whole speech and the fears of impotence it voices, particularly in the phrases "stand to, and not stand to," express the self-defeating quality of the actions he undertakes: the deed never "done"; the throne never secured; and the manhood barren of issue.[25] The futility of the "masculine" actions Macbeth undertakes to secure the crown might be paralleled to the sexual sterility at the heart of his identity as a man: they are complementary aspects of his plight. Some critics have claimed that he makes war on children because he cannot have any, but this is too literal a reading.[26] Rather, that "he has no children" is a metaphor for his failure to realize an authentic manliness that integrates his conscience and his feelings with his valor, a manliness fostering rather than merely destroying life.

Continuing the idea behind the pun on *spirits,* another pun runs through the play: *doing* as the sexual act and as murder, the "daring" deed that will make the hero a man.[27] It begins with the First Witch's line, "I'll do, and I'll do, and I'll do" (1.3.10): a terrifyingly vague litany of pure desire. As Matthew Proser argues in his excellent analysis of Macbeth's "manly image," the witches appeal to "desire alone . . . which then becomes a standard of action." Similarly, Lady Macbeth taunts her husband with his failure to be "the same in thine

---

if Lady Macbeth has psychologically "unsexed" herself and seeks to become a man through her husband's violence, then violence takes the place of intercourse, as a perverse consummation of their shared manliness.

25. Cf. the wordplay between Sampson and Gregory in *Romeo and Juliet,* 1.1.1–29, in which "to stand" first means "to be valiant," and then to have an erection and violate a maid; also *All's Well That Ends Well,* 3.2.40–41: "The danger is in standing to't; that's the loss of men, though it be the getting of children."

26. Notably, Barron (cited above) and Cleanth Brooks, "The Naked Babe and the Cloak of Manliness," in *Approaches to Shakespeare,* ed. Norman Rabkin (New York: McGraw-Hill, 1964), pp. 66–89.

27. M. M. Mahood, *Shakespeare's Word-Play* (London: Methuen, 1957), discusses wordplay on "done" in terms of nemesis and the hero's sense of time; for him, "the fatal moment is anticipated and recalled but never recognized as the *now*" (p. 133), while in the same vein, the terrible deed is never done in the sense of finished, but comes back to haunt him and then to punish him.

own act and valour / As thou art in desire" (1.7.39–40). This identification of women with arbitrary, insatiable, and inscrutable desire bespeaks a fear of engulfment or absorption by them; he who follows such desire in order to become a man becomes, in effect, a slave. The crown itself does not spur Macbeth and his wife on, nor the "greatness" broadly associated with it; rather, as Proser says,

> Duncan's murder, though in one light simply a means to the crown, in another is subconsciously understood by Macbeth as the act which will prove him worthy of it . . . as a kind of indelible stamp of valor.[28]

To *do* the murder is to *dare,* not merely to brave the rebels but to flout the holiest moral and political bonds. And the man who cannot "dare" in this fashion, Lady Macbeth declares, also reveals himself as less than a man sexually, impotent as a drunkard may be, timorous as a maid with green-sickness (1.7.35–38). Macbeth opposes her by saying,

> I dare do all that may become a man;
> Who dares do more, is none.
>
> (1.7.46–47)

In Shakespeare's rich irony he accepts her implicit notion of manhood as morally blind courage, but he also resists it, for the "more" he alludes to is the bloody pitilessness that makes man a beast. As we have just seen in his soliloquy on the wickedness of killing Duncan, Macbeth has within him what may indeed "become" (in both senses) a man: the moral sense that graces him as better than a beast.

But his wife, countering his resistance in phrases anticipating the Porter's speech, as much as calls Macbeth impotent:

> Nor time, nor place,
> Did then adhere, and yet you would make both:

28. Matthew Proser, *The Heroic Image in Five Shakespearean Tragedies* (Princeton: Princeton University Press, 1965), provides the most rigorous and incisive account I have found of Macbeth's psychological processes. It is particularly valuable in dissecting the stratagems by which he avoids taking conscious responsibility for acting on his desires and in defining the "manly image" of himself that he attempts to realize.

> They have made themselves, and that their fitness now
> Does unmake you.
>
> (1.7.51–54)

When she then "unsexes" herself in her vision of dashing the nursing child to the ground, his resistance crumbles. Intimidated by her valor and stung by her taunts at his virility, he "screws his courage to the sticking place" and "bends up his corporal agents" to the terrible feat. Shakespeare's language suggests a strained artificiality in this manliness similar to Coriolanus's, a body language that belies a lack of inward conviction.

When Banquo's ghost appears to fill his murderer with fear and unman him, another debate on the nature and limits of manliness arises between the hero and his wife:

> *Lady M:*   Are you a man?
> *Macb:*   Ay, and a bold one, that dare look on that
>   Which might appal the Devil.
> *Lady M:*   . . . .
>   . . . O! these flaws and starts
>   (Impostors to true fear), would well become
>   A woman's story at a winter's fire,
>   Authoris'd by her grandam. Shame itself!
>
> (3.4.57–59, 62–65)

Once again, she implicitly defines manhood as unblinking resolution, untouched by pity or fear, and he defines it as the courage to confront his own evil. And once again, she taunts him with effeminacy. When the ghost reappears, though, Macbeth no longer dares to look on him; he challenges the specter to a merely hypothetical combat as a way of replacing the gruesome vision with a comforting image of his own valor:

> What man dare, I dare.
> Approach thou like the rugged Russian bear,
> The arm'd rhinoceros, or th'Hyrcan tiger;
> Take any shape but that, and my firm nerves
> Shall never tremble: or, be alive again,
> And dare me to the desert with thy sword;
> If trembling I inhabit then, protest me
> The baby of a girl. Hence, horrible shadow!
>
> (3.4.98–105)

The hyperbolic feats of courage, the sheer fantasy of a second chance to prove himself a man against a ghost, the exaggerated self-deprecation by comparison not merely with a girl, but a girl's doll—Macbeth's rhetoric shows how desperate he is to make himself into his wife's kind of man, if only in words, and how he lacks any confidence in his own identity as a moral being. In fact, his word-magic works, and the ghost disappears, allowing his murderer to exclaim, "I am a man again" (3.4.107).[29] He can only feel himself a man when he has repressed what is most characteristically his—his moral feelings—and conformed to the one-dimensional manliness his wife shames him into, which gives him only brief respite from fear and leaves him still unsatisfied, which "makes" him but then "mars" him. The ultimate manly satisfaction in this play resides in fatherhood, and that he never achieves.

It is the issue of fatherhood that makes him Banquo's rival. When Macbeth calls attention to the difference between what the witches promise him and what they promise Banquo, immediately after he is named Thane of Cawdor (1.3.118–120), he does so in a comradely way, as though wishing to draw his fellow warrior into his own state of exultant hope. His letter to Lady Macbeth mentions only his prospective kingship, and the matter of Banquo's issue lies dormant till after Duncan's murder, when Banquo himself revives it, taking satisfaction from thinking that while Macbeth is king now, Banquo himself "should be the root and father / Of many kings" (3.1.5–6). Unlike Macbeth, he seems content merely with the prospect of transmitting a royal inheritance; the hope on which his brief soliloquy closes is not the hope of having the throne for himself, but of being known in posterity as the father of kings.[30] But though Macbeth thus lacks grounds for fearing Banquo, fear him he does—out of envy. Banquo combines "wisdom" with valor as Macbeth has not,

29. Arnold Stein, "Macbeth and Word-Magic," *Sewanee Review* 59 (Spring 1951): 271–284, explores how Macbeth uses language to avoid thinking and moral awareness, so as to act precipitately.

30. A. C. Bradley, on the other hand, believes that Banquo, by acquiescing in Macbeth's accession to the throne, expects to profit from it (*Shakespearean Tragedy* [Cleveland: World Publishing Co., 1964], pp. 306–307).

and acts in the "safety" that Macbeth has exchanged for fear; he is Macbeth's ideal self image, the man of conscience as well as courage; he is, finally, his rival. "Under him / My Genius is rebuk'd," says Macbeth grandly, and his soliloquy moves into a new key of fevered, anxious resentment rather than fear, an itching determination, as he remembers the witches' promise to his companion, not to let Banquo have what *he* cannot have:

> Upon my head they plac'd a fruitless crown,
> And put a barren scepter in my gripe,
> Thence to be wrench'd with an unlineal hand,
> No son of mine succeeding. If't be so,
> For Banquo's issue have I fil'd my mind;
> For them the gracious Duncan have I murther'd;
> Put rancours in the vessel of my peace,
> Only for them; and mine eternal jewel
> Given to the common Enemy of man,
> To make them kings, the seed of Banquo kings!
> Rather than so, come, fate, into the list,
> And champion me to th'utterance!
>
> (3.1.60–71)

If Macbeth in fact had a son, his existence could not guarantee the security of his father's throne, for it could still "be wrench'd with an unlineal hand"; Macbeth thought Malcolm the step lying in his way. What agitates the hero so deeply is the thought that his present honor, purchased at such great cost, will some day long after his death accrue, even indirectly, to his rival. Furthermore, "the seed of Banquo" attests, it seems, to a kind of greatness and power in him forever denied Macbeth—the power to procreate and specifically, to have sons. Sexually and socially, in Shakespeare's world, fatherhood validates a man's identity.[31]

31. Shakespeare even alters Holinshed so as to increase emphasis on fatherhood and lineal succession. The story of Duncan's reign begins with a brief genealogy in which it is established that he and Macbeth are cousins. Muriel Bradbrook, "The Sources of *Macbeth*," *Shakespeare Survey* 4 (1951): 35–49, notes that according to the ancient custom of Scotland, succession was determined by tanistry—election within a small group of kinsmen. Thus Macbeth had as good a chance at the throne as Duncan's two sons, and when Duncan appointed Malcolm his successor, Holinshed says Macbeth took offense,

ay does not bear out Freud's contention that the hero
ontent with the satisfaction of his own ambition, he
found a dynasty."[32] Rather, Macbeth envies Ban-
nasty primarily because it is Banquo's and not his,
and additionally because it constitutes "all that may become a
man"—the fulfillment of extending one's manly identity beyond one's own lifetime. In the soliloquy just quoted, Macbeth's rage does not come to rest on the cruelty of fate in
denying him sons. Though "fruitless crown," "barren
sceptre," and "no sons of mine succeeding" ring plangently
with disappointment, this tone is quickly succeeded by the
dominant tone of furious envy, *my* and *mine* repeatedly contrasted with *them* to stress the hero's competitive drive. The
speech concludes with a defiant challenge to "fate"; Macbeth
would personify his lack of issue in a chivalric opponent and
fight him to the death, as he fought Macdonwald and Cawdor. And in effect, that is what he does with Banquo, in the
ensuing scene with the murderers, displacing onto them his
own sense that Banquo holds him "so under fortune," urging
his own rivalrous envy onto them:

---

having a just quarell so to doo (as he tooke the matter) for that Dun-
cane did what in him lay to defraud him of all manner of title and
claime, which he might in time to come, pretend unto the crowne.
(Bullough, *Narrative and Dramatic Sources,* vol. 7, p. 496 [cited in
note 21])

Shakespeare, on the other hand, lets us assume that Duncan acts according to
established custom in naming his son as his successor, and his hero conceives
no "just quarell" against Malcolm, only the thought of eliminating him as
well as Duncan so as to secure the throne.
    32. Sigmund Freud, "Some Character-Types Met with in Psychoanalytic
Work," in *On Creativity and the Unconscious,* ed. Benjamin Nelson (New
York: Harper Torchbooks, 1958), pp. 84–110. Freud hypothesizes that during Macbeth's ten-year reign as recounted in Holinshed, his lack of issue
drove him to murder his rivals. In compressing the chronicle events into a
play, Freud argues, Shakespeare slurs over the long-drawn disappointment of
the hero and his wife that must have driven her to distraction and her husband
to defiance, and thus clouds explanation for the changes in their characters.
He nevertheless thinks it appropriate, in view of the murder of Macduff's
children, that Macbeth is "punished by barrenness for his crimes against geni-
ture." I take his barrenness, rather, as a metaphor for his unfinished, not fully
individuated, manly identity.

Are you so gospell'd,
To pray for this good man, and for his issue,
Whose heavy hand hath bow'd you to the grave,
And beggar'd yours for ever?

(3.1.87–90)

Macbeth feels more of a man when he has a man to struggle against—but here, even more than with Duncan, he hides from his own deed, hiring assassins and in addition hoodwinking them into thinking their motives are more than mercenary.

From this active enmity toward Banquo, Macbeth moves to passive identification with the mysterious, evil feminine powers who, his syntax suggests, will do his dirty work for him, as the murderers will.[33] Alone briefly with his wife after sending his hirelings to their task, Macbeth verbally conjures up the evil powers associated with her—Hecate, her nocturnal agents, the night itself—and hints at the murder of Banquo in terms of the "deeds" Lady Macbeth demands of him:

Macb: . . . there shall be done
        A deed of dreadful note.
Lady M: What's to be done?
Macb: Be innocent of the knowledge, dearest chuck,
        Till thou applaud the deed.

(3.2.43–46)

His language reveals his continuing dependence on her now internalized influence; only in a superficial sense does he act independently of her, by not telling her of his plans. He can "act" like a man only by concealing the knowledge of his actions from his better part, his moral self, and he uses both his identification with his wife and his rivalry with Banquo for this purpose.

Immediately after the banquet, when Banquo's ghost sits in Macbeth's place as if to mock his efforts to eliminate his rival, Macbeth notes Macduff's absence from the feast and announces that he will visit the Weird Sisters. Macduff will

33. Proser comments: "The 'black and deep desires' are acknowledged by Macbeth, but 'the eye' and 'the hand' seem detached from him, while the nameless deed itself 'is done.' It appears to do itself or is done by an act of prestidigitation" (p. 64).

soon take Banquo's place as masculine rival and spur to action, while the witches take Lady Macbeth's role as feminine powers on whom Macbeth can rely for inspiration and reassurance. The mood in which he seeks them shows to what extent he has changed into the resolute man his wife wished him to be:

> I will tomorrow
> (And betimes I will) to the Weird Sisters:
> More shall they speak; for now I am bent to know,
> By the worst means, the worst. For mine own good,
> All causes shall give way. I am in blood
> Stepp'd in so far, that, should I wade no more,
> Returning were as tedious as go o'er.
>
> (3.4.131–137)

"The worst" would be some confirmation of Banquo's preeminence through his issue, but again, such knowledge will not check Macbeth's pell-mell course of bloody action, which now takes on the monotonous and compulsive quality that palls his last stand in the besieged castle. Nothing the witches tell him can change him; he is already "bloody, bold, and resolute" and will manipulate whatever they say to sustain this attitude.

The apparitions, purely as visual symbols without their verbal mottoes, are richly overdetermined representations of the conflicting imperatives driving Macbeth toward his fatal manhood. The first, the armed head, suggests adult manhood and its warrior rivalries and combats: Macbeth heroically fighting the rebels in the first act and Macduff in the last act; Macbeth vanquished at the end, a bloody head on a pike dishonored and cast out by his country as his earlier opponent and namesake Cawdor was. The second, the bloody child, represents the infant man, bloodied at birth when nature separates him from his mother, the blood a sign of his link with women and his vulnerability as a human being dependent upon the human community. This child echoes Pity, the naked babe of Macbeth's great soliloquy, its helplessness paradoxically also its power, the power to move others to humane action. The third, the child crowned with a tree in its hand, symbolizes the paternity denied to Macbeth and reserved for the man able to refrain from action and wait for the seeds of time to grow, a man like Banquo—the kind of man Duncan began to "plant," when he honored Macbeth for bloody actions performed to protect the social order. The tree suggests a family tree, an organic union of male and female sustained from generation to generation.

Considered dramatically, as speaking personages to whom Macbeth responds, the apparitions perform like the witches and Lady Macbeth: they make him

> . . . spurn fate, scorn death, and bear
> His hopes 'bove wisdom, grace, and fear.
>
> (3.5.30–31)

In short, they pander to his infantile need for magical reassurance and utter certainty. And they do so in the way characteristic of the female influences in the play, by making and marring him, by setting him on with a spurious confidence and taking him off when the truth behind their equivocations becomes evident. The First Apparition is comparatively straightforward, confirming Macbeth's well-founded suspicion of Macduff, but it also reinforces the hero's irrational need to pit himself against another man in the attempt to solve inner conflict by external competition and combat. The Second Apparition's message cancels that of the first, as earlier the witches' promises to Banquo, so far as Macbeth was concerned, wiped out their promises to him. But here again Macbeth does not pause to puzzle out the discrepancy nor to ponder the meaning of the bloody child; instead, he seizes on the flattering image of himself as invulnerable that it implies:

> . . . laugh to scorn
> The power of man, for none of woman born
> Shall harm Macbeth.
>
> (4.1.79–81)

During the siege of the last act, he repeats the last sentence as if it were a charm to ward off the gathering army. Psychologically, it serves to make all other men seem effeminate compared to Macbeth, and sets him apart from women as well as from men. The Third Apparition's message also flatters his grandiose self-image, reinforcing the preceding message of invulnerability with a supernatural sanction.

Before bringing the play full circle to conclude with Macbeth's last heroic combat, Shakespeare takes pains to present Macduff and the two Siwards as touchstones of manhood and to set manhood in the context of procreation and the family.[34] Only in defense of the family as the basis of social order, he suggests, does violence properly authenticate a man.

By acquainting us with Macduff through his absence as father and husband, by showing us the terrible results of his flight to England, however necessary it is for the good of Scotland, Shakespeare suggests how deeply women and men can cooperate, in normal circumstances, for their mutual comfort and reorients the sexual terms that have thus far dominated the play. When Lady Macduff compares her family to a family of birds, she reminds us of Banquo's beautiful description of Macbeth's castle, the last statement of order based on love, before Duncan's murder and the end of order:

> This guest of summer,
> The temple-haunting martlet, does approve,
> By his loved mansionry, that the heaven's breath
> Smells wooingly here: no jutty, frieze,
> Buttress, nor coign of vantage, but this bird
> Hath made his pendent bed and procreant cradle:
> Where they most breed and haunt, I have observ'd
> The air is delicate.
>
> (1.6.3–10)

---

34. Malcolm, as he is presented in act 4, scene 3, is also, certainly, the embodiment of ideal manliness. The lines in which he drops his pose of viciousness reveal him as the moral opposite of Macbeth:

> I am yet
> Unknown to woman; never was forsworn;
> Scarcely have coveted what was mine own;
> At no time broke my faith: would not betray
> The Devil to his fellow; and delight
> No less in truth, than life.
>
> (4.3.125–130)

But since Shakespeare's main intention is to adumbrate Malcolm's virtues as king more than as man, he touches only lightly on his filial ties as "truest issue" of the Scottish throne.

Love, sexuality, and the divine are profoundly and sweetly one here. Their unity takes the natural shape of the family, with the traditional division of roles, the male providing and protecting, the female bearing and nurturing. Lady Macduff's family, in contrast, is disrupted and endangered by her husband's absence, and she argues—vociferously, vigorously—that even the female wren stays in her nest to fight the owl and protect her young ones. The father who leaves his family "wants the natural touch"; if he abandons them, he may as well be dead. Of course she speaks in ignorance of Macduff's praiseworthy motives for flight, but she is nonetheless right; had he stayed, he might have saved his "pretty chickens, and their dam."[35] The extremity of her situation and her uncompromising protest against it throw into relief the natural (in terms of the social order as Shakespeare knew it) dependency of women on men, contrasting with the perversity of Macbeth's dependency on his wife, and its perverse results—his slaughter of women and children.

When Rosse finishes his brief and terrible account of that slaughter, Macduff's first reaction confirms his wife's: "And I must be from thence!" (4.3.212). Then he gives rein to his grief, and in five lines Shakespeare sums up, with full impact and precise economy, the critique of masculinity expressed by the whole play:

> *Mal:* Dispute it like a man.
> *Macd:*   I shall do so;
> But I must also feel it as a man:
> I cannot but remember such things were,
> That were most precious to me.
>
> (4.3.220–224)

He must first assert his feelings as a father, his grief born of paternal love, before he will exercise his valor as a man. Then, courage and pity fused, he marches against Macbeth, his op-

35. David Barron (cited above in note 20) comments that Macbeth makes Macduff a man individuated through violence—separated from country and family because of Macbeth's cruelties—while Macbeth himself is enmeshed in "a female but unfeminine world." Paradoxically, though, Macduff's separation from Scotland is in the interest of family continuity through the royal succession, an interest so crucial as to outweigh his own family ties (p. 272).

posite in every sense, who kills pity in the name of courage, who kills children. This scene puts the final confrontation of the two warriors in a wholly different context from that of the combats described in act 1, and not just for the obvious political reasons. Macduff fights not only for honor or glory, not only to save his country or avenge his family, but in the broadest sense, to defend the continuance of human life itself as it devolves on love between men and women, procreation, nurturance, and pity.

Siward's stoic patriotism casts fatherhood in a stern, Roman mold to contrast with Macduff's deep personal feeling. The final battle is, for his son as for "many unrough youths, that even now / Protest their first of manhood" (5.3.10–11), a *rite de passage* which tests not only valor but loyalty. Young Siward's death is pure, uncomplicated by the brutality and excessive blood of Macbeth's early glories; "They say he parted well and paid his score," declares his father, for whom the criterion of manliness is simply bravery in the service of the state. The episode thus comments on Macbeth's errant path, for Young Siward seems to end where Macbeth began ("He only liv'd but till he was a man" [5.9.6]), and his father seems to attain through his child that sense of completion Macbeth can never know.

Like Coriolanus, Macbeth dies in combat as he lived, bloody to the last, at the hands of a man with whom he has a peculiar bond. That bond is an extension of his bond of rivalry with Banquo, not merely because Macbeth has projected his frustrations onto Macduff, but because Macduff represents and fights for the lineal continuity through fatherhood that Banquo also represented; he fights to avenge the "unfortunate souls that trace him in his line," as Macbeth called his family, and he fights to reinstate Malcolm as rightful heir. In doing so he asserts the alliance of political power with paternity, a "step" Macbeth has been unable to "o'erleap" as he had intended. What Macbeth feared and envied in Banquo he also fears and envies in Macduff, as his repeated invocation of the Second Apparition's motto indicates, being intended to charm that fear away.

When these mighty opposites finally meet, Macbeth first confesses his fear ("Of all men else I have avoided thee" [5.8.4]), but then has his last recourse to false reassurance from the female powers on which he has heretofore relied: "I bear a charmed life; which must not yield / To one of woman born" (5.8.12–13), he says. When his antagonist reveals that he does, after all, come from woman, though "untimely ripp'd," the hero responds, "It hath cow'd my better part of man" (5.8.18). This is the only use of "cow" as a verb in Shakespeare, and in this context it is richly suggestive. The OED states that the verb derives from O. N. *kúga*, to cow, force, tyrannize over. With fitting irony, then, it is Macduff's bond with the feminine which triumphs over Macbeth's manly valor, which cows him into his first cowardly refusal to fight. Furthermore, the cow as the most common milk-giving animal suggests the milk of human kindness, the naked babe of Pity, and the babe whose brains Lady Macbeth would dash to the ground—all those representations of nurturant tenderness that Macbeth's resolute dedication to violent deeds was supposed to extinguish. Finally, cow simply as a female animal suggests that Macbeth's "better part of man" has been feminized. This "emasculation" might be associated, on the one hand, with the unseaming of the rebel from the nave to the chops in act 1, and with the metaphorical unsexing of Lady Macbeth soon after, on the other.[36] Shakespeare's language suggests that when Macbeth loses his valor, he resembles a monstrosity, a womanish man. This meaning is reinforced when Macduff answers his opponent's refusal to fight:

> Then yield thee, coward,
> And live to be the show and gaze o' th' time:
> We'll have thee, as our rarer monsters are,
> Painted upon a pole, and underwrit,
> "Here you may see the tyrant."
> (5.8.23–27)

36. Seth Lerer directed my attention to the etymology of *cow* as a verb, and to the metaphorical connections between Macbeth and other monstrous figures.

All it takes to restore his courage, however, is the taunt of coward Lady Macbeth employed successfully before, and the threat of humiliation, a humiliation Macbeth perceives as submission to one embodying the lineal principle, the power of paternity, which he will die resisting: "I will not yield / To kiss the ground before young Malcolm's feet" (5.8.27–28). In this last battle, he fights for the first time without relying on feminine influences; the revelation of Macduff's birth has decisively shown their perfidy, and he blames them now for "juggling fiends." Trapped like an animal, he dies without remorse and, like Coriolanus, without the self-knowledge that might have ennobled his death. He fights as always, in fact, to avoid self-knowledge ("To know my deeds 'twere best not know myself"), having murdered his deepest self in the attempt to become a man.

Coriolanus begins and ends his tragic career as a "boy," lacking a developed and authentic manly self, but he at least realizes that self for one moment at Antium before reverting to his old pattern of anger and attack. Macbeth, in contrast, whose inner self is mature, richer, and more active than Coriolanus's, threatening him continually with "horrid images" of his guilt up to the last act, is impelled by its very strength to defend against it more. After the murder of Macduff's family, he fluctuates between two states, both designed to quell his real feelings. On the one hand, he is desperately brave and confident, laughing all to scorn; on the other, he is dead to feeling—weary with *tedium vitae,* empty of joy or sorrow. He who wanted to do "all that may become a man" has accomplished nothing.

CHAPTER SEVEN

The Providential Temp
and the Shakespearean F

Shakespeare rarely portrays masculine selfhood
without suggesting a filial context for it. Of all his
heroes, only Timon has neither kith nor kin—but as I
have argued, through his obsessive giving he tries
vainly to make all Athens his family, dependent on
him for nurturance. Even the most pathologically
solitary hero, Richard III, defines himself by
systematically exterminating his family and violating
its bonds in novel ways. It goes without saying that
Shakespeare portrays all his women characters as
sisters, daughter, wives, or mothers; Cleopatra is
only superficially an anomaly, for her milieu of
Egyptian fecundity binds her profoundly to the
human family through sexuality and procreation. Yet
at the same time, an intense ambivalence toward the
family runs through Shakespeare's works, taking the
familiar shape of a conflict between inheritance and
individuality, and between autonomy and
relatedness. As Meredith Skura observes, "The
family is so important that characters cannot even
imagine themselves without one, yet every family

must bring on its own destruction."[1] That is, characters must break out of their families in order to grow up, and when they have founded families of their own, they must learn both to accept and then to let go of their children.

In this final chapter, I will set the Shakespearean quest for masculine selfhood in the context of family and life cycle.[2] From the beginning of his career to the end, Shakespeare sought a dramatic and psychological strategy for dealing not only with our common ambivalence toward our families, but specifically with the male passage from being a son to being a father. He found it through the romance, in one of its typical patterns of action that I shall call "the providential tempest."[3] The five plays following this pattern are *The Comedy of Errors, Twelfth Night, Pericles, The Winter's Tale,* and *The Tempest,* all directly or indirectly based on narrative romance. They depict the separation of family members in a literal or metaphorical tempest, the resulting sorrow and confusion, and the ultimate reunion of the family, with a renewed sense of identity or "rebirth" for its members. This pattern is that of a journey, and suggests a passage through time as well as through space—the individual's passage from emotional residence within the family to independence and adulthood. As depicted in the plays, the tempest and shipwreck initiating the main action represent the violence, confusion, and even terror of passing from one stage of life to the next; the feeling of being estranged from a familiar world and sense of self without another to hang onto.[4]

1. Meredith Skura, "Interpreting Posthumus' Dream from Above and Below: Families, Psychoanalysts, and Literary Critics," in *Representing Shakespeare: New Psychoanalytic Essays,* ed. Coppélia Kahn and Murray Schwartz (Baltimore: Johns Hopkins University Press, 1980).
2. This essay also appears in the anthology cited in note 1, above.
3. See Frank Kermode's "Introduction" to the new Arden edition of *The Tempest* (Cambridge, Mass.: Harvard University Press, 1954) for a useful discussion of this motif in relation to its literary and historical sources.
4. Several Shakespearean critics have written perceptively on the tempest motif, first and notably G. Wilson Knight, in *Myth and Miracle* (London: E. J. Burrow, 1929) and in *The Shakespearian Tempest,* 3rd ed. (London: Methuen, 1960), who calls the storm "percurrent in Shakespeare as a symbol of tragedy" and sees the opposition of storm and music as central to the canon. Others are Northrop Frye, *A Natural Perspective: The Development of Shakespearean Com-*

The only female protagonists in these tempest plays are Viola and Olivia in *Twelfth Night,* and Viola plays a man's part in most of the action. Marina, Perdita, and Miranda of the romances are accessory to their fathers' development as characters, rather than characters developed for their own sakes, and their spheres of action are severely restricted. While Hermione is strongly defined, it is Leontes' identity crisis that the play stresses. Clearly, with the exception of *Twelfth Night,* the pattern of separation from and reunion with the family I am describing reflects a male passage, and the point of view within the five plays shifts significantly from that of son to that of father.

Reading these five plays as a group, we watch a process of identity formation highlighted in two significantly interrelated crises: that of the youth emerging from the family, more than a child but still not quite a man, and that of the father who has not yet fully accepted his fatherhood. Erik Erikson's division of the lifelong process of identity formation into stages can help us grasp the tempest action as a symbol for the way family relationships shape the growing self.[5] The great normative crisis of identity occurs in adolescence; it is then that instinctual and social imperatives for intimacy with the opposite sex, and pressures toward a settled choice of work and way of life, arise to create a crisis, defined by Erikson as "a necessary turning point, when development must move one way or another."[6] These imperatives and pressures create a recoil, a "regressive pull" back into the family, into the identifications of the early, pre-oedipal stage of ego building. In

edy and Romance (New York: Columbia University Press, 1965), and Douglas Peterson, *Time, Tide, and Tempest: A Study of Shakespeare's Romances* (San Marino, Ca.: Huntington Library, 1973). So far as I know, no one has pursued the psychological interpretation of the tempest that I will present here.

5. For the eight stages of psychosexual development, see his *Childhood and Society* (New York: W. W. Norton, 1974). I will be concerned here with three of the four stages succeeding latency: adolescence, characterized by a conflict between identity and role confusion; youth, by a conflict between intimacy and isolation; and maturity, by a conflict between generativity and stagnation.

6. Erikson, *Identity: Youth and Crisis* (New York: W. W. Norton, 1968), p. 16.

effect, the adolescent reexperiences separation and individuation, but not solely through his mother.

Peter Blos characterizes adolescence as dominated by two broad affective states: mourning and being in love.[7] Confronted with the great imperative of finding someone to love, the adolescent must give up the strongest ties of love he knows thus far, those he feels with his parents. To give them up, he must mourn them, and in mourning them, he has recourse to the usual mechanism of mourning: he identifies with them, or one of them. But he does this indirectly, by merging narcissistically with persons who can mirror him as that parent once did. In effect, he recapitulates the symbiotic merger with the mother preceding separation and individuation.[8] This recapitulation occurs in what Blos calls the transitory narcissistic stage of adolescence, which normally precedes the definitive stage, the search for a heterosexual object. It is characterized by an overwhelming object hunger in which the real identity of the object, the parent of the same sex, is denied. Whether it is positive or negative, identification with this same-sex object is necessary, as part of the mourning process, before heterosexual love can exist.[9] It is this process of mourning the loss of the parent by identification, and finding a new object of love after working through identification, then, that *The Comedy of Errors* and *Twelfth Night* depict.

The next three plays take up the process of maturing at a later turning point in which identity is again a generational issue. Though the father protagonists of the three romances have broken away from their families and formed families of their own, they return to fighting old battles with their internalized original families in the attempt to redefine themselves as fathers instead of sons. They struggle to accept their difference from and dependence on women, and to take parenthood as the measure of their mortality. Shakespeare resolves this crisis through the father-daughter relationship, using the daughter's chaste sexuality and capacity to produce

7. Peter Blos, *On Adolescence: A Psychoanalytic Interpretation* (New York: Free Press, 1962), p. 100, but see pp. 87–128, *passim*.

8. See the Introduction, pp. 4–5.

9. Blos (cited in note 7), pp. 90–91.

heirs as a bridge to the hero's new identity as father. In the history plays, it was the son on whom the father relied for a reaffirmation of his identity through the male line of succession. In these tempest plays, the patriarchal stress on lineage is softened, but not really changed; the daughter instead of the son carries on the father's line. But whereas the history plays bypassed the role of women in the definition of male identity, these plays recast it. The daughters do not inherit a patrimony in the same sense as the sons did; rather, they *are* the inheritance of female sexuality purified that the father-heroes pass on to their sons-in-law.

In the first group of plays, the fear animating the identity crisis is the fear of losing hold of the self; in psychoanalytic terms, the fear of ego loss. Often it is expressed as the fear of being engulfed, extinguished, or devoured in the sea or in some oceanic entity. The adolescent in the throes of establishing that continuity of self-image, that basic inner stability on which identity is based, fears losing his still emergent self in another through erotic fusion, which at the same time he ardently desires. What Erikson separates into two stages, adolescence and youth, Shakespeare treats as one in these comedies through courtship, the traditional comic action.[10] Courtship is a time of self-exploration through amorous adventure and testing that leads to the final choice of a mate, signifying the transition from youth to maturity.

The second group of plays, the romances, are more oedipally oriented than the first. In them, incestuous threat or wish motivates action rather than the fear of ego loss or identity confusion more closely related to pre-oedipal concerns. C. L. Barber characterizes the difference between the comedies and the romances thus:

> The festive comedies move out to the creation of new families; *Pericles* and *The Winter's Tale* move through experiences of loss to the recovery of family relations in and through the next generation. . . . where regular comedy deals with freeing sexu-

10. For a brief description of these stages, see *Childhood and Society* (New York: W. W. Norton, 1974), pp. 261–266; for a more extensive discussion, see *Identity: Youth and Crisis*, pp. 142–207.

ality from the ties of family, these late romances deal with free-
ing family ties from the threat of sexual degradation.[11]

That threat comes, in various ways, from the psychic remnants of old filial relationship, persisting into maturity and
preventing fathers from fully accepting the sexual powers of
women and their own implication in the cycle from birth to
death. *Pericles, The Winter's Tale* and *The Tempest* all mirror
anxiety and even disgust about desire, female sexuality, and
procreation.

Shakespeare also brings out the emotional structure underlying these crises of filial identity through a striking device of
repetition or doubling.[12] He first uses the twin as a double for
the self in relation to the mother; then the daughter, repetition
through generation, as a double for the self in relation to the
father; finally, in *The Tempest,* he uses revenge—repeating
what was done to you, but reversing it on to the other—and
the renunciation of revenge as a way of ending the contest of
the self against time and against its own children.

Any psychoanalytic discussion of doubling is of course indebted to Rank and Freud, who first described it in literature
as a neurotic manifestation of the oedipal complex.[13] Freud
discusses the double as an example of "the uncanny," a mental
representation of something familiar and homelike but at the
same time secret, strange, and sinful; a representation, in
short, of our earliest sexual feelings and wishes with regard to
our parents, which we later perceive as guilty and repress. The
double expresses the idea that these filial ties are inescapable
and will cling forever, no matter how hard we try to shake

11. C. L. Barber, " 'Thou that beget'st him that did thee beget': Transformation in *Pericles* and *The Winter's Tale,*" *Shakespeare Survey* 22 (1969):
59–68.

12. I am greatly indebted to John T. Irwin, *Doubling and Incest/Repetition
and Revenge: A Speculative Reading of Faulkner* (Baltimore: Johns Hopkins
University Press, 1975), for the ideas of the sibling as a double, of incest and
revenge as forms of repetition, and the relation of doubling, incest, and revenge to the sequence of generations within the family.

13. Otto Rank, *The Double: A Psychoanalytic Study,* tr. and ed. Harry
Tucker, Jr. (Chapel Hill, N.C.: University of North Carolina Press, 1971),
first published in 1914, expanded 1925; Sigmund Freud, "The 'Uncanny'"
(1919), *Standard Edition* 17, pp. 217–252.

them off. The double's typical activity in the literary sources cited by Rank and Freud is to pursue and unnerve the hero with his persistent, baffling presence that specifically prevents the hero from loving a woman. Intervening at crucial moments to poison the hero's attempts at intimacy, the double thus prevents him from becoming independent of his family.

Freud and Rank also stress the double's power to bind the hero to his oedipal past in another way. The double, they maintain, is a potential death-bringer, a projection of the castrating oedipal father, while at the same time he represents the hero's beloved, narcissistically overestimated self. The double makes the hero's life a torment, but the hero's life also depends on the double's existence. If the hero tries to kill his double, he too will die; they are symbiotically bound to each other.

By expressing his protagonists' struggles toward identity through doubles, Shakespeare brings out the fear of ego loss and the regressive narcissistic pull of the family that Freud and Rank stress. But he also uses the double as a means of negotiating the difficult passage from filial rootedness to independence, to suggest a normal resolution of identity crises. Defining himself in and then against his double, the Shakespearean protagonist discovers and affirms his sexual identity and loosens confining family ties, so that "Twinship and kinship are replaced by selfhood."[14]

I

Now, the twin-sibling plays, *Errors* and *Twelfth Night*. In each, the protagonist feels an intense affection for his twin that inspires his crucial actions, and the confusion caused by being mistaken for his twin leads ultimately not only to the desired reunion with the twin, but to a previously unsought union with a marriage partner. The double of these plays, the beloved twin, brings with him not just the morbid anxieties

14. Marjorie Garber, "Coming of Age in Shakespeare," *The Yale Review* (Summer 1977): 517–533.

Freud and Rank find, but also an ultimately benign confusion that catalyzes reunion, rebirth, and fulfillment. The twin is a compromise figure, a projection of contending desires; it is through the twin that the protagonist retains ties with the filial past, but also through the twin that he finds a mate and breaks with that past to create his own future. Searching for his twin and mistaken for him, Antipholus of Syracuse meets Adriana and falls in love; grieving for her twin and disguised as him, Viola meets Orsino and falls in love.

But in their searching and grieving, Antipholus S. and Viola are both regressing to the earliest stage of identity formation, identification with one perceived as the same as oneself, which is distinct from object choice, love for someone distinct from and outside the self, predicated on an already formed ego. Identification is first experienced at the mother's breast, when the infant fuses with one who is not yet perceived as not-me. It is also in infancy that the mother's face mirrors the child to himself, confirming his existence through her response to him before he has an inner sense of his separateness and permanence.[15] Thus the twin, as narcissistic mirror, represents the mother as the earliest, most rudimentary confirmation of the self.

In *Errors,* the twins' very names stress the idea behind the whole action, that identity is formed in relationship to significant others. Shakespeare changed the names from Menaechmus (in his source, Plautus's *Menaechmi*) to Antipholus, from the Greek *anti* + *philos:* love against or opposed to. The

15. See D. W. Winnicott's description of this process, "Mirror Role of Mother and Family in Child Development," in his *Playing and Reality* (New York: Basic Books, 1971), pp. 111–118; also Paula Elkisch, "The Psychological Significance of the Mirror," *Journal of the American Psychoanalytic Association* 5 (1965): 235–244, relates the need to see oneself in a mirror to narcissistic crises of identity; one who fears ego loss turns to the mirror for protection against it, trying to retrieve in the mirrored image his self, his boundaries. Morris W. Brody, "The Symbolic Significance of Twins in Dreams," *Psychoanalytic Quarterly* 21 (1952): 172–180, claims that twins in dream and folklore, whether of the same or opposite sexes, represent the dreamer and his or her mother in the fusion of the womb or of nursing; they symbolize the ambivalent wish to maintain union with the mother but at the same time not to be swallowed up in her, maintaining both separation through duplication of the self and union through sameness.

entire family, we realize as the play proceeds, has landed in Ephesus as either the direct or indirect result of storm, shipwreck, and separation. As each character is introduced, we see that he feels uprooted and alienated from himself because he has lost that other closest to him. The dominant metaphor for this collective psychic state is being lost in or on the sea— precisely the event that caused the state. Shakespeare thus internalizes the external and conventional events of the romance plot.

Psychological interest focuses on Antipholus of Syracuse, the melancholy, questing brother who comes to Ephesus in search of a self as well as a family. His first soliloquy crystallizes the interior action of the family romance:

> He that commends me to mine own content
> Commends me to the thing I cannot get.
> I to the world am like a drop of water
> That in the ocean seeks another drop,
> Who, falling there to find his fellow forth,
> (Unseen, inquisitive) confounds himself.
> So I, to find a mother and a brother,
> In quest of them, unhappy, lose myself.
>
> (1.2.33–40)

One might argue that Antipholus seeks to repeat an oedipal triangle, with his brother taking his father's place. But as the action focuses exclusively on his relationship to his brother, it seems, rather, that he wants to make a mirroring mother of his brother. He envisions extinction—total merger with an undifferentiated mass—as the result of his search. The image of a drop of water seeking another drop stresses his need for his identical twin, but also suggests the futility of this means of self-definition. As one half of a single drop of water, will Antipholus be more "content" or have more of a self? And the image of that one drop falling into a whole ocean conveys the terror of failing to find identity: irretrievable ego loss.

We cannot place much weight on Antipholus S. himself as a character with a complex inner world. Rather, his speech adds a powerful psychological dimension to the farcical action as a whole: it encourages us to see the incipient confusion and the ensuing descent into madness as fantasies of identity confusion and ego loss in adolescence, attendant on the break away from filial identifications and into adult identity. Erikson notes that when "identity hunger" is extreme, young people

> are apt to attach themselves to one brother or sister in a way resembling that of twins. . . . They seem apt to surrender to a total identification with at least one sibling . . . in the hope of regaining a bigger and better one by some act of merging. For periods they succeed, but the letdown which must follow the loss of artificial twinship is only the more traumatic. Rage and paralysis follow the sudden insight—also possible in one of a pair of twins—that there is enough identity only for one, and that the other seems to have made off with it.[16]

The irony for Erikson's adolescent and for Shakespeare's character is that seeking identity by narcissistic mirroring leads only to the obliteration, not the discovery, of the self.

That obliteration takes the form of the "errors," the comic confusions of identity, which provide the mirth of the play. The metaphorical and dramatic forms the errors take, however—metamorphosis, engulfment, and enchantment—allow for a psychological reading along with a farcical one and continue the theme of identity confusion and ego loss. Shakespeare shifts the scene of Plautus's comedy from Epidamnum to Ephesus in order to call on all the associations of that city with magic and witchcraft (well known to his audiences through St. Paul's visit to Ephesus) and gains a language in which he can express that theme.

Metamorphosis is first hinted at when Antipholus S., quite naturally fearing he has been robbed, voices deeper anxieties about the robbery of his very identity, by "dark-working sorcerers that change the mind, / Soul-killing witches that deform the body" (1.2.99–100). When at first he accedes, dazed and passive, to the new identity rather harshly attributed to him by his brother's wife, his response is parodied by that of his servant, who feels that he is being "transformed . . . both in mind and in my shape" to an ape; to one who only plays a part, who isn't really who he seems to be. Then, falling in love

16. *Identity: Youth and Crisis*, p. 178.

with Luciana when she persuades him more tenderly that he is someone else, Antipholus S. envisions her as a god, who would "create" him anew.

Calling her a mermaid and a siren, he picks up the oceanic imagery of his earlier soliloquy, and at this point the idea of metamorphosis shades into that of engulfment. Her sister would drown him, but she will rescue him; metaphorically, save him from that obliteration of self, that inauthentic metamorphosis into another person, which her sister promised:

> O, train me not, sweet mermaid, with thy note
> To drown me in thy sister's flood of tears;
> Sing, siren, for thyself, and I will dote;
> Spread o'er the waves thy golden hairs,
> And as a bed I'll take thee, and there lie . . .
> (3.2.45–49)

In raptures he continues, while she protests that he, as her sister's husband, ought to be saying such things to her sister, Adriana. Identifying himself ever more closely with Luciana, as "mine own self's better part, / Mine eye's dear eye, my dear heart's dearer heart," even saying, "I am thee," he asks her to marry him. But again parody questions this instant surrender of self to another, when Dromio of Syracuse wails, "I am an ass, I am a woman's man, and besides myself." He equates metamorphosis with possession by a woman, and possession by a woman with loss of self in the form of engulfment. In a hilariously disgusting blazon of the fat cook Luce, he identifies parts of her body with countries and continents; "spherical, like a globe," she gushes grease, sweat, and rheum, and "lays claim" to Dromio, believing he is his twin. Woman becomes identified with those engulfing waters in which Antipholus S. feared to "confound" himself in act 2. Dromio's fears of being lost in Luce prove contagious; by the end of act 3, Antipholus S. regards Luciana as a mermaid luring him to death by drowning and hastens to leave on the next ship.

The play now takes up a third metaphor for ego loss: possession by spirits. Antipholus of Ephesus's mistaken arrest for debt is described as seizure by "a devil," "a fiend, a fury," and

the Courtesan is called "the devil's dam" who appears, like
Satan, as "an angel of light" to gain men's souls. Metaphor
becomes dramatic reality when the conjurer Dr. Pinch arrives
to exorcise Antipholus E. But his efforts, of course, are vain.
The real deliverance from the bonds of error is by angelic
power. Pauline wordplay runs through the scenes focusing on
Antipholus E.'s arrest; mistakenly and to no avail, he seeks
deliverance from the sergeant's bonds with the coins—
angels—which will pay his debt.[17] These echoes of Paul's
miraculous deliverance from prison prepare us for the denouement at the abbey, wherein the evil powers of Lapland
sorcerers and Circe's cup show themselves to be providence
in disguise.

Counterpointing this series of metaphorical and dramatic
projections of what it is like to lose or "confound" one's identity, one's relationship to others, and one's grasp of reality in
general, are two other senses of reality. Both involve a sense
of time. As an aspect of its concern with the development of
identity as process rather than fixed state, *Errors* fittingly
stresses the importance of time in two ways. First, from the
beginning of the play, it is the means by which the network of
obligations and relations in ordinary life is maintained, allowing people to experience and reaffirm their identities constantly. When the twins are mistaken for each other, ap-
pointments are broken, people are late, and the network
breaks down. Much of the comic action depends on this precise and mundane sense of time. Contrasted with it is the idea
that time is an organic process analogous to conception, birth,
and growth; it proceeds at a proper pace toward a destined
goal, can neither be hurried nor stopped, and is controlled by
God, like the tempest itself. Emilia's final lines firmly link this
sense of time with a sense of identity as growth in time—the
serious and realistic theme underlying the farce:

17. Antipholus S.'s hoped-for redemption from arrest by money in the
form of angels parodies the liberation of Peter from prison in *Acts* 12:1–11,
and adds a spiritual dimension to the subsequent liberation of Antipholus
from the errors of mistaken identity and domestic dissension plaguing him.

Thirty-three years have I but gone in travail
Of you, my sons, and till this present hour
My heavy burden ne'er delivered.
                                    (5.1.400–402)

Identity grows through time, and through loss, confusion, and challenge. Errors are part of a process whereby youth grows into and out of the family to find itself.

In *Errors,* the twin provides an affective bridge from filial to individual identity; seeking the twin, the hero finds his mate, but only when he is able to distinguish himself firmly from his twin. In *Twelfth Night,* we move a step further from the family, and the twin and other doubles function at first as projections of emotional obstacles to identity and then, in Viola and Sebastian, as the fulfillment of a wish for a way around the obstacles. The play abounds in images of engulfment and devouring connected with the sea and love; often it is suggested that love, like the sea, is boundless and voracious, swallowing up the lover. As John Hollander points out, the play is saturated in waters of various sorts, just as two of the main characters (and several of the minor ones) are suffused by their desires.[18] Images of the sea (reinforced by allusions to ships, sailing, and sea-trading), of tears, rain, liquor, urine, and the humors appear frequently. First stated in Orsino's famous opening speech—

O spirit of love, how quick and fresh art thou,
That notwithstanding thy capacity
Receiveth as the sea, nought enters there,
Of what validity and pitch soe'er,
But falls into abatement and low price,
Even in a minute!
                                    (1.1.9–14)

—the idea is reiterated in the succeeding image of Orsino, like Actaeon, being torn apart by his desires. Though Orsino reverses the image in comparing his love to a woman's, saying,

    18. John Hollander, "*Twelfth Night* and the Morality of Indulgence," *Sewanee Review* 67 (1959): 222–235.

> Alas, their love may be call'd appetite,
> No motion of the liver, but the palate,
> That suffers surfeit, cloyment, and revolt;
> But mine is all as hungry as the sea,
> And can digest as much,
>
> (2.4.98–102)

everything about him proclaims that it is he who is consumed by desire, and not the opposite. Skittish, giddy, "a very opal" of erotic whim, he himself is like the mutable sea. Similarly, when love comes stealing upon Olivia like the plague, her self-mortifying dedication to a dead brother vanishes instantly, and she becomes a bold wooer. When Orsino and Olivia love, they lose themselves in desire.

Interacting with this tendency to lose the self in surrender to eros, however, is the attempt to retain identity, through a narcissistic mirroring similar to that Antipholus S. sought in *Errors,* and through distancing oneself from the object of desire. Viola copes with the supposed loss of her twin brother by, in effect, becoming him; when she disguises herself as a man, she is another Sebastian, her twin's twin. Viola is paralleled and contrasted with Olivia, another grieving sister; "to season a brother's dead love" she vows to water her chamber once a day with tears. Sequestered with the memory of her brother, she rejects Orsino's constant suit and punishes the world by withdrawing her beauty from it. When Viola falls in love with Orsino, she devotes herself to a martyrdom similar to Olivia's. As long as her disguise proves convincing, she can never confess or consummate her love, and as Orsino's page, can only express it by furthering his suit to Olivia, her rival. Viola's disguise, it must be said, is to some extent necessitated by her circumstances, and unlike Olivia's attachment to her brother, is a conscious assumption of a different identity that she maintains in tandem with her real one. Both move, however, from loving dead brothers to loving unattainable male figures, maintaining a love whose distance does not threaten their persistent ties to the family through their brothers.

Orsino's love parallels theirs in the sense that his object is hopelessly unattainable, and in the exacerbated self-consciousness and distance it involves. His desire for Olivia

Olivia followed nature in loving a woman, for a short and perhaps necessary period, before actually marrying a man.[22] Similarly, Orsino perhaps needed to see Viola as a girlish boy before he could accept her as a real and ardent woman. The dramatic device of identical opposite-sex twins allows Orsino and Olivia to navigate the crucial passage from identification to object choice, from adolescent sexual experimentation to adult intimacy, from filial ties to adult independence, without even changing the object of their desires.

Feste's song, "When that I was and a little tiny boy," which concludes the play, states in its offhand, colloquial, cryptic way the conception of a man's life-cycle in terms of psychosexual stages that underlies the action of *Twelfth Night*. Several interpreters have suggested that the "foolish thing" of the first stanza is the *membrum virile*.[23] Before the speaker comes to "man's estate," sexuality can be like a toy, playful and open to experimentation, fluid, spontaneous, and uncommitted; but man's "estate" in the second stanza implies status, responsibility, wealth, and property, which "knaves and thieves" may cheat him out of; he must leave sexual play behind, and in the third stanza, take himself a wife. Now the issue is "swaggering," the pretense and display of courtship, as we have seen it in the play through Orsino's elegant embassies of love and Sir Andrew's pathetic attempts at valor, neither of which "thrive." The song skips over marriage and parenthood, coming to rest in the puzzling fourth stanza at the last stage of life, a decline into drunkenness and sleep,[24] before ending with a sigh at the perpetual recurrence of the cycle: "A great while ago the world began. . . . But that's all one, our play is done." *Twelfth Night* traces the evolution of sexuality as related to identity, from the playful and unconscious toy-

22. C. L. Barber, *Shakespeare's Festive Comedy: A Study of Dramatic Form and Its Relation to Social Custom* (Princeton: Princeton University Press, 1959), makes this suggestion.

23. Hollander, *op. cit.*, p. 236; Leslie Hotson, *The First Night of Twelfth Night* (New York: Macmillan, 1954), p. 173.

24. Furness and Halliwell in the *Variorum*, and Craik and Lothian in the new Arden edition, cite Sir Thomas Overbury's *Characters* for "beds" as denoting old age.

can never be satisfied. Even though Orsino, like Olivia when she falls in love with Cesario, gives himself over to passion, that he chooses an unyielding object with whom real intimacy is impossible argues his fear of losing himself in passion.

Thus while all three characters fall madly in love, they all, in different ways, defend against eros as a threat to the integrity and stability of the self. It is the narcissistic mirroring in which Viola and Olivia engage, however, that is most relevant to the Shakespearean family romance. The twin and the sibling, for Viola and for Olivia, are versions of a need for primary ontological reassurance; like the mother, they are not fully differentiated from the self (they look the same, or similar, and are of the same blood) and thus they reaffirm the self at the most basic level, but keep it from developing further.

Mirroring is sought from a double of the opposite sex, however, which focuses the issue specifically on sexual identity rather than on identity *per se* as in *Errors*. The errors of *Twelfth Night* are not merely those of mistaken identity as in the earlier play, but errors that create an aura of doubt about the characters' sexual identity, for *us* rather than for them. *Twelfth Night* is frequently read as a play about masking, about the conscious and unconscious assumption of false identities and about levels of self-knowledge and self-deception;[19] this theme is played out prominently through Viola's transsexual disguise.

For the greater part of the play, until act 5, scene 2, each of the three major characters is wholly certain of who it is that he or she loves: Orsino, unaware of his growing attachment to Cesario, ardently pursues Olivia; Olivia gives herself passionately to a man she knows as Cesario; and Viola is constant to Orsino. Viola's transsexual disguise, until she and Sebastian are mistaken for each other in the duel with Sir Andrew, works on us more deeply and disturbingly than it does on the characters it fools, precisely because it fools them and doesn't fool us. As we watch Viola mediating between Olivia and

19. See L. G. Salingar, "The Design of *Twelfth Night*," *Shakespeare Quarterly* 9 (1958): 118–135, and Joseph H. Summers, "The Masks of *Twelfth Night*," in *Shakespeare: Modern Essays in Criticism*, ed. Leonard F. Dean (New York: Oxford, 1961), pp. 128–137.

Orsino, inhabiting one sex with them and another with us, we are forced to conceive of novel and conflicting ways in which sexual identity might be detached from personal identity; we are cut loose from our habitual assumption that the two are inextricable, that the person is defined by his or her sex. In effect, we experience that state of radical identity-confusion typical of adolescence, when the differences between the sexes are as fluid as their desires for each other, when a boy might feel more like a girl than like a boy, or a girl might love another girl rather than a boy.[20]

Consider these several possibilities. Olivia believes Cesario to be a man, but we know he is not and are titillated by the suggestion that Olivia, loving a woman instead of a man, is not the woman she should be. Similar doubts arise with Orsino, who has unclasped his bosom so readily to a charming boy. At the same time, Shakespeare lets us see that both Olivia and Orsino are drawn to Viola because they find in her those characteristics of the opposite sex to which they are attracted. Orsino says,

> For they shall yet belie thy happy years,
> That say thou art a man. Diana's lip
> Is not more smooth and rubious; thy small pipe
> Is as the maiden's organ, shrill and sound,
> And all is semblative a woman's part.
> I know thy constellation is right apt for this affair
>
> (1.4.30–35)

while Olivia, musing on Cesario's statement that he is "a gentleman," declares

> I'll be sworn thou art;
> Thy tongue, thy face, thy limbs, actions, and spirit
> Do give thee five-fold blazon. Not so fast: soft! soft!
> Unless the master were the man.
>
> (1.5.295–298)

20. Blos explains that in adolescence the withdrawal of love from the parents, or from their object representations in the ego, deflects love onto the self; the adolescent thus enters into the "transitory narcissistic stage" mentioned on p. 196 that precedes attachment to a heterosexual object. In the boy, this narcissism may lead to a same-sex object choice based on an ego ideal. Blos cites Tonio Kröger's crush on Hans Hansen as an example; Mann says that Tonio "loved him in the first place because he was handsome; but in the next because he was in every respect his own opposite and foil" (quoted in

At some level, Cesario is a homosexual object choice for each of them; at another, a heterosexual one. Yet "she" or "he" is the same person, one person. Creatures whose sexual identity is not simply and clearly male or female—hermaphrodites or eunuchs—threaten the binary opposition on which sexual identity, and much else in culture, is based. Without the strict differentiation of male from female, sexual integrity disappears and chaos impends. When Viola refers to herself as a "poor monster," she only touches on the fearsome aspects of her disguise that have been evident to us as she moves ambiguously from Orsino to Olivia.

Yet in the delicate comic irony of the scenes between Viola and each of the other two, Shakespeare reminds us through Viola's poignant double entendres of what Viola herself never forgets: that no matter how the duke and countess see her, she is not androgynous, but irreducibly a woman. The fluid sexual proclivities of youth promise to clash with the reality principle, for that "little thing" she thinks she lacks of being a man is crucial.

The early introduction of Sebastian into the play, however, assures us that all will end properly with a mate of the opposite sex for both Orsino and Olivia. When Sebastian and Viola recognize each other as brother and sister in the last scene, and Olivia is reprieved from the shadow of our doubt that she might have been in love with a woman, Sebastian says,

> So comes it, lady, you have been mistook.
> But nature to her bias drew in that.
>
> (5.1.257–258)

Nature's bias is usually regarded as a heterosexual one, but the line is actually ambiguous;[21] "nature's bias" can mean that

Blos, p. 80). Helene Deutsch describes "a strongly bisexual tendency" in girls in early adolescence, which leads them to stress masculine traits, to suffer the same kind of homosexual crushes as boys do, or to have bisexual fantasies about a brother (often a twin) endowed with all the qualities the girl herself would like to have, or blamed for the impulses she represses and rejects (The Psychology of Women: A Psychoanalytic Interpretation, 2 vols. [New York: Grune and Stratton, 1944; rpt. Bantam Books, 1967], vol. 1, pp. 88–89).

21. The editors of the new Arden Shakespeare Twelfth Night, J. M. Lothian and T. W. Craik, comment, "Nature followed its inborn tendency, to mate female with male and so undo the effects of Viola's misleading disguise."

ings of youthful courtship, through a period of sexual confusion, to a final thriving in which swaggering is left behind and men and women truly know themselves through choosing and loving the right mate.

II

With *Pericles*, written six or seven years after *Twelfth Night* and toward the end of Shakespeare's career, the family romance moves to its second stage: the protagonist as father, and his daughter as a different kind of double than the twin, one who repeats but reverses his experience and lifts him decisively out of the oedipal family of his past. Through her he becomes a father anew, accepting his fatherhood as his identity, and stops trying vainly to deny his mortality.

Pericles begins by plunging boldly into a representation of the oedipal family. The hero, seeking the hand of a princess, must win her by answering the riddle her father Antiochus has devised, or else lose his head. The riddle simultaneously proclaims and hides the incest between father and daughter:

> I am no viper, yet I feed
> On mother's flesh, which did me breed.
> I sought a husband, in which labour
> I found that kindness in a father.
> He's father, son, and husband mild;
> I mother, wife, and yet his child:
> How they may be, and yet in two,
> As you will love, resolve it you.
>
> (1.1.65–72)

Riddles occur at points of life crisis in folklore and literature because the riddle structure offers an expressive model for the reconciliation of essential dualities. It creates confusion and then establishes clarity, reaffirming the rules and essential distinctions on which social life depends.[25] Underlying the riddle in *Pericles* is the ancient image of the *uroboros*, the mythical

---

25. Phyllis Gorfain, "Riddles and Tragic Structure in Shakespeare," *Mississippi Folklore Register, Special Issue: Shakespeare and Folklore*, ed. Philip C. Kolin, 10 (Fall 1976): 187–209.

snake swallowing its own tail, nourishing itself from its own substance. In a Jungian sense, the *uroboros* is

> an expression of the archetypal domination of nature and the unconscious over life . . . in this phase the Archetypal Feminine not only bears and directs life as a whole, and the ego in particular, but also takes everything that is born of it back into its womb of origination and death.[26]

It signifies the mystical and perhaps sinister unity of life and death in woman, a mortal creature who gives birth to another creature that will also die. In the specific context of incest that the riddle traces, however, this mystical continuity of life and death is perverted; the union between the princess and her father denies the ongoing process of producing life from one generation to the next; her womb, receiving the seed from which she herself was generated, is a haven of sterility and death instead of the source of life. The *uroboros* suggests the incestuous oedipal family doubling back upon itself, consuming generational differences instead of sending forth new generations. The riddle and the Antioch experience as a whole are thus a negative analogue for "the family romance in *Pericles* [that] brings together a separated father, mother, and daughter only to divide the generations again for reproduction and rule."[27] In particular, the riddle stresses the destructive confluence of father and daughter, which will be canceled out by the role Marina is to play as one who figuratively and positively "gives birth" to her own father.

Clearly the father–daughter incest of the riddle is a projection of the son's desire to possess the mother, and is associated with Pericles as a son. Whether he answers the riddle or feigns ignorance, he is helpless in Antiochus's hands, and through the rest of the play he is dogged with miseries though he does nothing to deserve them. Not his character, but the action of the providential tempest demands that he suffer punishment for a guilty desire not dramatized as his. Antiochus's riddle

---

26. Erich Neumann, *The Great Mother: An Analysis of the Archetype* (Princeton: Princeton University Press, 1972), p. 30.
27. Phyllis Gorfain, "Puzzle and Artifice: The Riddle as Metapoetry in *Pericles*," *Shakespeare Survey* 29 (1976): 11–20.

scheme impressively depicts the castration threat (the stage is decked with the heads of failed suitors) while Pericles' meek, passive response to it represents the son's desire to renounce his phallic challenge to the father and regain his love, in effect taking the mother's place.

Pericles' episodic voyages from place to place and his successive experiences of loss are symbolic confrontations with oedipal desire and oedipal fear. The father figures he repeatedly encounters represent his continuing difficulty in resolving his image of the father and his position in relation to him. Simonides, on whose shores Pericles is washed up half-dead after the first tempest, is a jolly, generous, nurturant figure who at first delights in playing the possessive father as a joke, then gives his daughter Thaisa to Pericles with his blessing. Cleon, the governor of a kingdom decimated by famine, is aided by the hero with gifts of food; out of gratitude, he takes in his daughter Marina after the second tempest when her mother Thaisa supposedly dies. But Cleon proves spineless before his envious, scheming wife, who arranges for the girl's death, and thus he betrays Pericles' trust. Cerimon, a holy, wise, and kindly magus, restores Thaisa to life by his art. Lysimachus, the governor of Mytilene whom Marina redeems from carnal vice, charitably reunites her with her father, and becomes his son-in-law. Collectively, these figures bear an array of ambivalent traits: generous and impoverished, powerful and powerless, ascetic and fleshly. Throughout his encounters with them, Pericles can only bow his head, suffer, and endure. Only once does he show initiative and act a hero's part—whereupon the second tempest hits him. He is pointedly enjoined to learn patience, the virtue analogous to renunciation of the oedipal project. Unable to do so, he withdraws from the world in a deathlike trance, from which only his daughter can save him.

The shift from twin to daughter as the figure through whom the hero gains his final identity is crucial. What it means is that he breaks out of time conceived as a repetition of oedipal patterns and breaks into the future through his daughter and his own, new family. The twin is the hero's physical and temporal double; born at the same time and looking just like him, he represents the hero's ties to the pre-oedipal past. But the daughter, of the opposite sex, born from the hero, the product of his union with a woman, is not his mirror image but his successor and opposite. Her fruitful chastity is the opposite of his mother's problematical oedipal sexuality, and (in *Pericles* and *The Winter's Tale*) reunion with her precedes reunion with his wife. Thus she validates his separateness from his own father, his fatherhood, his uniqueness.

Pericles falls conspicuously into two halves, the first tracing the hero's adventures, the second beginning some years later when his daughter approaches maturity and centering on her. Her life recapitulates his in that she too suffers several "tempests": threatened with death by her foster mother, captured by pirates, finally delivered to a brothel to become a whore. Her name and her character make her a walking symbol of the tempest action:

> Ay me! poor maid,
> Born in a tempest, when my mother died,
> This world to me is as a lasting storm,
> Whirring me from my friends
>
> (4.1.18–20)

and her oblique, cryptic, enigmatic mode of speech links her to the riddling, incestuous princess of Antioch. Plainly enough, her relationship with Pericles in the reunion scene is the reverse of the father-daughter incest of the play's beginning, her redemptive chastity paradoxically more truly fruitful than the princess's lust; Pericles calls her "Thou that beget'st him that did thee beget" (5.1.195). Her purity banishes the shadow of oedipal sexuality, and brings the hero back to his wife and to the world.

In an illuminating essay, C. L. Barber says, "The primary motive which is transformed in *The Winter's Tale* . . . is the affection of Leontes for Polixenes, whatever name one gives it."[28] Though Leontes is a mature man—king, husband, father—the nine-months' visit of his boyhood friend reveals

28. C. L. Barber, "'Thou that beget'st him that did thee beget'" (see note 11), p. 65.

THE PROVIDENTIAL TEMPEST   215

that he is still split between two identities, the boy of the past and the father of the present. Following J. I. M. Stewart (who follows Freud) in interpreting Leontes' jealousy, I would argue that the hero's belief that his wife loves his best friend is his way of defending against the horrified realization that he too still loves that friend, his way of saying, "Indeed, I do not love him, she loves him!"[29] Recall the appealing imagery used to describe the affection "rooted" between Leontes and Polixenes in their boyhoods. It portrays a paradise of sameness and oneness, the complete untroubled identity of each with the other:

> We were as twinn'd lambs that did frisk i' th' sun,
> And bleat the one at th'other: what we chang'd
> Was innocence for innocence: we knew not
> The doctrine of ill-doing, nor dream'd that any did.
> (1.2.67–71)

Clearly, Polixenes is Leontes' double, one of the same sex and age who only mirrors him; loving Polixenes is depicted as guiltless, Edenic, and asexual, as opposed to loving a woman. It is also a love which denies time; Leontes and his friend were

> Two lads that thought there was no more behind
> But such a day to-morrow as to-day, and to be boy eternal.
> (1.2.63–65)

The homosexual implications of this nostalgic fantasy are less important than what it suggests about Leontes' attitude toward his mature sexuality, his manliness. He would like to escape and repudiate it, because being a husband and father means entrusting one's sexual dignity to a daughter of Eve, ceding the future to one's children, and facing death. Being "boy eternal," on the other hand, means being free of sexual desire, with its risks, its complications, and its implication in the procreative cycle, and being, though only in fantasy, immortal. In Polixenes' idyllic picture of boyhood, childish

---

29. J. I. M. Stewart, *Character and Motive in Shakespeare* (London and New York: Longmans, Green, 1949), p. 34. See also Sigmund Freud, "Some Neurotic Mechanisms in Jealousy, Paranoia, and Homosexuality" (1922), *Standard Edition* 18, pp. 221–233.

innocence is contrasted with adult sinfulness, and that sinfulness is then specifically associated with the women he and Leontes married, the "temptations" later "born to" them. The association of sin with the carnal pleasure legitimized by marriage betokens a guilt-ridden reluctance to accept, let alone appreciate, the natural desire of men for women; a reluctance soon rationalized in the violent misogyny through which Leontes voices his jealousy, the conviction that women are false through and through.

Having lost the mirror of his masculine identity in Polixenes, Leontes then seeks it in Mamillius, as he normally would in the patriarchal Shakespearean world. But his jealousy provokes him, ironically, to misinterpret the strong physical resemblance between himself and Mamillius. While Shakespeare makes it clear that this resemblance is the legitimate confirmation of Leontes' sexual union with Hermione, and the proof of her fidelity, Leontes finds Hermione's assertion of it another indication of female treachery:

> . . . they say we are
> Almost as like as eggs; women say so,
> (That will say anything).
>
> (1.2.129–131)

In several significant ways, Shakespeare makes Mamillius a symbol of the union of male and female. While his name associates him with the maternal function of nursing, and he is shown in the female company of his mother and her attendants, he is also "a gentleman of the greatest promise" and universally acknowledged as the future ruler of Sicily, Leontes' heir. The news of his death arrives immediately upon Leontes' denial of the oracle, an act which spells Hermione's doom. That is, Mamillius dies when Leontes denies most absolutely his natural and legitimate sexual union with the feminine, with Hermione, of which Mamillius is the sign and seal. And he is driven to deny it because he cannot sustain it. Despite his age, his kingship and his fatherhood, emotionally he is stuck at the developmental stage preceding the formation of identity, the stage of undifferentiated oneness with the mother, on which his oneness with Polixenes was modeled,[30] He cannot sustain a relationship with a woman based on the union of his and her separate identities, in which trust and reciprocity mediate that separateness.

Fittingly, Mamillius's death, in robbing Leontes of an heir, deprives him of a supremely important aspect of his male identity. Just as Macbeth cannot rest content with kingship so long as he lacks heirs to pass it on to, so Leontes is incomplete without an heir, and his lack of one is the direct result of his inability to accept his dependence on feminine power and to sustain a trusting union with Hermione. With the deaths of Mamillius and (seemingly) Hermione, Leontes' delusion lifts, and he enters into a period of realization and repentance. At this point Shakespeare makes explicit, through the figure of Time, connections between the human experience of time in the life cycle, women, and the formation of masculine identity that have been implicit in the first half of the play.

Inga-Stina Ewbank shows how Leontes, crazy in his jealousy, acts with feverish haste, "goes against time and is therefore blind to truth." In the tradition of Renaissance iconography appropriated by Shakespeare in this play, time is a father, an old man, just what Leontes does not want to be. Ironically, in defying Father Time, he denies his own fatherhood and deprives himself of a son and a future. He is plunged into seemingly endless mourning for his past actions. As Ewbank says, now Leontes "has to become aware of truth in a

---

30. See Sigmund Freud, "Leonardo da Vinci and a Memory of His Childhood," *Standard Edition* 11; "On Narcissism: An Introduction," *Standard Edition* 14; and Murray Schwartz, "Leontes' Jealousy in *The Winter's Tale*," *American Imago* 30 (Fall 1973): 250–273, and "*The Winter's Tale:* Loss and Transformation," *American Imago* 32 (Summer 1975): 145–199. Arguing that Leontes is motivated by a "fear of separation from idealized others" and that he attempts "to reunite himself with a fantasized ideal maternal figure," Schwartz analyzes the paranoia of the hero's jealousy as a radical denial of separation, and sees the second half of the play as a successful reconstitution of continuity and union rooted ontogenetically in the mother-son symbiosis. His interpretation of the play's psychology is rigorous, comprehensive, and brilliant; I am greatly indebted to it.

wider sense . . . through subjection to Time the Revealer."[31]
It is in this second half of the play that women, Paulina and
Perdita, gain effective dramatic power to nurture men; while
concurrently, time becomes the revealer, whose daughter is
truth, rather than the destroyer, *tempus edax,* who seized
Mamillius and Hermione. The play moves to "a world
ransomed"—Bohemia, and through a number of parallels in
dramatic structure and action, Shakespeare keeps alive his
"primary motive," Leontes' feeling for Polixenes, now
changed into the wide gap of enmity dividing the once
"twinn'd" brothers. But this time the younger generation, the
sons and daughters, are to redeem or, in Shakespeare's
metaphor, "beget" their fathers, restoring them to new identities as fathers.

Camillo's plot to present Florizel as his father's ambassador
to Leontes provides the middle term by which the breaches
between father and son, and brother and brother (Leontes and
Polixenes), can both be healed at once. As Murray Schwartz
argues, "By impersonating his father, Florizel can replace him
without really replacing him."[32] But more important for the
play's main action, the transformation of Leontes' affection
for Polixenes, Florizel in the latter's place bridges the gap between the two men and makes them friends again, not as
"twinn'd lambs" but as men who have erred, suffered, and
lost. The king's greeting to his future son-in-law makes this
change clear:

> Your mother was most true to wedlock, prince;
> For she did print your royal father off,
> Conceiving you. . . . .
> . . . Most dearly welcome!
> And your fair princess—goddess! O! alas,
> I lost a couple that 'twixt heaven and earth
> Might thus have stood, begetting wonder, as
> You, gracious couple, do; and then I lost
> (All mine own folly) the society,

31. Inga-Stina Ewbank, "The Triumph of Time in *The Winter's Tale,*" in
Shakespeare's Later Comedies, ed. D. J. Gordon (Harmondsworth, England:
Penguin, 1971).
32. Schwartz, "*The Winter's Tale:* Loss and Transformation," p. 178.

Amity too, of your brave father, whom
(Though bearing misery) I desire my life
Once more to look on him.
(5.1.123–125, 129–137)

Florizel and Perdita represent complementary modes of
mediating separation and difference from significant others, a
crucial task in identity formation. He fights his father; then
reconciles with him. Perdita, on the other hand, does not
fight, but subsumes opposites into a transcendent reality. On
the sexual level, she reconciles virginity and erotic appeal,
modesty and abandonment; mythically, through the imagery
and ambiance of Bohemia, she is associated with "things dying" and "things newborn," with mother earth, the womb
and tomb of all. She combines the qualities of the chaste
preoedipal mother and the sexually desirable oedipal mother, symbolically uniting Leontes' divided attitudes toward
women.

Significantly, though, Leontes' recognition of Florizel precedes his recognition of Perdita; he gains a son before he regains a daughter, thus recasting his relationship with his
"brother," Polixenes, before he goes on to recognize and recast his relationship with the feminine in Perdita and then
Hermione. This sequence of reunions recapitulates the sequence of identity development for which I am arguing. The
total identity of like with like Leontes found with Polixenes
was an effort to repeat the mother-child symbiotic unity and
to avoid male identity. When Leontes "takes" Florizel "for"
Polixenes as well as "for" Mamillius, he is accepting paternity, his and Polixenes', as the crucial component of his male
identity—and paternity is equally based upon his separateness
from the feminine and his union with it. To acknowledge
Perdita as his daughter is to accept the sexuality he had
wanted to repudiate; to acknowledge her as his heir is to accept the mortality he had wanted to escape. It is fitting that
Leontes, as he clasps Hermione's hand (that crucial gesture
again), characterizes his reunion with her in terms of the most
primitive, elemental human activity, begun at the mother's
breast:

> O, she's warm!
> If this be magic, let it be an art
> Lawful as eating.
> (5.3.109–111)

The island setting of *The Tempest* and the centrality of Prospero as demiurge make it a fantasy of omnipotence. Prospero not only controls; he creates. He devises scenarios of his deepest wishes and causes them to be enacted, redesigning his world so as to rectify or compensate for his past. The play's several interwoven actions—the courtship of Ferdinand and Miranda, the ordeal and illumination of the court party, the usurpations attempted by Antonio and Sebastian, and by Caliban, Stephano, and Trinculo—are all foreseen or overseen by Prospero. They are his attempts to work through his oedipal past, to complete himself. As such, they are only partly successful. He redefines himself as man rather than magician, and regains his dukedom. But while he gives up his omnipotence in the end, he never recognizes and accepts his sexuality and his relationship to women as Leontes does. Unlike *Pericles* and *The Winter's Tale, The Tempest* does not depict the rebirth of a family as well as of a man, and thus Prospero's final identity lacks the fullness of that achieved by the other heroes.[33]

Unlike them, Prospero has no wife; strangely, he doesn't even allude to his duchess's fate in the otherwise detailed account of his past that he gives Miranda. Moreover, his only mention of his wife is highly ambivalent, at once commending and questioning her chastity: "Thy mother was a piece of virtue, and / She said thou wast my daughter" (1.2.56–57). In addition to Miranda, the only other woman in the play is Sycorax, the "foul witch" and bad mother who penned Ariel in a cloven pine and gave birth to Caliban the freckled whelp. Marina and Perdita as doubles of their fathers grow up inde-

---

33. Carol Thomas Neely, in "Women and Issue in *The Winter's Tale*," *Philological Quarterly* 57 (1978), firmly distinguishes Shakespeare's treatment of sexuality in that play from its treatment in the other romances, which "hover uneasily between the extreme idealization of sex and its extreme degradation," while in *The Winter's Tale,* "fully developed women characters play central roles" to free men from distorted sexual attitudes. I came upon her paper after writing this essay, to discover that its view coheres with my own at many points.

pendently from them, their qualities and powers developing spontaneously and freely. They then function as mothers to their fathers by "delivering" them to new identities as fathers. They also serve as doubles of their mothers, uniting chastity with fertility and countering their mothers' oedipally tinged sexuality. Miranda, on the other hand, has never left her father. She is his creation, exclusively nurtured, tutored, and controlled by him on the island. Her sexuality, like that of the other daughter-doubles, is firmly allied with the divine order behind nature. But it is Prospero who defines and guards that sexuality, subsuming it into his larger project for the settling of old scores and the resumption of his role in Milan.

On a larger scale, Prospero's subjugation of sexuality in Miranda is figured in the antithesis between Ariel and Caliban. Spirit and flesh, air and earth, god and beast: these facets of human existence, it is implied, are decisively sundered in Prospero as in his underlings, whom he keeps separate by anxious, vigilant control. Ironically, neither character is actually as distinct from the other or as one-dimensional as Prospero thinks he is; each has potential that the magus is too busy with his task of defensive control to notice. Though Ariel is not human and cannot feel, he knows what sympathy and love are and, moreover, values them as a human would:

> Ariel: The King,
> His brother, and yours, abide all three distracted,
> And the remainder mourning over them,
> Brimful of sorrow and dismay. . . . .
>   . . . Your charm so strongly works 'em
> That if you now beheld them, your affections
> Would become tender.
> Prosp: Dost thou think so,
>   spirit?
> Ariel: Mine would, sir, were I human.
> Prosp: And mine shall.
> Hast thou, which art but air, a touch, a feeling
> Of their afflictions, and shall not myself,
> One of their kind, that relish all as sharply,
> Passion as they, be kindlier mov'd than thou art?
>   (5.1.11–14, 16–24)

Prospero, who is human, has to be reminded that he has a heart by one who lacks it. The terms of endearment with which he plies Ariel and no one else are wasted on the spirit, who nonetheless has a touch of humanity. On the other hand, the salvage and deformed slave on whose nature, Prospero claims, nurture will never stick, reveals a touching sensitivity to beauty and a capacity for wonder to which his master is oblivious. Caliban gives his heart, however foolishly, to Stephano and Trinculo, but at least he has affections. All that matters to Prospero, though, is that Caliban tried to rape his daughter; it was then that the magician abandoned the task of educating his creature and removed him from the cell to imprisonment in a rock (1.2.346–364). In the last scene, Prospero hardly gives Caliban's moral enlightenment its due, though he hints he will pardon him and directs him back to the cell instead of the rock. Ariel finally gains his freedom, as Prospero gains his in renouncing revenge, but Caliban is likely to remain confined on the island, as Prospero's sexuality remains confined in himself and in Miranda's chaste marriage.

Essentially, in coming from Milan to the island, Prospero went from childlike, self-absorbed dependency to paternal omnipotence, skipping the steps of maturation in between. Whether he surrendered the cares of state to Antonio or whether Antonio stole the state for himself (Prospero's self-contradictory account suggests both; see 1.2.66–132), Antonio in effect served as his brother's parental provider before casting him out.[34] Then, assuming dominion over the island, Prospero became free to pursue his studies in a boundlessly nurturant environment, without significant rivalry. The island was his virgin space: he was the first man on it. Having previously withdrawn from all competition in the world of men, under these special conditions he was given a second chance to eradicate his father's preeminence and priority in time, and become his father's equal, through preeminence and priority on the island. As Harry Berger argues, the island is like a child's microsphere, where he makes a model of his painful experiences so as "to play at doing something that was in reality done to him," and thus "redeems his failures and

---

34. Karl M. Abenheimer, "Shakespeare's *Tempest*: A Psychological Analysis," *Psychoanalytic Review* 33 (1946): 399–415, suggests this interpretation.

strengthens his hopes."[35] This "playing" is a magical, wish-
fulfillment form of delayed growing up for Prospero.

Specifically, he plays out rivalries that he never fully confronted before, using his brother as a stand-in for his father.
He does so through a brilliant compromise between revenge
and charity, which allows him to have his cake and eat it too.
When Providence brings his treacherous brother and his
brother's confederate Alonso to the island in a tempest, he
recreates for them his own near-fatal voyage "in a rotten car-
cass of a butt" years before. He subjects Alonso to the threat
of usurpation and the seeming loss of his son, again versions
of their actions against him. These trials would add up to a
tidy revenge were they not sheer illusion, the product of
Prospero's strenuous art, and were they not perpetrated for
the sake of arousing "heart-sorrow and a clear life ensuing."
They are and are not revenge. For Prospero to take revenge in
reality would be to repeat what was done to him and become
mired in the family past, in a cycle of successive revenges, but
not to take revenge would be passivity and impotence. By not
really taking revenge, by living wih his own anger in the
realization that "the rarer action lies in virtue than in vengeance," he breaks out of repetition, out of the revenge cycle,
and out of his oedipal past. But he also fails to recreate in any
mature sexual relationship the lifegiving love experience first
known with the mother.[36]

Delineating the centrality of the rival sibling motif to the
Shakespearean conception of masculinity, Joel Fineman argues that "branching pairs of siblings, real or virtual, male and
female, rooted together in synonymous rivalry" are crucial to
male identity. For since the male's first sense of self is implicated with the mother, in order to define himself he must

35. Harry Berger, "Shakespeare's Miraculous Harp: A Reading of Shakespeare's *Tempest,*" *Shakespeare Studies* 5 (1970): 253–283, makes this point.
36. Hans W. Loewald, *Psychoanalysis and the History of the Individual* (New
Haven: Yale University Press, 1978), remarks: "Ego development does not
proceed in a straight line, does not consist in a movement further and further
away from id. . . . One might come close to human time by saying that it
consists in an interpretation and reciprocal relatedness of past, present, and
future. . . . an ascending spiral in which the same basic themes are reexperienced and enacted on different levels of mentation and action" (p. 23).

separate decisively from her; he must establish a crucial difference. Fineman sees fratricidal rivalry as the adult rephrasing of
this original differentiation and regards it as essential to the
next step in masculine identity formation, the oedipal conflict
and its resolution.[37] Among Shakespearean rivals, Prospero
neither fights his brother to the death, as Claudius does King
Hamlet, or Hal Hotspur, nor reconciles with him as does
Oliver with Orlando, or Proteus with Valentine. Rather, he
effects the unique compromise I have described. But that
compromise brings him no closer to acknowledging his sexuality or to uniting with the feminine, because he has still not
fully worked through his oedipal past, or perhaps because he
has sublimated it too well in his art.

Presumably, Prospero's years on the island were devoted
to two ends: perfecting his art and perfecting Miranda. Her
chastity, like Marina's and Perdita's, functions as a denial of
her father's past desires. By giving her to Ferdinand, the son
of his brother's partner in crime, and insuring legitimate heirs
to his regained dukedom, he symbolically resolves his old
rivalries and validates his new identity as duke. The summit
of Pericles' and Leontes' lives is reunion with their daughters
and then with their wives: recovery of what they denied and
lost before. In contrast, the triple crown of Prospero's life is to
give up revenge, then to give his daughter away, and finally,
to give up his art.

A final question suggests itself. All through the play Shakespeare stresses in Prospero a superb combination of power
and control. There are signs of strain in his tetchiness with
Ariel, his disgust with Caliban, his obsession with Miranda's
virtue, his hatred of Antonio. But on the whole, he commands his art in the service of giving vent to but transcending
his violent feelings. Why must he renounce his art? Why can't
he keep it and hold his dukedom too, since it has served his
worldly and his personal aims so well? He gives it up because
he does not need it any more, because with its aid he has accomplished the project of emerging from the family and be-

37. Joel Fineman, "Fratricide and Cuckoldry: Shakespeare and His Sense
of Difference," Psychoanalytic Review 64 (Fall 1977): 409–453.

coming his own man, the Duke of Milan. The cost of this achievement, however, is sexual and social isolation.

A romance is a fiction of wish-fulfillment. The plays I have discussed are all romances, by virtue of their sources, or their nature as dramas, or both. They articulate the ambivalent wish to get free of the family and find a self outside it, while at the same time to stay within it, nurtured by its loves. All these plays seek a compromise between the two conflicting urges, and the compromise turns on finding a mate. From the male protagonist's point of view, this means that it turns on his ability to accept woman and sustain intimacy with her. She is at once the seal of his male identity and the obstacle to it; he fears her and he needs her. Without her, he can neither leave his family of origin and find himself, nor father his own family and play his part in the patriarchal world. At the cost of great suffering, Leontes wins the fullest acceptance of woman, and *The Winter's Tale* presents the richest vision of male identity defined within the family. Leontes is both, and equally, husband and father. Significantly, though, the family romance concludes with *The Tempest*, in which woman is most strongly repressed. Prospero's identity is based entirely on his role as father, and his family is never united or complete. The Shakespearean family romance, then, remains closer to the imperfect realities we live with than to the wishes we cherish.

Index

Actaeon, 148, 149
Adelman, Janet, 154, 162
Adolescence, 3, 21–45; crisis of
    identity, 22, 195–196; ego
    loss, 202; of girls, 93–94;
    identity confusion of, 208; and
    mourning, 196; and
    narcissism, 22, 23, 31; passage
    to adulthood, 82, 83–84, 85,
    93, 96, 101–103; passage from
    boyhood, 70–80, 82; rebellion
    against maturity, 73; rejection
    of love and sexuality, 18, 21,
    28–29, 33, 38–45, 82,
    206–207; *rite de passage* in
    reverse, 18, 21; separation and
    individuation reexperienced
    in, 196
Adonis. See *Venus and Adonis*
Adultery, 133, 137, 138
Aggression, 43, 61, 86; and
    competitiveness, 168–169; and
    dependency, 154, 160, 162;
    imagery of bloody men, 155;
    masculine identity expressed
    by, 49–50, 86, 90, 93. See also
    Violence
Alexander, Franz, 71–72
All's Well That Ends Well, 123,
    124
Aristotle, 13
Ass, 129
As You Like It, 123–124
Auden, W. H., 72, 143

Balint, Michael, 25
Barber, C. L., 197, 210n, 214

Barthes, Roland, 48, 50, 53, 54
Bastards, 128
Beasts: and cuckoldry, 122, 125,
    127; men as, 149, 150, 151, 180
Beauvoir, Simone de, 106
Behavior norms for men and
    women, 104, 109
Berger, Harry, 222
Bettelheim, Bruno, 102
Bevington, David, 55
Birth, 92, 93, 97, 186, 191, 212;
    and alienation from the
    mother, 64
Bloody child, symbol of, 186,
    187
Bloody men, imagery of, 155,
    173
Blos, Peter, 196, 208n
Boar symbol, in *Venus and
    Adonis,* 38–44
Bond: created by cuckoldry,
    144–145; of hate, 163, 170;
    with the mother, 159, 160,
    161, 163, 170, 172; of rivalry,
    19, 190
"Boy eternal," 71, 215
"Boy of tears," 158, 171
Boys: friendship between,
    214–215; men as, 44, 151, 158,
    171, 172, 192
Breast feeding, 3, 34, 45, 153,
    200, 216, 219. See also Nursing
    babe imagery
Brooke, Arthur, 94–95, 96
Brotherhood of married men as
    potential cuckolds, 124–125
Brothers, 201–202, 206

Cade, Jack, in the history plays,
  56, 58
Castration: fear of, 11, 43;
  psychosocial, 132; threat of,
  213
Chastity: of daughters, 140–141,
  214, 221, 224; of wives, 121,
  126, 150, 220
Childbearing, 64, 94, 97; of male
  children, 156; and murder, 177
Childhood, 2–3, 64–65, 155–156
Chivalric masculinity, 52, 74,
  111
Chodorow, Nancy, 10n, 11n
Clemen, Wolfgang, 63
Cleopatra, 193
"Closed heart," 41–42
Coleridge, Hartley, 95
Comedies by Shakespeare, 167;
  compared to the history plays,
  62; compared to the romances,
  197–198; cuckoldry in, 123;
  love in, 114; marriage in, 119
Comedy of Errors, The, 19, 194,
  196, 199–205; time in,
  204–205; twins in, 199–205
Coriolanus, 1, 17, 19, 151–172;
  character transformation in,
  170–171; childhood in, 2–3,
  155–156; masculine identity
  formed by the mother,
  156–163, 165–166, 170, 172;
  motif of engulfment and
  isolation in, 160–161; revenge
  against Rome, 166–167, 170,
  172
Counteridentification with the
  father, 11, 16–17, 18
Courtship, 119, 197, 210
"Cow," used as a verb, 191
Cuckoldry, 19, 119–150;
  brotherhood of men, 124–126,

140, 144, 150; castration by,
  132; defined, 120; double
  standard in, 121, 146, 147,
  149–150; in Hamlet, 19,
  132–140; male possession of
  female sexuality, 121, 124,
  126, 131–132; masculine
  fantasy of feminine betrayal,
  120, 140; in Merry Wives of
  Windsor, 19, 128–130, 131,
  147–150; and misogyny, 121,
  133, 137, 146, 147; in Othello,
  19, 127–128, 138, 140–146;
  and patriarchal marriage, 121,
  146, 147, 150; rivalry and
  competitive aspects of, 126,
  131, 142–143; stigma and
  shame of, 119–120, 121–122,
  129, 131, 145; symbolism of
  horns, 122, 123–125, 127, 128,
  130, 143, 145, 147–150; wife's
  viewpoint of, 146
Cymbeline, 126–127

Daphne, 30
Daughters: chastity of, 140–141,
  196, 214, 221, 224; as doubles,
  211, 220–221; heirs by, 94,
  197; identity of fathers
  achieved by, 196–197,
  211–214, 220–221; reunion
  with, 214, 224
Death, 98–99; and doubles, 199;
  vs. eros and narcissism, 22, 42;
  and sexual fusion, 45,
  102–103; unity of father and
  son in, 54
Defense against love and
  sexuality, 26, 32–33, 38–45,
  83, 206–207
Dependency: on the mother,
  154, 160, 162; need for, 22; and

paternal omnipotence, 222; on women, 17, 173, 174, 185, 191, 196, 217
Disguise, transsexual, 207
Doubles, 169; daughters as, 211, 220–221; described, 198–199; of the opposite sex, 207; of the same sex, 215; twins, 199–200, 205, 213
Dreams, 91–92, 101

Echo, 31–32
Ego ideal, 19; in the mother-son relationship, 157, 159; and rivalry, 152, 174
Ego loss, 197, 199, 201–202; metaphors for, 202–204
Emasculation, 44, 86, 166, 191
Emulation of the father, 49, 52, 80; rivalry in, 50, 51, 53–54
"Enemy twin," 152
England, imagery of, 67–68, 69
Engulfment, 205; ego loss caused by, 203; fear of, 16, 180, 197; and isolation, 161; by the mother, 11, 23, 48
Enmity, 185, 218
Envy, 168, 182, 184
Erikson, Erik, 3, 44n, 86n; on stages of identity formation, 195, 197, 202
Eros and love, 205; absence of maternal love, 64–65; adolescent, 196; in comedies by Shakespeare, 114; by cuckolded husbands, 139; and death, 22, 32, 98–99, 102–103; fear of, 45; vs. manhood proved by violence and aggression, 90–91, 93; between men, 79–81, 168, 169; and narcissism, 21–46;

Ovid's concept of, 26–28, 30–31; rejection of, 26, 32–33, 38–45, 206–207; ridicule of, 40, 91; Shakespeare's concept of, 42; and twins, 200
Estates, inheritance of, 16
Evil feminine powers, 177, 185
Ewbank, Inga-Stina, 217–218

"False-self system," 158
Falstaff, in the Henry IV plays, 70, 77; character of, 71–73; death of, 80; sexuality of, 72–73
Falstaff, in The Merry Wives of Windsor, 128–129, 130, 131, 147–150
Family, 2; ambivalence toward, 193–194; collective self of, 63; defense of, 86, 188–189; destruction of, 66; influence on masculine identity, 188–189, 193–225; patriarchal power in, 12–14, 48; separation from, 83; status of servants in, 87; status of women in, 156, 189
Fantasy: of betrayal by women, 120, 140; of male dominance, 116–117
Farce, 116
Fate, 84, 99
Father: anteriority of, 50, 53; avenging of, 57, 58, 61, 65, 139; bond with the son, 69–71; changed father–son relationships, 61, 69; counteridentification with, 11, 16–17, 18, 138, 139; cuckolded, 133–140; emulation and rivalry with, 49–54, 63; identity achieved

Father: (continued)
via the daughter, 211–214,
220–221; incest with the
daughter, 211–212, 214;
inherited identity of the son,
48, 49, 50, 57–58; loyalty to,
49, 63, 83; patriarchal power
of, 12–16, 48; rebellion and
submission by the son, 76;
role in the separation–
individuation process, 8,
47–48; surrogate, 96. See
also Patriarchy
Fatherhood, 13; and masculine
identity, 175, 179, 182–190
passim, 211–214, 220–221;
passage to the status of, 194,
195, 196–197, 215–219
Fear of ego loss, 197, 199
Feminine identity, 10, 96–97
Feminine, the, 10, 92; bond with,
191; in Falstaff, 72–73;
imagery of, 176–177; sexual
union with, 216, 224
Feuds: manhood proved by, 86,
87–88, 89, 90; in patriarchal
society, 84, 86, 87, 90, 95; role
in Romeo and Juliet, 83, 84–91,
95, 98, 99
Filmer, Robert, 14
Fineman, Joel, 152, 223
Fratricidal rivalry and violence,
50, 152, 224
Freud, Sigmund, 1, 92, 122n,
215; on castration fear, 11;
concept of gender identity, 9,
11; concept of narcissism, 24;
doubles discussed by,
198–199; on emulation of the
father, 50–51; Macbeth's lack
of children interpreted by,
184; on role of the father in
child development, 47

Frey, Charles, 62
Friendship between men, 79–81,
167–168, 215
Frye, Northrop, 114, 194n

Gender awareness, 9
Gender identity, 3; ambivalence
of, 152–153; defined, 9;
detached from personal
identity, 208–211;
development in boys, 9–12,
47–48; female identification
with masculine behavior, 19,
151, 154–155, 157, 159, 173,
181; metaphorical unsexing,
181; in the separation–
individuation process,
9–12, 47
Goddard, Harold, 73, 84
Gohlke, Madelon, 132
Grief, 93
Guilt, 74, 77, 79, 136

Hal, Prince, in the history plays,
18, 69–81 passim, 224; ego
ideal of, 152; inherited identity
of, 49; kingship of, 77–79, 80;
marriage of, 79, 82; passage
from boyhood to manhood,
69–81 passim; rebellion and
submission by, 73, 76;
relationship with Falstaff,
72–73, 75, 77, 80; relationship
with his father, 69–71, 73–74,
75–77
Hamlet, 132–140, 172, 224;
cuckoldry in, 19, 133–140;
Oedipus complex in, 2
Hate, 163, 168
Heart metaphors, 41–42
Heirs, 94, 197; legitimate male,
13; role in masculine identity,
217

Henry IV plays, 49, 69–81; comparison of Henry and Hal as kings, 77; *1 Henry IV*, 77; *2 Henry IV*, 70, 77, 78; father–son bond in, 69–71, 73–74, 75–76; motif of the Prodigal Son, 75–76; succession in, 70, 71, 75, 76–77

Henry V, 49, 51, 77, 79–81; father–king in, 56, 60; friendship and love between men in, 79, 80, 81

Henry VI plays, 49, 51–62 *passim*, 70, 81; character of Henry VI, 51–52, 56, 60; decline of paternally defined identity, 57; *1 Henry VI*, 51–52, 62; *2 Henry VI*, 52, 56; *3 Henry VI*, 56, 62, 64, 65; relationship between Talbot and his son, 52–55; succession in, 57–62; women in, 55–56

Hermaphrodites, 209

Hermaphroditus, 26, 29, 30, 31, 37, 44

Heroes, Shakespearean, 17, 42, 163, 167, 193

Hibbard, George, 107

History plays, 47–81; basis of masculine identity in, 57, 66, 79; emulation of the father, 49–54, 63; father–son bond in, 52–55, 69–71; kingship and identity in, 67–69, 73, 77–79, 80; role of the father in masculine identity, 47–55, 61, 63, 197; role of the mother in forming masculine identity, 63–65; succession in, 49, 57–62, 66, 70, 71, 75, 81, 197; warrior bonding in, 54;

women in, 47, 55, 62, 72–73, 79, 80, 81

Hollander, John, 205

Homosexuality, 24, 28, 142n, 145, 209, 215

Honor, and cuckoldry, 121, 124, 126, 128, 131, 136

Horns, symbolism of. *See* Cuckoldry

Hubler, Edward, 41–42

Hunting, 123; vs. love in *Venus and Adonis*, 38–44, 83

Husbands: authority of, 83; role as property owner, 110–111, 121

Iago, 42, 127, 138, 140–145

Ibsen, Henrik, 114

Icarus, 53, 54, 56

Identification, 44; with the father, 11, 16–17, 18, 48, 52, 54, 82, 133, 139; with mother England, 67–68, 69; with the same-sex object, 196; in the separation–individuation process, 5–6, 10, 12

Identity, 2; collective identity of English men, 56; confusion of sexual identity, 208–211; crisis, 22, 195, 197, 198, 199; defense against eros, 26, 30–34, 38–45, 206–207; feminine, 9–10, 96–97; filial, 198, 201–202, 205; ideal self, 172, 183; influenced by feuds, 85–86; and the family, 85–86, 193–225; and narcissism, 22, 25, 36, 43–44, 202; negative, 44; obliteration of self, 202, 203; relationship to significant others, 200–201, 219; warrior self, 158, 160, 165, 166, 172

Identity formation, 3–17; of

Identity formation (*continued*)
boys and girls, 9–12; stages of,
3, 195–196, 200, 216–217
Impotence, 178–179, 180–181
Incest, 28, 133, 137, 197;
between father and daughter,
211, 212, 214
Individuation, 3–12; through
violence, 152. *See also*
Separation–individuation
process
Inheritance, 16, 57, 85; as basis of
masculine identity, 79; of the
father's identity, 48, 49, 50,
57–58, 63; of wealth, 106
Initiation into manhood, 82
Intimacy, 195, 199, 207, 225;
development of the self by, 33;
and isolation, 21; sexual,
31, 34
Jacobson, Edith, 3, 6n, 153n
James I, King, 15
Jealousy, 215; and cuckoldry,
127–130, 140, 143, 144; and
misogyny, 216
Joan of Aire, 55
Jonson, Ben, 114

Kate, in *Taming of the Shrew*, 1,
83, 104; capitulation and
freedom of, 112–114, 115;
speech on her status as a
woman, 108; submission to
Petruchio, 18; as a victim of
the marriage market, 105;
violence of, 107–109
Kierkegaard, Søren, 7
Killing, justification of, 58–59
Kings, fatherhood of, 182
Kingship and identity, 67–69,
73, 77–78
Kissing, 34–37, 38n, 45

Knight, G. Wilson, 176, 194n
Knox, John, 14

Laertes, in *Hamlet*, 140
Laing, R. D., 158
Lawrence, D. H., 160
Lear, 42
Legend of the Wild Prince, 75
Leontes, in *The Winter's Tale*, 1,
2, 20, 125–126, 214–219, 225;
boyhood friendship of,
214–215; horns of, 128, 129
Life stages, 82, 194, 195
Love. *See* Eros and love
Love's Labour's Lost, 123
Lucrece, 37, 128, 132
Lust, 34, 37

Macbeth, 1, 19, 42, 151–153,
172–192; apparitions in,
186–188; imagery of bloody
men in, 155, 173; compared to
Coriolanus, 172, 174, 175, 190,
192; fatherhood in, 175, 179,
182–190; lack of heirs,
183–184, 217; masculine
identity created by women,
172–173, 178, 181–182, 185,
186; nursing babe imagery in,
153–154, 176, 181
McCanles, Michael, 164
Mahler, Margaret, 3, 4n, 4–9,
7n, 153n, 154n; on role of the
father in child development,
47–48, 47n
Male dominance, 104; fantasy of,
116–117; in marriage,
110–118
Man's estate, 210
Margaret of Anjou in the *Henry
VI* plays, 55, 56, 60–61
Marriage, 56; arranged, 94–96;

and cuckoldry, 19, 119–150; and friendship between men, 145, 167–168; male dominance in, 15, 110–118; money in, 106–107; passage to manhood by, 18, 79, 82; vs. patriarchal loyalty, 82–83, 86, 89–90, 93, 95–96, 98; to produce heirs, 13, 94; as a test of manhood, 83; wife as an animal, 111–112; wife as property of the husband, 110–111, 121; yoke of, 19, 125, 150. See also Cuckoldry

Martial valor, 50, 57, 176

Masculine identity: achieved via the daughter, 196–197, 211–214, 220–221; aggression for the father vs. love of a woman, 86–87, 89–91, 93; basis in the history plays, 57, 66, 79; defense against love, 26, 32–33, 38–45, 206–207; dilemma of, 2, 17, 20, 87, 89–91, 93, 98, 160–161, 172; emulation of the father, 49–54, 63; vs. engulfment by women, 11, 23, 48, 180; in the family and life cycle, 193–225; by fatherhood, 175, 179, 182–190 passim; formed by the mother, 63–64, 156–163, 165–166, 170, 172; formed by women, 172–173, 178, 181–182, 185, 186, 192; influence of the father–son bond, 70–71, 74, 75–76; inherited, 48, 49, 50, 57–58, 63; male dominance in marriage, 104, 109–118; passage from being a son to fatherhood, 16, 194, 195,

196–197, 215–219; reciprocal process between father and son, 71, 74; in the separation–individuation process, 9–12, 17, 47–48, 172–173; and sibling rivalry, 223–224; weakened by cuckoldry, 119, 121–122, 129, 132, 136–137, 138–139

Masculinity: authenticated by female submission, 117–118; dependent on sexual property in women, 131–132; feelings of pity and love, 151, 170–171, 172, 189; feminization of, 191; and morality, 180, 181, 182, 185; problems in achieving, 17; proved by the phallic violence of feuds, 86, 87–88, 89, 90; and self-knowledge, 192; vulnerable to women, 17, 119, 132

Merry Wives of Windsor, The, cuckoldry, jealousy, and marriage in, 19, 128–130, 131, 147–150

Metamorphoses. See Ovid

Metamorphosis, 202–203; in Venus and Adonis, 44–45, 46

Mirroring: and adolescence, 196; by brothers, 201; and character of Richard III, 64; defined, 5; in male friendships, 215, 216; narcissistic, 200, 202, 206, 207; by twins, 200

Misogyny, 19, 55n; and cuckoldry, 121, 133, 137, 146, 147; in Hamlet, 133, 137; and jealousy, 216

Monsters: and jealousy, 143, 144; men as, 119, 137, 145, 150, 151, 191

Mortality, 94, 211
Mother: adolescence terminated by motherhood, 93–94; bond with, 159, 160, 161, 163, 170, 172; England as, 67, 69; father cuckolded by, 136–140; "good enough," 7, 8; identified with the state, 160, 163, 167, 170; masculine ego ideal of, 157, 159; masculine identity of sons, 63–64, 156–163, 165–166, 170, 172; nurturance by, 45; reengulfment of the son, 48; separation of the child, 3–12, 17, 47–48; Venus as, 34, 45. See also Mirroring; Symbiotic union with the mother
Mourning by adolescents, 196
Much Ado about Nothing, 82, 125
Murder, 177, 179, 180, 185

Narcissism: concept and context of, 23–26; and dominance, 46; emotional isolation of, 21; fear of losing the self, 36, 43–44; and identity crisis of youth, 22; and mirroring, 200, 202, 206, 207; murder of self, 44, 45; of Richard II and Richard III, 66–67
Narcissus: allegorized story of, 24; Ovid's account of, 22, 29, 31–32, 33
Negative identity, 44
Neill, Michael, 64, 67n
Nevo, Ruth, 90
Nursing babe imagery, 153–154, 159, 181; and "valiantness," 160, 162
Nurturance, 45, 46, 191

Obesity, 72
Oedipal complex, 47, 197, 201, 224; desire and fear, 213; and doubles, 198, 199; in Hamlet, 2, 134; incest, 197, 211, 212, 214
Omnipotence, 4, 5, 7, 220, 222
Oral imagery: in Coriolanus, 162; in Venus and Adonis, 34–38, 42–43, 45
Oral threat, personification of, 42
Othello, 17, 42, 126, 172; bond between Iago and Othello, 140, 144–145; cuckoldry in, 19, 127–128, 138, 140–146; Iago cuckolded by Othello, 141, 143
Ovid: concept of eros, 26–28, 30–32; influence on Shakespeare, 22, 26, 28, 29, 31, 32; Metamorphoses, 22, 23, 26–27, 53

Patriarchy: and cuckoldry, 121, 146, 147, 150; family loyalty vs. marriage, 82–83, 86, 89–90, 93, 95–96, 98; in the family structure, 12–16; feuds in patriarchal society, 84, 85, 86, 87; inherited identity of the son, 48, 49, 50, 57–58, 63; and masculine identity, 12–13, 15, 16, 17, 47–49; role of daughters, 94–96, 140–141, 197; in the social order, 13–14; subjugation of women, 96–97
Penis, 9, 47, 122
Pericles, 20, 194, 198, 211–214, 220; riddle in, 211–212
Petruchio in Taming of the Shrew,

18, 83; male dominance of, 104, 109–118; as property owner and knight-errant, 110–111; violence of, 107, 109–110, 111

Phaeton, 53, 56–57

Phallic: role of avenger, 139; symbol, 122

Phallocentrism, 9

Procreation, 33, 34, 188, 193, 198

Prodigal Son motif, 75–76

Property: sexual property in women, 131–132; wife as, 110–111, 121

Proser, Matthew, 179, 180

Prospero, in *The Tempest,* 20, 220–225

Providential tempest, 212; defined, 194

Psychoanalytic theory, 2. *See also* Blos, Peter; Chodorow, Nancy; Erikson, Erik; Freud, Sigmund; Jacobson, Edith; Mahler, Margaret; Winnicott, D. W.

"Psycho-sexual moratorium," 86

Puns, 88, 89, 177, 179

Puritan fundamentalism, 15, 120n

Rank, Otto, 198–199

Rape, 36–37, 80, 132, 222

Revenge, 61; for cuckoldry, 121, 127, 130, 133, 136, 139; repetition and doubling, 198; among siblings, 223–224. *See also* Rivalry

Richard II, 49, 57–58, 60; compared to *Richard III,* 66–67; images of England in,

67–68; kingship and identity in, 67–69

Richard III, 42, 49, 50, 62–66, 70; alienation from the mother, 64; character of Richard III, 63–66; family in, 65–66, 193; women in, 62

Riddles, 211–212

Riggs, David, 51, 52n

Rite de passage, 164; in battle, 190; feuds as, 84; of male adolescents, 18, 21

Rivalry: bond of, 19, 190; in cuckoldry, 126, 131; and ego ideal, 152; and emulation of the father, 50, 51, 53–54; and masculine identity, 152, 168–169, 174–175, 182–185; between siblings, 223–224

Roberts, Jeanne Addison, 148

Romeo and Juliet, 18, 82–103; arranged marriage of Juliet, 94–96; conflicting definitions of manhood in, 87, 89–91, 93, 98; feud in, 83, 84–91, 95, 98, 99, 100; marraige vs. patriarchal loyalty, 82–83, 86, 89–90, 95–96, 98, 100; Mercutio in, 89–92; Queen Mab speech in, 91–92; tragedy in, 84, 85, 86, 87, 93; Tybalt in, 87–90, 92, 94, 95

Salic Law, 79

Salmacis, 37

Satyrs, 135

Scapegoats, 147–148

Schizophrenic personality, 158

Schwartz, Murray, 153–154, 218

Self-knowledge, 192

Self-love, 24. *See also* Narcissism

Separation–individuation process, 3–12; of adolescent youths, 21, 23, 196; gender identity in, 9–12; and masculine identity, 9–12, 17, 20, 34, 47–48, 153, 172–173; role of the father, 8, 47–48; reexperienced in adolescence, 196; symbiotic union with the mother, 3–6, 8, 48

Servants: beating of, 111; role in feuds, 87–88; status of, 87

Sex roles, 20; in the family, 189; polarization of, 12, 152, 156, 157

Sexual: consummation in death, 102–103; desire, 28, 34, 149, 179–180, 205–206; fusion, 45; imagery in battle, 80; penetration, 135; rivalry, 140, 142, 148; theft, 140–141

Sexual identity. See Gender identity

Sexuality: acceptance of, 220, 224; avoidance of sexual maturity, 72–73; collective violence against women, 81; of daughters, 140–141, 221; of Falstaff, 72–73; of Hamlet's father, 135, 138–139; male possession of female sexuality, 121, 124, 126, 131–132; oedipal, 214; vs. protection of the self, 32–33; rejection of, 18, 21, 28–29, 33, 38, 40–41, 43, 82; union of male and female, 45, 216; of women, 97, 138, 198

Shakespeare, W., 48, 72–73, 144, 145; ambivalence toward the family, 193, 194; approach to

inherited masculine identity, 49; attitude toward male comradeships, 81; attitudes toward women, 55n; concept of love, 42, 114; conclusions on the masculine dilemma, 20; critique of masculinity, 189; on defense of the family, 188; father–son bond presented by, 70–71; interest in masculine identity, 12, 17; and marriage to produce heirs, 94; psychological insight of, 1–2; source material used by, 22, 26, 31, 32, 75, 94–95; on status of women in marriage, 110, 112; use of time by, 204–205, 217–218; use of verse in *Henry VI,* 54

Shrews, 104, 105, 107, 108, 115

Skura, Meredith, 193

Sibling rivalry, 223–224

Slater, Philip, 31n, 156

Smith, Gordon Ross, 99

Smith, Thomas, 14

Society, entrance into, 82

Sonnets by Shakespeare, 22, 41–42

Spirits, 176–178, 179; possession by, 203–204

Stewart, J. I. M., 215

Stockholder, Katherine, 160

Stoller, Robert, 10–11

Stone, Lawrence, 14–16

Succession, 18, 49; challenges to, 57–58; and fatherhood, 183–184, 190, 192; in the *Henry IV* plays, 70, 71, 75, 76–77; of Henry VI, 59–60; and political order, 59, 61; problematic nature of, 81;

slaughter and vengeance
justified by, 58–59, 61–62, 66;
and virility, 56
Supernatural power of
women, 55
Symbiotic union with the
mother, 16, 48, 54n; and
adolescence, 196; attempt to
reestablish, 8, 216–217, 219;
friendship between men, 80;
in the separation–
individuation process, 3–6,
10; and warrior bonding,
54–80
Symbolic characters, 63
Symbols of manhood, 186–187

Talbot, John, in *Henry VI*,
52–54, 70; chivalric
masculinity exemplified by,
52; compared to Joan of Aire,
55; compared to Prince Hal,
76; death of his son, 53, 80;
loyalty of his son, 50, 52–53;
warrior bonding of, 79
Taming of the Shrew, 18,
104–118; animal metaphor in,
111–112; love in, 114; male
dominance in, 104, 109–118;
marriage as a test of manhood
in, 83; taming motif in, 104,
109–110, 112–114, 115, 117;
violence of Kate and Petruchio
compared, 107–110. *See also*
Kate; Petruchio
Tempest motif, 194, 214
Tempest, The, 20, 194, 198,
220–225; doubles in, 220–221;
revenge and sibling rivalry in,
223–224
Tillyard, E. M. W., 111

Time, and identity development,
204–205, 217–218
Timon, in *Timon of Athens*, 17,
193
Tragedy: in *Coriolanus*, 160, 172;
in *Romeo and Juliet*, 85, 86,
87, 93
Transitional object, 6
Treason, 69, 70
Troilus and Cressida, 131–132;
emulation in, 50n
Twelfth Night, 19, 194, 195, 198,
205–211; identification in,
196; sexual identity in,
207–211; twins in, 199–200,
205
Twins, 1, 198, 199–205; and
doubles, 198, 199–200, 211;
and identity achieved via
daughters, 213–214; of
opposite sex, 210
Tyndale, William, 14

Uroboros, 211–212

Vendetta, 57, 61
Vengeance, and succession,
61–62
Venus and Adonis, 17–18, 21–46,
91, 102; characterization of
Venus, 33–38, 43; death of
Adonis, 42, 43–45, 102; flower
metaphor in, 22, 29–30, 32,
44–45; hunting vs. love in,
38–44, 83; metamorphosis of
Adonis, 44–46; oral imagery
in, 34–38, 42, 45; rejection of
sexuality and love in, 18, 21,
28–29, 33, 38, 40–41, 43, 82;
separation crisis in, 21, 47;
source of, 22, 26, 28, 29, 31

Violence: to achieve manhood, 19, 86–88, 151, 154–155, 174–175, 179, 185; compared between husband and wife, 107–110; to defend the family, 86, 87, 188–189; of feuds, 83, 86; individuation achieved by, 152; unity of men in, 83. *See also* Aggression

Virginity, 97, 101, 219

Virility, 150; as divine power, 147; and succession, 56

Volumnia, in *Coriolanus,* 19, 154; ego ideal of, 157, 159; manhood and identity of her son, 156–163, 165–166, 170, 172

War, 82

Warrior: bonding, 54, 79, 80; self, 158, 160, 165, 166, 172

Wealth, 106

Whores, 121, 132, 145–146

Winnicott, D. W., 3, 200n; and mirroring, 5, 64; and the transitional object, 6

Winter's Tale, The, 20, 194, 214–220, 225; cuckoldry in, 125–126; "boy eternal" motif in, 70–71, 215; and symbiotic union with the mother, 216–217, 219

Witches, 173, 174, 176, 186; and sexual desire, 179

Wittol, 129

Womb, 100–101

Women: betrayal by, 120, 131, 132, 140, 144; compared in the comedies and in the history plays, 62; as dangerous to men, 55; engulfment by, 11, 16, 23, 48, 161, 180; fear of, 23, 140; fidelity of, 13, 146, 216; frailty of, 135; freedom of, 113–114, 115; identification with masculine behavior, 151, 154–155, 157, 173, 181; male attitudes toward during feuds, 86, 88, 89, 92; male fantasy of the untamed woman, 117; manhood authenticated by, 12, 117–118; masculine identity formed by, 151–153, 156–163, 165–166, 170, 172, 174, 178, 181–182, 185–186, 192, 202–203, 225; narcissism as a defense against, 23; power of, 176–178; responsibility for cuckoldry, 137, 139; role of wife and mother, 96–97; as sexual property of men, 131–132; subjugation of, 15, 104, 108, 110–112, 117

Yoke, emblem of marriage, 19, 125, 150

York vs. Lancaster, 57–58, 60

Designer:	Randall Goodall
Compositor:	Interactive Composition
Printer:	Thomson-Shore
Text:	VIP Bembo
Display:	VIP Bembo
Paper:	50lb. P&S offset B32

Amanda Jacobson